Medicine for Medical Students

The Complete Guide to Both OSCE & Written Exams

Second Edition

Dedicated to my mom, dad and brother, without whom I would not be the man I am today and to my girlfriend Aimee for her continual support, understanding and encouragement

For this second edition I decided to do something new, different, and exciting, something that would result in a much more comprehensive educational textbook for the reader. I had the idea to ask my friends and colleagues to help me write or read over those chapters in areas within which they specialise, making this book an amalgamation of knowledge and experience. I would like to take this opportunity to thank them all for their help in creating such a unique book.

Miss Aimee Dempsey	Nursing
Mr Tom Watcyn-Jones	Urology
Dr David McGouran	Gastroenterology
Dr Paul Burgess	Obstetrics & Gynaecology
Mr Dan Cocker	General Surgery
Mr Simon MacLean	Orthopaedics
Dr Vicky Plested	Haematology
Dr Andrew Davies	Ophthalmology

To find out more information about myself and the above co-authors please visit my website **www.themedicalstudent.com**

Also if you have any ideas and wish to contribute to future editions of this textbook, which is great fun and will look amazing on your CV, or have any comments about the book, good or bad, please contact me via **info@themedicalstudent.com**

Chapter	Contents	Page
	Introduction & Before You Start (IT IS IMPORTANT TO READ THIS FIRST)	**i - vi**

Introduction

First of all I would like to say well done for purchasing this book, you have made a fantastic decision in doing so and will be rewarded when it comes to your OSCE and written exams.

I honestly believe that a large proportion of what you read and are taught when studying medicine is not needed for examinations. Trying to learn and memorise all of these random facts over complicates your revision and clutters your mind. I know this because I fell into the same trap, I bought book after book, spending a small fortune and countless hours trying to remember the most obscure facts only to find that when it comes to real life, i.e. your exams and eventually practicing medicine, it is the basics that really count. I decided long ago that I wanted to teach medicine to others how I, due to my own experiences, believe it is best taught, by cutting out all of the unnecessary jargon and waffle, focusing only on the information that is important for you to pass your exams and become a good junior doctor.

You are probably thinking, "Who the hell is this guy?" Well I am just someone who has been through exactly what you are going through and has successfully come out the other side and learnt what is important along the way. Because of this I believe I have a unique view on what students want, what they need, and more importantly what they do not need to pass medical examinations. I remember reading through countless books and going to lecture after lecture whilst all the time thinking how much time I was wasting. I did all of this because I was scared, scared to miss out on any random bit of knowledge that might just pop up in a question on the exam.

I always wished I could stumble upon a book that would stop wasting my time and tell me everything I needed without the extra waffle. Unfortunately I did not, it is not good business for publishing houses to sell you just one book when they can sell you ten, so I decided to write my own!

'Medicine for Medical Students' has been designed and written with medical students in mind. It contains not only revision sections for virtually all of the main specialties in medicine that are invaluable for your written tests but also details the histories, clinical examinations, clinical skills, and investigation interpretation that you will need to pass your OSCEs and when you start work as a junior doctor. It is this combination of information that makes this book so different to all of the other text books currently on the market.

I really do hope that you find this book useful during your medical studies. I am really proud of it, and as I have already mentioned this is exactly the kind of book I would have loved to own when I was a student. It places all of the knowledge you need to become a well rounded junior doctor into the palm of your hands, the other ingredients such as hard work, commitment and courage come from you.

Wishing you the best of luck

Dr. Marc A. Crutchley BSc MBChB

P.S. if you wish to find out more about myself, my work, this book's accompanying lecture series, or you wish to get involved and contribute to future editions of 'Medicine for Medical Students' please check out **www.themedicalstudent.com**, also I would be very grateful if you would email any comments or thoughts you have about the book to **info@themedicalstudent.com**

Before You Start

I am now going to explain how the book works and how to get the most out of it. First of all, it is arranged by the main medical specialties, each of which is further split into history taking, clinical examination and revision sections. The book also contains detailed steps how to perform all the important clinical skills and has extensive appendices that have all sorts of invaluable information, for example how to interpret blood results, ECGs, X-rays, ABGs, & much more. Also each page has been set out with a large column on the left hand side that is virtually empty, this is for you to write your own notes in, making the book interactive and user friendly, many people have commented how useful this setup is.

History taking

Being able to take a good history is probably the most important part of being a doctor. Most diagnoses can be made from history taking alone before even laying a finger on the patient. Because of this you will be examined on your history taking ability in your OSCEs over and over again, so it is extremely important that you practice and get very good at this skill.

The trick to mastering history taking is to keep things simple. If you look at any of the histories in this book you will see that only the 'presenting complaint' section changes, the start (introduction) and the end (past medical/family/social history + smoking, alcohol, medications & allergies) are always kept virtually the same. OCSEs are tremendously stressful, you panic, your mind goes blank and the few seconds it takes you to think what question to ask next seems to last forever. Keeping as many questions the same as possible for every history you do will pull you through these stressful moments and will make your performance seem well structured and slick.

1. **Introduction**: I cannot stress how important this part of the history taking process is. You need to begin every OSCE station by approaching the patient, introducing yourself politely and obtaining their personal details. I know this sounds easy but I can guarantee that you will forget to do this at least once if not a number of times during your OSCEs, I know I did. Passing exams is all about scoring points, so make sure you score maximum on the easy ones. To do this formulate an introduction that you can use every time you meet a patient and use it even when you are practicing with friends. For example, "Pleased to meet you, my name is Marc, I am a medical student, would you mind me asking you some questions about why you are here today? First of all can I get your name, date of birth and occupation (or past occupation if you have retired)?"

2. **Presenting complaint**: once you have introduced yourself and gained permission the next step involves working out what is wrong. As I mentioned above this should be the only section that changes between histories. A good way to start this section is by asking an open-ended question like, "What seems to be bothering you?" or "How can I help you today?" There are a number of symptoms you must enquire about depending on the type of history being asked. For example, when performing a cardiovascular history on a patient complaining of palpitations, you first ask about the palpitations then work your way through the other cardiovascular symptoms one after another, i.e. chest pain, shortness of breath, intermittent claudication, loss of consciousness, ankle oedema and fatigue. That is all you need to do for this part of the history, simple ay? The only hard part is remembering these questions whilst you are feeling anxious in your OSCE. The trick I used, and continue to use to this day, is to come up with some kind of mental image that includes a trigger for each symptom. I have included in the book the images that I use and I hope that they

will help you too. Alternatively you could come up with your own. I promise that you will thank me for this tip when your exams are over, as it helps not only with remembering what questions to ask, but also doing so in an organised fashion.

3. **Past medical history**: once you have covered the presenting complaint you need to ask about the patient's general health. I always start this section with another open question like "Tell me about your general health. Do you suffer with any illness or have you seen a doctor about anything in the past?" Some patients (or actors as many are in OSCEs) are great and tell you everything, others will not. Therefore, at this point you do a quick systematic review, I use the 'DEAR J SMITH' mnemonic for this. All you have to say is "I'm going to ask you whether you suffer from or have suffered with the following conditions, just say yes or no to each." Then work your way through the mnemonic (Diabetes, Epilepsy, Asthma, Rheumatic fever, Jaundice, Stroke, MI, TB, Hyper/hypo tension/thyroid/cholesterol). This will take you about 10 seconds and again looks slick and structured. If you have time at the end you can cover a more in-depth systematic enquiry *(see 'Systematic Enquiry' in the appendix).*

4. **Medications, allergies, smoking & alcohol**: another guarantee I will make to you is that you will forget to enquire about at least one of these subjects, I know I did many a time before I come up with this very simple way of remembering them. All you have to do is link all four together in your head, so when you ask one of them you ask the rest straight after each other. You are probably thinking "That's obvious!" Well yes it is, but by doing so you will never miss out on scoring these very simple points and, as I already mentioned, that is what OSCEs are all about.

5. **Family history**: as you all know many diseases have a genetic factor to them, if someone in your immediate family has a certain condition you have a higher risk of developing the same thing. You do not need to go over the top when assessing family history, you just need to know about any conditions that run in the immediate family, i.e. brothers/sisters, mom/dad and at a stretch aunts/uncles. A good line to use is "Can I enquire as to whether your parents are still alive?" If they are, ask whether they suffer from any diseases. If they have passed away say "Sorry to hear that, can you remember at what age they died and what they died of?" Expressing sympathy with the patient is very important, not just in this instance, but also throughout the entire history to show compassion and to build rapport. Some patients may also mention pain or disability, if they do it is crucial that you show understanding and empathy. This is certainly the case in your OSCE, so using obvious sentences such as "That must be hard for you" can put the patient at ease and help you to gain those all important points.

6. **Social & occupational history**: this is the last section of your history, but that does not mean it is not important. There are lots of points to be gained by taking a good social history as it shows that you are thinking of your patient as a whole, not just their disease. The two main things you need to find out are; who lives at home with them (also is the person able to care for the patient or are they ill themselves), and how is this condition affecting their life. It may be totally disruptive to their normal life or conversely, it may hardly affect them at all, this will help you to decide on a treatment/management plan. Also at this point it is good practice to expand on their occupational history, i.e. do they work with any hazardous materials. As I already mentioned, I always ask the patient's occupation during the introduction, this is a real help in some OSCE stations. For example, if you are doing a respiratory history and from the start you know that the patient was a coal miner you can tailor you history to suit, instead of finding that out at the very end.

Because it is paramount that as good doctors we are good communicators and that we show empathy with the patient's feelings there is another issue that needs to be addressed at some point during your history taking. This is called 'ICE' and stands for Ideas, Concerns and Expectations. Just ask the following questions either one after another at the end, or blend them into your history separately.

- Ideas: "Do you have any idea what you could be suffering with?" Patients can be very good at self diagnosis.
- Concerns: "Is there anything that is worrying you about your condition?" It is human nature to think the worst, you will find that a lot of people, especially in your OSCEs, will be worried about something. Cancer is at the forefront of most patients' minds for a number of presenting complaints. If someone says "Do you think I've got cancer?" handle it tactfully by saying "Why do you think that?" then try and put the patient at ease and say something like "I can understand that you are worried, but at this time it is too early for me to answer that question, I would like to run a few tests to try and rule that out." On the other hand some patients are the exact opposite and think nothing can affect them.
- Expectations: "What are your expectations about your condition, what would you like us to do for you?" You need to find out whether this condition is bothering them to the extent that they want something done about it. For example, certain conditions can only be cured by surgery, an older patient may not want that. For expectations you also need to find out what the patient's thoughts are about their condition. What they have may be incurable which is something they need to come to terms with.

Most OSCE examiners ask you to summarize your findings once the history is completed. Just start with something like "This is Mr. Smith, he is a 45 year old electrician and has presented with chest palpitations" Then work your way through your findings, including the negatives, in an organised fashion.

That is basically it for history taking, as I said keep it simple, only change the presenting complaint section and you will pass the history section of your OSCE without a problem.

Clinical Examination

I would love to be able to tell you that I have some 'tricks of the trade' when it comes to performing clinical examinations, unfortunately I do not. All you need to do is practice them over and over again on patients and on your friends. What my friends and I would do was write down all of the examinations on pieces of paper and draw them randomly out of a hat. This gives you less time to prepare and ensures that you practice all of the examinations an equal number of times.

As you will see, most examinations start at the hand, work up the arm to the head, then down the body. Examiners make it a little harder in OSCEs by saying things like "Perform a focused cardiovascular chest examination". This can be confusing so ask the examiner what they mean, say something like "For all cardiovascular exams I would start at the hands and work my way to the chest, is that what you would like me to do?" They may say "No just focus on the chest", or if they are being harsh they may say "Do what you would usually do". In this case start at the hands and they may prompt you after a few moments to move to the chest. It is a waste of your precious time doing something in an OSCE if you are not scoring points for it.

The only other piece of advice I can give you is that when practicing, always perform the whole examination. For example, when examining the respiratory system most students, including myself, do the steps for the front of the chest but do not bother practicing on the back. This is a mistake, you need to get used to moving the patient in a confident and slick way. Also by not practicing certain steps when it comes to the OSCE, your lack of experience will show and you will only panic more.

Revision sections

Put simply, these sections contain in-depth knowledge covering most of the specialities you will cover as a medical student. They also contain hints and tips throughout to help with your understanding of the subject. They really do cut out the waffle found in other books, making them an invaluable source of information not only for your written exams, but also as a reference in your junior doctor years.

When learning about certain diseases and their management look for similarities. For example, learn all of the investigations for each speciality instead of for each disease, this results in less to remember and gives you a better idea as to why each test is being performed. Also try to link similar disease types as the underlying physiology and management will also be similar. For example, rheumatoid arthritis, inflammatory bowel disease, hyperthyroid, pericarditis, etc. although are from different specialities they are all 'inflammatory' diseases, therefore many of the investigations performed and treatments used will be the same.

One last tip concerning patient management is to ensure that when considering treatment always mention 'lifestyle changes'. Just talk for a few seconds about diet, smoking, alcohol, and regular exercise, examiners love this.

Presenting investigations

When interpreting or presenting any investigation, be that an ECG, an X-ray, or blood results, the most important tip I can give you is to have a simple, logical, step-by-step approach and always stick to it. I know it is temping to just focus on the most obvious diagnosis, but to assess the investigation correctly you must begin with the patient's details and work your way through stating the negative results as well as the positives. The investigations covered in this book each have simple step by step instructions which, if followed, make interpreting and presenting results simple.

Clinical procedures

In this second edition I have added a section that covers all the important procedures you will be asked to perform as a medical student. As with clinical examinations there is no trick to help you perform these, you just need to practise them over and over until you feel comfortable. My only advice is once you get to a level where you feel comfortable practise them several more times, because performing these on fake arms or on a fake penis will not prepare you for the stress you will encounter when you have to perform them in your exams or on a real person. I still remember the first time I ever inserted a urinary catheter into a patient, it was on my first day of work and was an experience for the both of us!

Final thoughts

Studying medicine isn't easy but it's not as difficult as everyone says either. During your years at medical school you will experience a number of highs and lows, that's OK, every doctor I know had moments as a student when they felt overwhelmed by the task ahead. The thing I found most difficult was committing to memory the mountain of random facts you are expected to learn. Unfortunately my memory has never been great so I gradually became frustrated and disillusioned and started to lose interest in the subject. I remember my third and fourth years at university being difficult for this reason, then during my final year everything started to come together. Once this happened I started seeing links between different diseases and it was at this point that the interest and excitement I had for medicine when I first started returned.

So my final advice is this: when presented with a patient the most valuable tool you have is taking a good history, use the techniques from this book to gather the required information from the patient, after which you can identify the systems you need to examine, then using your problem solving skills come up with a differential diagnosis. The next step is to order whichever investigations you need to prove or disprove each diagnosis. Finally you share what you have found with the patient and discuss with them the treatment options.

Now, the above techniques do not come together over night, it takes a long time to become competent and a lifetime to perfect so don't worry if you feel slightly overwhelmed. Keep setting yourself goals and split these larger goals into small manageable steps. Remember, the university is not expecting you to be amazing in every field of medicine, no one knows everything which is why doctors specialise. So just focus on learning the basics, practising your history taking and examination skills alongside revising the subject and in time everything will come together. As I said medicine is not difficult, just be safe, logical, and ask for help when required.

I wish you all the best.

Cardiovascular History

Introduction	- approach politely and introduce yourself - patient's name, DOB & occupation

Chest pain	- SOCRATES can be used whenever pain is mentioned, it can also be adapted for many other presenting complaints - <u>S</u>ite - <u>O</u>nset: during exertion/rest, exercise tolerance (how far can you walk on flat/hill/stairs without discomfort) - <u>C</u>haracter: sharp, dull ache, crushing - <u>R</u>adiation: arm, back, jaw - <u>A</u>ssociated with: sweating, N&V, SOB, palpitations, LOC, etc. - <u>T</u>iming: when is it worst, go through the whole day (morning to night + waking up from sleep) - <u>E</u>asing/aggravating factors: rest, GTN spray, worse in the cold, influenced by meals, etc. - <u>S</u>everity: grade from 1 to 10, where 10 =very severe
Short of Breath (SOB)	- during exertion (how far can you walk on flat/hill/stairs before symptoms occur) - how many pillows do you sleep with (L heart failure $\Rightarrow$ fluid build up in lungs =pulmonary oedema $\Rightarrow$ orthopnoea =SOB when lying flat due to fluid redistribution over a greater surface area of the lungs) - do you wake at night SOB (paroxysmal nocturnal dyspnoea = worsening orthopnoea/heart failure) - at rest (can also be due to L heart failure) - associated symptoms: cough, wheeze, sputum, haemoptysis (pulmonary oedema $\Rightarrow$ pink frothy sputum), pain on inspiration (pleuritic pain, if sudden onset need to rule out PE, *see 'Respiratory' section*)
Intermittent claudication	- pain in calves, thighs or buttocks when walking & relieved by rest - how far can you walk on flat/hill/stairs before getting symptoms - is due to peripheral vascular disease - NB. legs are 5-10 times more susceptible to vascular disease than arms, due to the legs having a less developed blood supply
Palpitations	- mode of onset, frequency, duration & regularity - use of: caffeine, alcohol & recreational drugs - NB. can ask if possible for patient to tap out heart beat
Syncope =loss of consciousness (LOC)	- what happened before, during (eye witness account) & after episode important causes: 1. drug related (e.g. anti-hypertensives) 2. stokes-adams attacks = syncope due to arrhythmias (AF, bradycardia, VT, etc.) 3. left ventricular (LV) outflow obstruction (aortic stenosis, cardiomyopathy) - *N.B. these are the cardiac causes of syncope, other causes can be found throughout the book*
Ankle/pitting oedema	- due to R heart failure (inability of R side of heart to pump blood away quick enough $\Rightarrow$ fluid builds up in lower limbs)
Fatigue	- recent illness or fever (e.g. infective endocarditis)

PMH	- list PMH + ask the following (DEAR J SMITH):
	- Diabetes
	- Epilepsy
	- Asthma
	- Rheumatic fever
	- Jaundice
	- Stroke
	- MI
	- TB
	- Hyper tension/thyroid/cholesterol & Hypothyroid
	- any recent dental work (can ⇒staph aureus infection ⇒endocarditis)
Medications, allergies, smoking & alcohol	- if ex smoker ask smoking history
FH	- are parents/brothers/sisters alive, if so do they suffer from any diseases, if they have passed away (say "sorry to hear that") ask age & reason of death
Social/occupational history	- who is at home & how does this condition effect your life
	- expand on occupation

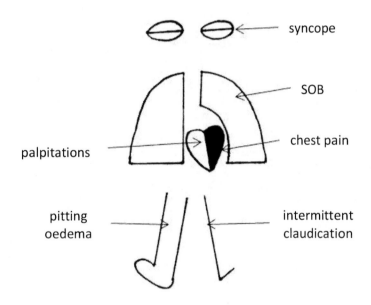

visual mnemonic of the cardiovascular history, start at the head and work down

Cardiovascular Exam

Introduction	- wash hands
	- approach politely and introduce yourself
	- patient's name & DOB
	- explain to patient what you are going to do & obtain verbal consent
	- expose patient after asking
	- position on bed at 45°
Inspection	- comment on patient & surroundings
	- SOB, obvious pain, general health, surrounding apparatus/medications/O_2 etc.
Hands	- clubbing = chronic disease (in cardiovascular this is mainly due to heart disease & infective endocarditis)
	- spoon shaped nails (koilonychia = anaemia)
	- splinter haemorrhages (infective endocarditis)
	- osler's nodes & janeway lesions (infective endocarditis)
	- muscle wasting
	- peripheral cyanosis (pale/bluish)
	- red, warm & clammy palms (CO_2 retention)
Radial pulse	- use 3 finger tips to assess
	comment on:
	1. rate: HR <40 = bradycardia, >100 = tachycardia
	2. rhythm: regular, regularly irregular (e.g. heart block), irregularly irregular (e.g. AF)
Collapsing pulse	- due to aortic regurge ⇒backflow of blood into L ventricle ⇒↓diastolic pressure ⇒wide pulse pressure ⇒ "slapping" pulse
	- place 4 fingers across wrist & raise the patient's arm above their head to illicit sign
	- NB. ask patient about shoulder pain before performing
Radial-radial & radial-femoral delay	- checks for arterial occlusion (usually due to atherosclerotic plaques)
	- radial – radial: due to subclavian artery coarctation, may compromise CABG operations
	- radial – femoral: due to coarctation of aorta
BP	- it is good practise to do both lying & standing BPs
JVP	- equivalent to pressure in R atrium
	- the JVP will collapse if palpated
	- it can be made more prominent by applying pressure to the stomach (ask if patient has any abdomen pain first)
	- normal = <4cm up neck (i.e. not above mediastinum, when patient lining at 45°)
	- causes of ↑JVP: right ventricular failure (heart failure), tricuspid stenosis & regurgitation, fluid overload, pericardial effusion or constrictive pericarditis
	JVP has a double pulse wave:
	1. 'a' wave = atrial systole/contraction (↑'a' wave =tricuspid stenosis, also there is no 'a' wave in AF)
	2. 'v' wave = just before tricuspid valve opens (↑=tricuspid regurge)
Carotid pulse	- use your thumb (do not palpate both sides at same time or patient may collapse)
	- comment on volume & character
	- small volume = low output (aortic/mitral stenosis, pericardial effusion or peripheral vascular disease)
	- large volume = diastolic overload (aortic/mitral regurge) or fluid overload (↑BP)
	- character: slow rising = aortic stenosis
	- N.B. pulsus paradoxus =↑vol on expiration & ↓vol on inspiration (>15mmHg is pathological = severe airway obstruction or pericardial tamponade)

Eyes & Mouth	- eyes: anaemia (pale conjunctivae), jaundice (yellow sclera), hyperlipidaemia (corneal arcus =white/yellow band around iris), hypercholesterolemia (xanthelasma =yellow skin around eyes)
	- mouth: central cyanosis (blue lips), dental hygiene, high palate (marfan's syndrome can ⇒mitral valve prolapse & aortic regurge, *see 'Syndromes' section in appendix*)
	- malar flush (rosy cheeks with blue tinge, due to pulmonary hypertension & low cardiac output e.g. mitral stenosis)

Focused Chest Exam

Close inspection	- comment on scars, feel for thrills (palpable murmurs) & find apex beat
	- thrills: feel with palm of hand over each valve (aortic, pulmonary, tricuspid & mitral = <u>A</u>ndy, <u>P</u>andy, <u>T</u>eddy & <u>Me</u>)
	- apex beat: start at mid axillary line and work towards centre of chest, it is normally found at the 5th intercostal space mid clavicular line
Auscultation of chest	1. listen over each valve (see diagram): <u>A</u>ndy, <u>P</u>andy, <u>T</u>eddy & <u>Me</u> (feel pulse at same time to coordinate beat with heart sound, S1-beat-S2) - 1st heart sound (S1) = ventricular valves opening (mainly the aortic), best heard at apex - 2nd heart sound (S2) = blood slapping back against the ventricular valves after they have closed (mainly the aortic) 2. roll on L side, ask patient to breath out & hold on expiration, listen at apex with bell (best position to hear mitral stenosis) 3. sit patient forward, ask to hold on expiration, listen over aortic valve with diaphragm (best position to hear aortic regurge) - listen for murmurs, 3rd & 4th heart sounds, clicks/snaps (e.g. artificial valves) & for a pericardial rub, *see murmurs section in 'CV revision'* - NB. the bell hears low pitched sounds better (e.g. mitral stenosis)
Auscultate lungs	- whilst patient is sitting forward, listen to lungs & inspect the back for sacral oedema
do quick CV exam of abdomen & legs if you have time or say "I would end this examination by inspecting the abdomen & peripheral vasculature" (for more info see 'Peripheral Vascular' section)	
Abdomen	- palpate/percuss for liver boarders, palpate for spleen & blot kidneys - feel for AAA (= an expansile pulsation, *see 'Gastroenterology Examination' section*)
Inspect & palpate legs	- pitting oedema = right heart failure - DVTs, varicose veins & ulcers
Check leg/foot pulses	- dorsalis pedis, posterior tibial & popliteal on both legs

Cardiovascular Revision

↑Blood Pressure (BP)	- BP = cardiac output × peripheral resistance - cardiac output = HR × stroke volume types of ↑BP: 1. primary/essential hypertension = genetic + lifestyle factors cause 95% of cases 2. secondary to: renal disease/failure, ↑steroids, coarctation, ↑renin secretion, diabetes, vascular disease, pregnancy (pre-eclampsia) - can ⇒cerebrovascular incidents, coronary artery disease (atherosclerosis), LVH, retinopathy, renal failure (glomerular vasculature damage ⇒proteinuria) - tests: bloods (inc. U&Es =renal function), ECG, CXR, echo + USS kidneys - treatment (=ABCDs): ACE inhibitors, β blockers, Ca channel agonists, diuretics, statins + LIFESTYLE changes (stop smoking/alcohol, ↓weight/salt intake, exercise, etc.) - N.B. hypertensive retinopathy = arterial nipping (arteries cutting across veins), silver wiring (↑arterial musculature), flame haemorrhages (blood explodes out of capillaries due to ↑BP), cotton wool spots (areas of ischaemia), papilloedema (swelling around optic disc ⇒optic disc ischaemia) - *more information on drugs can be found in the 'Cardiac Medications' section*
Lipids	- ↑cholesterol/lipids ⇒atherosclerosis - cholesterol is obtained from the diet + created (from acetate) & destroyed by the liver then excreted as bile salts - triglyceride (a lipoprotein) is the form in which the body stores/transports dietary fat - types: VLDL (rich in triglyceride) transports lipids from liver to tissues where it is catabolised into LDL (bad in blood as rich in cholesterol), HDL is the good form as it carries cholesterol from tissues to the liver for disposal - treatment for hyperlipidaemia: lifestyle (diet), statins (inhibit HMG-CoA reductase ⇒↓cholesterol synthesis by liver & ↑cholesterol uptake from blood by liver) - N.B. when giving statins for the first time monitor LFTs closely
Cardiac enzymes	- certain enzymes are released from cardiac muscle cells when they are damaged, their presence in the blood is therefore used to diagnosed MI - creatine kinase CK (found in brain, skeletal & myocardial muscle), peaks day 1, high for 3 days - CK-MB (myocardial bound CK, specific to heart), peaks day 1, high for 3 days - Troponin T (specific to myocardial damage), peaks day 1, high for 7 days - aspartate transaminase AST (also in RBCs, kidney, liver & lung), peaks day 2, high for 3 days - lactate dehydrogenase LDH (also in RBCs, liver & skeletal muscle), high from day 2-7, peaks day 3 - N.B. Troponin T is the test normally used to diagnose MI, its levels are measured 12 hours post onset of chest pain, generally a level >0.03 = positive, but this maybe higher in a patient with renal failure due to ↓ability to expel waste products from blood

Acute coronary syndrome (ACS)	-	this encompasses a range of diseases that are all due to $\downarrow O_2$ reaching the heart via the coronary arteries, usually due to a blockage within them
	types:	
	1.	unstable angina
	2.	non ST elevation MI (NSTEMI)
	3.	MI (with ST elevation)
	-	think of ischaemic heart disease as a scale of 1 to 10, stable angina (not an ACS) would be at 1-2, unstable angina about 4-5, NSTEMI about 7-8 & MI at 10
	-	tests: ECG straight away, bloods (inc. FBC for anaemia, glucose, U&Es for electrolyte imbalance) + chest X-ray (to rule out respiratory causes, aortic dissection, cardiomegaly, etc.), N.B. check cardiac enzymes 12hrs post attack (trop T)
	-	all ACS is treated initially the same: resus, O_2, aspirin (300mg) + clopidogrel (300mg), GTN, analgesia = IV morphine (via titrated dose, usually 5-10mg + antiemetic) +/- heparin (clexane = 1mg/kg)
	-	mnemonic: MONAC = Morphine, Oxygen, Nitrates, Aspirin, & Clopidogrel
	-	general post event treatment: lifestyle + rehab advice, daily aspirin, β blockers (to reduce heart's O_2 demand), exercise ECG +/- echo
	-	long term treatments if required: lifestyle improvements, ACE inhibitors, aspirin, β blockers or Ca channel blockers, GTN (when needed), statin, coronary angioplasty (balloon dilatation of coronary arteries) & CABG surgery
Chronic coronary syndrome (stable angina)	-	rupture/erosion of coronary artery plaque $\Rightarrow$thrombosis $\Rightarrow$partial occlusion $\Rightarrow$myocardial ischaemia
	-	symptoms: central tight/heavy chest pain (brought on by exertion relieved by rest & GTN), can radiate to jaw/neck/arm, associated symptoms (SOB, nausea & sweating)
	-	tests: as ACS above + ECG (can $\Rightarrow$ST depression) & Trop T = -'ve (no myocardial damage)
	-	immediate treatment: ACS protocol (MONAC), do not need thrombolytics
	-	post event treatment & long term treatment as ACS above
Non-ST elevation MI (NSTEMI) & Unstable angina	-	severe ischaemic chest pain can radiate to jaw/neck/arm + sweating, nausea + may have history of angina
	-	tests: as ACS
	-	possible ECG changes: ST depression &/or T wave inversion
	-	can differentiate between them as only NSTEMI $\Rightarrow\uparrow$cardiac enzymes =myocardial damage, angina is only a partial arterial blockage so it does not $\Rightarrow$myocardial damage
	-	treatment: ACS protocol (do not need thrombolytics)
	-	post event treatment & long term treatment as ACS above
	-	NB. unstable angina = symptoms begin when at rest & with $\uparrow$frequency + severity = high risk of MI
Myocardial infarction (MI)	-	rupture/erosion of coronary artery plaque $\Rightarrow$thrombosis $\Rightarrow$total occlusion $\Rightarrow$ischaemic necrosis $\Rightarrow$ECG changes (ST elevation)
	-	if not treated (by thrombolysis) can $\Rightarrow$Q wave/full thickness MI
	-	symptoms: severe central crushing chest pain (can radiate to jaw/neck/arm) lasting >20mins (not relieved by GTN/nitrates) + SOB, sweating, N&V
	-	tests: as ACS + exclude aortic dissection & pericarditis
	-	treat as ACS + consider thrombolytics or immediate coronary angioplasty if possible (artificial dilatation of coronary arteries via balloon/stent), β blockers,

	<ul><li>diuretics, catheterize (to monitor urine output), admit to coronary care unit</li><li>post MI treatment & long term treatment as ACS above</li><li>complications (immediate, early, late): ventricular arrhythmias (VF/VT, due to ↓K, hypoxia & acidosis), AF, reinfarct, papillary muscle rupture/ischaemia (⇒valve incompetence ⇒regurge, usually mitral), DVT/PE (initially treat with high dose heparin then with warfarin for 3-6 months), chronic heart failure, dressler's syndrome (self limiting autoimmune pericarditis, bloods = ↑inflammatory markers)</li></ul>
Aortic dissection/aneurysm	<ul><li>chronic ↑BP + atherosclerosis ⇒tear in intima layer of vessel wall ⇒bleed into aortic wall ⇒raising flap ⇒interruption of blood supply to vital organs</li><li>symptoms: abrupt extreme pain in chest or back + ↑BP (different in each arm)</li><li>type A: tear in ascending aorta, tracks to heart, can occlude carotid artery ⇒stroke, coronary artery ⇒MI, stretch the aortic valve ⇒aortic regurge & rupture into pericardium ⇒tamponade, has poor prognosis, patient needs emergency surgery</li><li>type B: tear in descending aorta, tracks distally, can occlude renal artery ⇒renal failure, celiac/mesenteric artery ⇒gut ischaemia & iliac arteries ⇒leg ischaemia, type B has a better prognosis, treated with surgery if severe</li><li>both can rupture, which is usually fatal</li><li>imaging = CXR & CT scan</li></ul>
Heart failure	<ul><li>inability to maintain cardiac output (CO) ⇒compensatory mechanisms, e.g. ↑vasoconstrictor release (renin, angiotensin II, catecholamines) ⇒salt & water retention (↑BP) + ↑cardiac afterload (↓diameter of vessels means ↑force/work is needed to pump blood = ↑strain on heart) ⇒↓LV emptying ⇒further ↓CO ⇒more & more compensation ⇒continual decline (this system is now mechanically inefficient, NB. starling's law)</li></ul> types:<ol><li>acute failure = L heart failure quicker than compensatory mechanisms can develop ⇒SOB due to acute pulmonary oedema (worse when lying)</li><li>chronic failure = R heart failure (can be 2° to lung disease) ⇒peripheral overload, ↑JVP & ascites/pitting oedema</li><li>congestive heart failure = L ⇒pulmonary hypertension ⇒R ⇒peripheral overload</li></ol><ul><li>causes: ischaemic heart disease, post MI, valve disease, rhythm disorders, fluid overload, myocarditis</li><li>X-ray findings: cardiomegaly, pulmonary oedema, pleural effusions, engorged veins & kerley B lines (show fluid level of small pockets of fluid in lungs)</li><li>ECG = LVH +/- ischaemic changes</li><li>treatment: lifestyle, diuretics, ACE inhibitor, angiotensin II inhibitors, β blockers, digoxin & anticoagulation</li><li>N.B. during lung auscultation fluid sounds like fine crackles at the lung bases</li></ul>
Murmurs	<ul><li>1st heart sound = ventricular valves opening (mainly the aortic)</li><li>2nd heart sound = blood slapping back against the ventricular valves after they have closed (mainly the aortic)</li><li>systole = ventricular valves open, atrial valves closed</li><li>diastole = ventricular valves closed, atrial valves open</li></ul> a good way to remember murmurs:<ul><li>stenosis happens when valves are open, regurge happens when valves are closed</li><li>systolic murmur = aortic valve open (aortic stenosis) &/or mitral valve closed</li></ul>

	- (mitral regurge) - diastolic murmur = aortic valve closed (aortic regurge) &/or mitral valve open (mitral stenosis) - NB. 3rd & 4th heart sounds can happen when valves become uncoordinated e.g. bundle branch block
Aortic stenosis S1 S2	- due to calcification of aortic valve (usually due to rheumatic fever or wear & tear), quicker onset if also ↑cholesterol - symptoms: effort SOB, angina, syncope & sudden cardiac death - signs: harsh ejection systolic murmur (heard most in aortic valve region) radiating to carotids + slow rising pulse (low systolic = narrow pulse pressure), can ⇒absent 2nd heart sound + LVH (due to obstructed emptying) - can also ⇒L heart failure & ischaemia ⇒angina - investigations: bloods, ECG (shows LVH), echocardiography (shows ↓emptying velocity of L ventricle) & CXR (enlarged heart, dilated ascending aorta +/- calcification on the aortic valve) - treatment: anti endocarditis advice (antibiotic prophylaxis), β blockers (↓angina), anticoagulation +/- valve replacement
Aortic regurge S1 S2	causes: 1. disease effecting valve (rheumatic heart disease, endocarditis, SLE) 2. disease dilating aortic root & therefore effecting the valve ring (aortic dissection/aneurysm or connective tissue disorders e.g. marfan's) - symptoms: SOB + palpitations, can ⇒L heart failure (due to backflow into the L ventricle ⇒LVH, which can ⇒ischaemia ⇒angina) - signs: early diastolic murmur (heard best when patient leaning forward), collapsing pulse (due to wide pulse pressure, i.e. low diastolic) & displaced apex (due to volume overload) - investigations: bloods, ECG (shows LVH) + cardiac echo + CXR (enlarged heart + dilated ascending aorta) - treatment: ACE inhibitors, diuretics, anticoagulation +/- surgery (valve replacement) - N.B. wide pulse pressure can also ⇒corrigan's sign (visible carotid pulsation), musset's sign (head bobbing) & quincke's sign (nail bed pulsation)
Mitral stenosis S1 S2	- usually due to previous rheumatic fever - can result in AF (can ⇒thromboemboli) and L atrial hypertrophy (⇒pulmonary hypertension/oedema ⇒RV hypertrophy ⇒R heart failure) - signs: mid diastolic murmur with opening snap, tapping apex beat, malar flush (cyanotic cheeks), low volume pulse & signs of heart failure (↑JVP and oedema) - tests: bloods, echo, ECG & CXR (atrial enlargement) - treatment: diuretics (↓preload), digoxin (if suffering with AF), anticoagulation, antibiotic prophylaxis +/- surgery
Mitral regurge S1 S2	causes: 1. valve disease (rheumatic heart disease, endocarditis or damage to papillary muscles) 2. secondary to LV dilatation ⇒mitral ring stretching - symptoms: effort SOB, angina, syncope, can ⇒R heart failure due to L atrial hypertrophy *(see mitral stenosis)* - signs: pansystolic murmur radiates to axilla & a displaced apex (due to volume overload), can ⇒AF - treatment: ACE, diuretics, anticoagulation +/- surgery - N.B. aortic valve disease ⇒LVH, mitral ⇒LAH, RVH & AF

Cardiomyopathy	- various diseases of the heart muscle, types:
	1. dilated: large volume heart (systolic dysfunction) ⇒mitral regurge (due to stretched mitral valve ring) + AF, usually genetic or due to alcohol excess
	2. hypertrophic: genetic (autosomal dominant, affects young), a thick myocardium (especially the septum) ⇒LV outflow obstruction ⇒aortic stenosis symptoms
	3. restrictive: diastolic dysfunction ⇒heart failure, commonly due to amyloid deposition (multiple myeloma)
Acute pericarditis	- inflammation of pericardium
	- symptoms: pleuritic chest pain (sharp stabbing pain radiates to neck/shoulder relieved by sitting up), pericardial rub & general fever/fatigue
	- ECG shows saddle shaped ST elevation
	- causes: viral, post MI, autoimmune dressler's syndrome (post MI), post cardiac surgery, bacterial & vasculitis (rheumatoid disease, SLE)
	- treat cause: NSAIDs, steroids, antibiotics & analgesia
Pericardial effusion	- fluid in pericardial space, can be:
	1. transudate (↓protein = heart/liver failure or nephrotic syndrome)
	2. exudate (↑protein = acute pericarditis, malignancy)
	3. blood (haemopericardium = aortic dissection, trauma)
	4. purulent (bacteria)
	- if cardiac filling compromised ⇒cardiac tamponade (↓CO ⇒tachycardia & ↓BP)
	- signs: quiet heart sounds, apex beat difficult to palpate, ECG (shows low voltage trace), CXR (large globular heart), & kussmaul's sign (↑JVP when inspiring)
	- treatment: surgical drainage (pericardiocentesis)
Constrictive pericarditis	- fibrosis due to chronic/relapsing pericarditis
	- often due to TB, RA or radiotherapy
	- symptoms: pericardial knock (loud diastolic sound), exercise SOB, AF, oedema & ascites
	- diagnosis: cardiac catheterisation, blood (infective/inflammatory markers), ECG
	- treatment: lifestyle advice, diuretics, digoxin (if AF), β blockers, & aspirin
Infective endocarditis	- usually due to strep, staph aureus/epidermis or enterococci, commonly infected during dentist visit
	- effects heart valves ⇒mainly aortic, but also mitral regurge
	- signs: signs of infection (fever, N&V, etc.), splinter haemorrhages, osler's nodes (painful lesions on finger pulps), janeway lesions (lesions on palms & soles, non-tender), & roth spots on retina (retina haemorrhages with pale centres)
	- can result in cardiac failure, pericarditis, haemolytic anaemia, meningitis, emboli & renal failure
	- diagnosis: 3 separate blood cultures (before antibiotics given), bloods (signs of infection/inflammation & chronic disease e.g. anaemia), ECG, CXR & echo
	- treatment: IV antibiotics, lifelong antibiotic prophylaxis (before surgery or dental work) +/- surgery (valve replacement)
	- NB. IV drug users ⇒tricuspid valve infection
Myocarditis	- inflammation of heart muscle
	- causes: infection, autoimmune or radiation (e.g. radiotherapy)
	- ⇒ tachycardia out of proportion to heart failure & ↑cardiac enzymes
	- tests: bloods (signs of infection and inflammation), ECG & CXR
	- treat cause
Acute rheumatic fever (RF)	- group A strep infection (usually in throat) ⇒immune response ⇒RF
	- usually occurs at 5-15 yrs of age, approx. 50% ⇒valve disease in later life
	- treat with aspirin & lifelong antibiotic prophylaxis

Peripheral Vascular Examination

Due to it being less developed the leg vasculature is 8 times more likely to be effected by disease than the arms

Introduction	- wash hands - approach politely and introduce yourself - patient's name & DOB - explain to patient what you are going to do & obtain verbal consent - expose patient after asking
Arterial system examination	- inspect the limbs for ischaemic changes (colour & temp), pitting/peripheral oedema & scars - assess capillary refill time in finger tips (normal < 2secs) - palpate radial pulse (comment on rate & rhythm) & carotid (volume & character) - check BP in both arms (if different = coarctation) - assess radial – radial delay (if delay detected = subclavian coarctation, may effect CABG surgery) - abdomen: palpate for a AAA (expansile pulsation, *see 'Gastroenterology Exam' section*) & an enlarged liver + listen for renal & abdominal artery bruits - assess radial – femoral delay (if delay detected = coarctation of aorta) - inspect leg pulses: femoral (volume & character), popliteal (in popliteal fossa), posterior tibial & dorsalis pedis - listen for murmurs/bruits over femoral arteries - feet: capillary refill time (normal < 2secs), assess temp (with back of hand) then closely inspect between each toe & bottom of feet - buerger's test: elevate legs off bed, ischaemic legs will look pale at 15-30° - NB. femoral vessel position mnemonic (NAVY): <u>N</u>erve, <u>A</u>rtery, <u>V</u>ein, <u>Y</u>-fronts
Venous system examination	- inspect for colour change, swelling, superficial venous dilatation & tortuosity (twisting & turning) + scars from previous surgery - assess temp (with back of hand down both legs, feel for temp change) - haemosiderin: brown pigmentation (= oxidized iron deposited in the skin), due to ↑venous pressure - lipodermatosclerosis: chronic ↑venous pressure ⇒fibrin deposited into skin ⇒sclerosis of skin - inspect for venous ulcers *(see 'Peripheral Vascular Revision' section)* - trendelenburg test (investigates cause of varicose veins): elevate and milk blood from leg, put pressure over saphenofemoral junction (finger or tourniquet), ask patient to stand, if the varicosed veins are due to saphenofemoral junction incompetence they will not refill until the pressure is removed, if the veins refill whilst the tourniquet is applied the defect is below the saphenofemoral junction anatomy: - long saphenous vein path = medial aspect of calf & thigh, joins with femoral vein at saphenofemoral junction (2-3cm lateral of pubic tubercle) - short saphenous vein path = posterior aspect of calf, joins with popliteal vein behind knee at saphenopopliteal junction

Peripheral Vascular Revision

Intermittent claudication	- due to insufficient arterial blood supply - mainly affects calves but can ascend to thighs & buttocks (can ⇒impotency) - symptoms: calf pain during exercise, disappears at rest - associated symptoms: ↓skin temp, ↓/absent foot pulses, ↓hair on calves, arterial bruits, muscle weakness & ↓sensation - tests: investigate whole cardiovascular system + bloods (inc. clotting profile), doppler USS & ABPI (ankle:brachial pressure index, should be > 1 when lying flat), angiography (radio-opaque contrast injected & X-ray taken) - treat cardiac symptoms + lifestyle changes, aspirin, balloon angioplasty, re-vascularisation/grafting surgery - NB. claudication can also be venous (⇒oedema & varicose veins) or neurogenic (spinal stenosis ⇒bilateral leg pain)
Limb ischaemia (6Ps)	- symptoms = 6Ps: pulse less, pallor, perishing cold, paraesthesia, paralysis, pain - can ⇒hair loss & +'ve buerger's test, *see 'Peripheral Vascular Exam'* causes: 1. embolus (fragment of blood clot) ⇒acute & profound ischaemia, check for AF/prosthetic valves/trauma, usually no history of claudication, pulses usually present in other leg 2. thrombosis (gradually grows in vessel): insidious onset & less severe ischaemia, history of claudication, pulses often absent in both legs - tests: investigate whole CV system + bloods (inc. clotting profile), doppler USS & ABPI (ankle:brachial pressure index, should be > 1 when lying flat), angiography - treatment: anticoagulation (high dose heparin short term, convert to warfarin if needed for 6 months or longer), analgesia, thrombolysis (dissolves clots if used within 24hrs) - surgical treatment: for emboli =embolectomy, thrombosis = angioplasty or bypass surgery
Deep vein thrombosis (DVT)	- mainly in legs but can also affect axillary vein of arm - risk factors: recent bed rest/operation/long flight, history of DVT/trauma to leg, pregnancy, smoking, FH of thrombosis types: 1. partially occluded thrombus: pain, calf tenderness, no swelling, slight localised ↑temp, normal superficial veins, high risk of PE (blood flow past thrombus could dislodge a small emboli) 2. occlusive thrombus: pain, calf tenderness, swelling/erythema, pitting oedema, localised ↑temp, distended superficial veins, low PE risk - if swollen measure circumference of each leg & compare - tests: d-dimer (fibrin breakdown product, is not specific as raised in other diseases, but -'ve result is usually conclusive = no DVT), doppler USS, venography (venous X-ray with dye) - prevention: stop oral contraceptive pill, mobilize, TED stockings, aspirin &/or heparin/warfarin - treatment: high dose heparin then warfarin (aim for INR 2-3 for 6 months), if recurrent DVTs then lifelong warfarin DVTs are due to one or more of virchow's triad of factors: 1. venous stasis = recent long journey, immobility & prolonged pressure 2. vessel damage = surgery & trauma 3. ↑coagulation = thromboembolic disease, COCP & pregnancy

Leg ulcers	types: 1. venous: caused by DVT or varicosed veins, mainly effects women, 40-60 yrs old, usually on lower limbs, have irregular margin with neo epithelium (new skin formation, whiter than mature skin), pulses are present 2. arterial: caused by atherosclerosis, thrombi/emboli & diabetes, usually afflicts men >60 yrs with history of peripheral arterial/cardiovascular/cerebrovascular disease, risk factors (smoking, diabetes, ↑BP, ↑cholesterol), cause severe pain (unless neuropathic diabetes), usually found on pressure areas, have regular margins, green/black coloured with no granulation (no signs of healing), limbs are cold & their pulses absent 3. neuropathic: usually due to diabetes (⇒peripheral nerve damage, *see 'Endocrine Revision' section*) 4. those caused by burns & trauma - treatment: local (clean area, elevate & apply compressive bandage unless leg is ischaemic), systemic (↑blood supply, oral antibiotics, anticoagulation), surgery (skin graft)
Varicose veins	- dilated superficial leg veins - due to defects in muscle pump system & vein valves (e.g. sapheno-femoral junction) - symptoms: pain, itching, swelling, worse after prolonged standing - treat with lifestyle changes, TED stockings & surgery (if severe)
Thrombophlebitis	- inflammation due to thrombosis of superficial veins ⇒trauma +/- infection of vessel - treat with antibiotics if needed
Raynaud's	- colour, sensation & temp changes when hands & feet exposed to cold - overtime the disease ⇒muscle wasting & can ⇒gangrene at finger tips types: 1. primary = raynaud's disease, due to digital artery vasospasm 2. secondary = raynaud's syndrome, due to digital artery obstruction, connective tissue disease (sclerosis) or vibration injury - if unilateral & patient >40 yrs old check for peripheral arterial disease - treat by keeping hands warm + nifedipine medication (a vasodilator)

ECG Interpretation + Arrhythmias

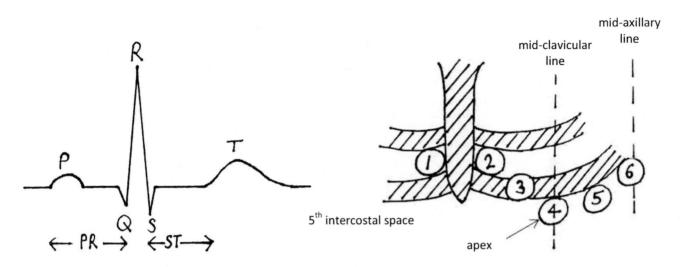

normal ECG tracing & where to place the chest leads for a '12 lead ECG'

ECG anatomy	- P wave (atrial depolarization) = electrical impulse created in the sinoatrial node propagates via the atria to the atrioventricular node, if P wave present is known as sinus rhythm - PR interval = time from sinoatrial node impulse until AV node impulse, the AV node stores charge until there is enough to create a full ventricular impulse, this time also allows the atria to empty all their blood into the ventricles - QRS complex (ventricular depolarization) = release of the electrical impulse from the AV node →down the bundle-of-his/purkinje fibres →bundle branches→ventricles ⇒ventricles contract from the bottom up - ST segment = period from the end of ventricular depolarization to the beginning of ventricular repolarisation - T wave = repolarisation/recovery of the ventricles
Reporting steps	- patient's name & DOB, date ECG recorded, rate, rhythm, *axis*, P wave, PR interval, QRS complex, ST segment, T wave
Rate (bpm)	- normal settings: large square = 0.2seconds, small square = 0.04seconds - beats per minute (bpm) = 300 divided by large squares between QRS peaks - bradycardia (<60bpm) = heart block, inferior MI, hypothyroid, hypothermia, sinoatrial node disease, drugs (β blockers, digoxin, verapamil) or can be normal in very healthy individuals - tachycardia (>100bpm) = anxiety, fever/infection, pregnancy, shock, anaemia, PE, thyrotoxicosis, heart failure, medication/drugs (salbutamol) + many more, basically this is a sign something maybe physiologically wrong
Rhythm	- types: regular, regularly irregular (e.g. 2nd degree heart block), irregularly irregular (AF = no p waves present) - sinus rhythm = p waves present (signifies normal atria depolarisation) - to assess rhythm trace a number of QRS peaks onto the edge of a piece of paper then move the paper along the ECG, if the distance between the marks continues to match other QRS peaks = regular rhythm

Tachy arrhythmias	types: 1. narrow (QRS) complex = supraventricular (due to signals arising from above ventricles), arrhythmias arise in atria or AV node, the impulse propagates normally through the ventricles via the bundle-of-his 2. broad (QRS) complex = due to arrhythmias that arise within the ventricles, are caused by ectopic foci (firing faster than the SA node) or due to re-entry circuits, and impulse starting in the ventricles, all these abnormal impulses do not propagate as fast as those via the bundle-of-his $\Rightarrow$a broad complex QRS (N.B. broad $\equiv \uparrow$time, so a broad complex = full impulse takes longer to propagate) - symptoms: chest pain, palpitations, dizziness, syncope/LOC, $\downarrow$BP & death - tests: bloods (inc. FBC, LFTs, U&Es, Ca, Mg, TFT), ECG (normal, exercise & 24hr tape), CXR & echo - treat underlying cause - N.B. usually tachycardia arise because cardiac output needs to be maintained, this puts stress on the heart & increases its O_2 demands, making the system inefficient
Supraventricular tachycardia, SVT (narrow complex QRS)	causes: 1. natural i.e. due to a raised heart rate (see causes of tachycardia above) 2. the AV node usually has a relatively slow depolarisation & refractory period but a re-entrant circuit in the node overrides this - $\Rightarrow$regular narrow QRS complex tachycardia (150-200 bpm) + regular p waves - type 1 = treat underlying cause, type 2 = vagotonic manoeuvres, IV adenosine, β blockers or surgery (radiofrequency ablation destroys circuit pathway)
Atrial fibrillation, AF (narrow complex QRS)	- in this case the atria depolarize at 300bpm but the AV node limits ventricular depolarisation due to its refraction period $\Rightarrow$irregular irregular beat with no visible p waves - causes: cardiac (ischaemic/valvular heart disease, $\uparrow$BP), respiratory (PE), hyperthyroid, alcohol, infection, metabolic & many more - treat underlying cause + anticoagulation, if chronic consider β blockers first line followed by digoxin (a rate stabilizer), if continues consider amiodarone (converts back to sinus rhythm) or DC cardioversion
Atrial flutter (narrow complex QRS)	- micro re-entry circuit moving clockwise inside the R atria $\Rightarrow$300bpm atrial depolarization, but due to AV node only a 'specific fraction' are passed to the ventricles - typically $\Rightarrow$150bpm (2:1), 100bpm (3:1), etc. - ECG: regular narrow QRS complexes + 'saw-tooth' appearance (=atrial depolarization) - treat as AF
Wolff-parkinson-white syndrome (narrow complex QRS)	- defect in the atrial-ventricular wall $\Rightarrow$electrical impulse via direct accessory pathway from atria to ventricle bypassing the AV node - $\Rightarrow$part of the ventricular myocardium depolarizes before the normal contraction wave propagates via the bundle-of-his & through the ventricles - $\Rightarrow\downarrow$PR interval & slurred start of QRS + narrow complex tachycardia - treat with cardiac medication & surgical ablation to destroy accessory pathway

Ventricular tachycardia (VT) & ventricular fibrillation (VF) (broad complex QRS)	- these are the only shockable rhythms - can be due to: MI, ↓/↑potassium, heart failure, & many more VT types: 1. monomorphic VT = uniform (120-190bpm), due to re-entrant circuits within the ventricles caused by scarring usually from a previous MI 2. polymorphic VT = less regular + has torsades de pointes (varying height of QRS complexes), usually due to abnormal ventricular triggering caused by metabolic changes, ischaemia, or drugs - treatment: resus (ABCs) + cardiac arrest algorithm, need to establish & treat underlying cause - VF is also due to a number of heart diseases, it results in a broad complex tachycardia that is chaotic (whereas VT is more ordered & uniform), treat as VT
Axis	- this is an imaginary line passing through the heart's apex calculated from the sum of all the electrical impulse vectors picked up by an ECG, in healthy patients it points between 0-90° (imagine a clock face, 0° = 3 O'clock & 90° = 6 O'clock) - there are a number of technical ways to calculate the axis using vector analysis, but a short cut for recognising deviation is: - normal: I & aV_F = +'ve - L deviation: aV_F = −'ve (i.e. the ECG tracing in aV_F has more points below the imaginary x-axis than above it) - R deviation: I = −'ve causes of deviation: 1. Left = LBBB, LVH, cardiomyopathy 2. Right = infancy, RBBB, RVH, lung disease, PE, pulmonary stenosis - N.B. if I was you I would skip this step when reporting ECGs, unless you are specifically asked to calculate it, it takes too long to calculate & is not required at junior level
PR interval	- for a healthy heart this should be between 0.12-0.2seconds (3-5 small squares) - if increased/widened think heart block - N.B. PR segment depression may indicate atrial injury or pericarditis
Heart block	- causes: disease of AV node, bundle of his, or purkinje fibres - the later stages of the disease usually result in bradycardia because less electrical signals are passing to the ventricles types: 1. 1st degree: ↑PR interval, treat by observation 2. 2nd degree (mobitz 1/wenckebach): each beat results in a progressively increasing PR interval ⇒a missed beat, which then resets the PR interval & the cycle beings again, patient may need a pacemaker 3. 2nd degree (mobitz 2): not all P waves are conducted, PR interval can be normal, always ⇒complete heart block, pacemaker needed 4. 3rd degree (complete heart block): no P waves conducted to the ventricles, no connection between P & QRS, P wave & ventricular escape rhythms become independent + QRS complex can look widened due to improper ventricular conduction, urgent pacemaker needed - N.B. imagine heart block as increasing degrees of damage to the conducting fibres between the atria & ventricles, with complete heart block being total destruction of these fibres ⇒no signal can pass

QRS complex	- corresponds to depolarisation of the ventricles
	- should be <0.12seconds (3 squares)
	abnormalities:
	1. widened = bundle branch block (BBB)
	2. tall = ventricular hypertrophy (VH) diagnosed when distance between tallest R & deepest S >35mm = 7 large squares
	- NB. ventricular hypertrophy usually signifies increased muscle in the wall of the ventricles due to increased demands on the heart, the more muscular the heart the more blood/O_2 supply it requires, if this demand is not met can $\Rightarrow$angina-like symptoms
Left ventricular hypertrophy (LVH)	- ECG: $V_{5/6}$ = tall R wave + $V_{1/2}$ = deep S wave
	causes (any disease that requires the L ventricle to pump harder $\Rightarrow\uparrow$muscle over time):
	1. $\uparrow$L ventricular outflow resistance: $\uparrow$BP, AAA, aortic stenosis, hypertrophic cardiomyopathy
	2. $\downarrow$emptying of L ventricle: aortic/mitral regurge
	3. $\uparrow$L ventricular requirements (high output states): thyrotoxicosis & anaemia
Right ventricular hypertrophy (RVH)	- ECG: V_1 R wave > S wave
	causes:
	1. $\uparrow$ R ventricular outflow resistance: pulmonary artery hypertension (lung diseases), pulmonary valve stenosis
	2. $\downarrow$ emptying of R ventricle: pulmonary/tricuspid regurge
	3. $\uparrow$ R ventricular filling: high output states, $\uparrow$blood volume (too much fluids, kidney failure)
Left bundle branch block (LBBB) WiLliaM	- damage/interruption to left bundle branch conduction
	- ECG: V_1 Down & Left
	- remember neumonic = V_1 WiLliaM V_6, V_1 looks like a W & V_6 looks like a M)
	- causes: ischaemic heart disease, LVH, aortic valve disease, cardiomyopathy, myocarditis
	- N.B. think of BBB in the same way as heart block, but in this case the damaged conducting fibres are in the bundle branches $\Rightarrow$widened QRS instead of PR interval
Right bundle branch block (RBBB) MaRroW	- damage/interruption to right bundle branch conduction
	- ECG: V_1 Up & Right ($\equiv V_1$ MaRroW V_6, V_1 looks like a M & V_6 looks like a W)
	- causes: RVH, RV strain (PE), ischaemic heart disease, congenital heart disease (e.g. septal defects), myocarditis
ST segment	- elevation = acute MI
	- depression = ischaemia, recent MI, posterior MI, digoxin, $\uparrow$BP, $\downarrow$K
	- saddle shaped = pericarditis
MI regions	- assessing the heart region that has been infarcted can be simple, just work out which leads show ST elevation & remember where they are positioned on the body (see diagram at start of this chapter)
	- first do this horizontally: is the elevation anterior ($V_{1\rightarrow3}$) or lateral ($V_{4\rightarrow6}$)
	- then vertically: inferior (aV_F) or superior (aV_L &/or aV_R)
	- N.B. if MI is posterior there maybe ST depression in the V leads
	these are some of the coronary arteries involved depending on the MI region:
	- anterior = L ant. descending
	- inferior = R coronary artery
	- posterior = R coronary or circumflex
	- lateral = circumflex or diagonal branch of L ant. descending

T wave	- represents the repolarisation of the ventricles
	- inverted: is usually due to MI or ischaemia
	- an inverted T wave is normal in lead aVR
	- tall T waves = ↑K (also if more severe ⇒no P wave and wide QRS)
	- N.B. ↓K = ST depression, flat T & U wave (*see 'renal revision' section*)
U Wave	- U waves are thought to represent repolarisation of the papillary muscles or purkinje fibres
	- can be due to a number of diseases e.g. ↓K, ↑Ca, thyrotoxicosis, digoxin
Review	when reporting an ECG comment on the following:
	- rate (bpm): normal, tachycardic or bradycardic
	- rhythm: regular, irregular regular, irregular irregular (AF)
	- p wave: if present = sinus rhythm
	- *axis (I would leave out unless you are specifically asked to calculate)*
	- PR interval: ↑ = heart block (if ↓ think of wolff-parkinson-white syndrome)
	- QRS complex: wide = BBB, tall = hypertrophy
	- ST segment: elevated = MI, depressed = ischaemia
	- T wave: tall = ↑K, flat = ↓K, inverted = MI or ischaemia
	- N.B. if you have the opportunity always compare the current ECG with past readings to assess whether the changes are acute or chronic

CV Medication

Miscellaneous	- **angiotensin-converting enzyme (ACE) inhibitors** (e.g. ramipril): used to ↓BP, works on both arteries & veins by blocking angiotensin II (a vasoconstrictor) & ⇒↓aldosterone production (an antidiuretic), side effects (can ⇒renal failure if patient has renal artery stenosis)
	- **β blocker** (e.g. atenolol): used for HR control, also ⇒↓BP, works by inhibiting β_1 receptors (part of sympathetic/fight or flight system) ⇒↓HR ⇒↓cardiac output =↓work performed by heart ⇒↓O_2 demands, do not use if patient has asthma (lungs contain β_2 receptors that work opposite to β_1, i.e. β blockers ⇒bronchial contraction/spasm), side effects (cold peripheries & can ⇒heart failure)
	- **calcium (Ca) channel blockers** (e.g. amlodipine): used to ↓BP by dilating arteries (including the coronary arteries) ⇒↓afterload (↓force heart needs to push against ⇒reduces hearts workload ⇒↓O_2 demands), has less side effects than β blockers but can ⇒dizziness & hypotension
	- **nitrates** (e.g. GTN): peripheral vessel dilators ⇒↓preload (=↓pressure exerted on heart by blood flowing into it)
	- **dopamine**: activates β_1 receptors (does opposite to β blockers) ⇒↑HR, ↑BP, etc.
	- NB. ↓venous resistance ⇒↓preload, ↓arterial resistance ⇒↓afterload
Anti-arrhythmic drugs	- the sympathetic system stimulates noradrenaline which affects the pacemaker cells in the heart ⇒↓action potential ⇒more frequent signal conduction ⇒↑HR
	- the parasympathetic/vagal system stimulates acetylcholine (ACh) which ⇒↑action potential in the same pacemaker cells ⇒↓HR
	- supraventricular arrhythmias arise in the atria or AV node, ventricular arrhythmias arise in the ventricles, they are all caused by ectopic foci (firing faster than the SA node) or re-entry circuits
	- β blockers are good for stress related ↑HR (e.g. emotions, excitement, thyrotoxicosis, MI)
	- **atropine**: used in bradycardia, works by antagonising/reducing parasympathetic stimulation ⇒↑HR
	- **amiodarone** & **quinidine** are general arrhythmic drugs that act on all heart muscle cells, the AV node & purkinje fibres, quinidine acts by increasing both action potential threshold & refractory period, amiodarone increases repolarisation time & prolongs action potential, both ⇒↓HR & HR stabilization
	- **lignocaine** is also used for ventricular arrhythmias, it blocks Na^+ channels
	- N.B. amiodarone is the drug given in VT/VF arrests, if this is not available give lignocaine
	- **adenosine** causes transient heart block in the AV node, it is used for supraventricular tachycardia (SVT)
	- **digoxin** is used for supraventricular arrhythmias (e.g. AF): it blocks Ca^+ channels (slows conduction & ↑refractory period) in AV node & bundle of his, digoxin is also used for heart failure because ⇒↑cardiac force/muscle contraction, high concentrations of digoxin are toxic
Anticoagulation	- **heparin** (injection, usually given S/C = just under the skin): fast acting & short lasting (~24hrs), works on clotting mechanism
	- **warfarin** (oral): slow acting (~2days) & long lasting (~5days), works on clotting mechanism by blocking the action of vitamin K, patients need regular monitoring, aim for INR of 2-3seconds in most cases (3-4secs for prosthetic heart valves), to reverse its action give vitamin K or fresh frozen plasma (concentrated clotting factors)

	- **aspirin**: irreversible blockage of platelet activation sites, is slow acting & long lasting (have to wait for new platelets to be created), **clopidogrel** works in much the same way - **streptokinase** (fibrinolytic drug) ⇒destruction of fibrin bonds ⇒thrombi breakdown, used for MI & stroke, for best results use within 3 hours of disease process, is not beneficial after 24 hours - main side effect for all anticoagulants is haemorrhage - N.B. anticoagulants need to be stopped before any surgical procedure
Diuretics	- ⇒↓blood volume ⇒↓preload & after load ⇒↓CO (reduced strain on heart) - **thiazides** (e.g. bendrofluazide): safe but weak, inhibit NaCl reabsorption in distal tube (via osmosis this ⇒↓water absorption into the bloodstream) - **loop** (e.g. frusemide): strong, fast acting (IV or oral) & short lasting, inhibits reabsorption of NaCl in loop-of-henle - **potassium (K) sparing** (e.g. spironolactone): weak, usually used in combination with above, can ⇒↑K - side effects: electrolyte imbalances (e.g. ↑U&Es, *see 'Blood Test Interpretation' in appendix*), ↓BP, ↑uric acid & ↓K (unless K sparing) - NB. aldosterone (an antidiuretic) ⇒↑reabsorption of NaCl in distal tube, ⇒↑water reabsorption & at same time ⇒↑K secretion
Treatments (for chronic conditions)	- **lifestyle changes**: ↑activity, ↓weight/alcohol/smoking, ↓salt intake - **hypertension** (ABCD): ACE inhibitor, β blocker, Ca channel blocker, diuretic - **angina**: aspirin/clopidogrel, β blocker & Ca channel blocker, nitrates (GTN = during acute attack &/or isosorbide mononitrate regularly) - **heart failure**: diuretics, ACE, β blocker, as disease progresses give digoxin - **anti-arrhythmic**: general (amiodarone & quinidine), AF (start with β blocker then move onto digoxin), SVT (adenosine), VF/VT (amiodarone +/- cardiac shock conversion) remember the equation BP=CO×PR, where CO=HR×SV, drug effects: - ↓HR = β blocker - ↓SV (stroke volume) = β blocker + diuretics - ↓PR (peripheral resistance) = Ca channel blocker, ACE inhibitors, nitrates, angiotensin II blockers

Respiratory History

Introduction	- approach politely and introduce yourself - patient's name, DOB & occupation

Cough	- onset (how long had symptoms), frequency, timing (worse in morning/day/night), severity & character types: - from larynx: whooping cough, tumour, laryngitis, croup (harsh/barking and persistent) - from bronchi: COPD (usually dry but can be productive when infected, worse in mornings), asthma (dry or productive when infected, worse at night), carcinoma (persistent +/- haemoptysis), pneumonia (productive), fibrosis (dry), pulmonary oedema (worse at night because lying flat results in the oedema/fluid settling over the back of the lungs $\Rightarrow\uparrow$ surface area covered, can $\Rightarrow$ pink frothy sputum)
Sputum	- amount, character, viscosity, taste/odour types: - serous (watery & frothy) = benign or pulmonary oedema (if pink looking) - mucoid (clear, grey/white, frothy) = bronchitis, asthma, COPD - purulent (yellow/green/brown) = bacterial infection/abscess - rusty = pneumococcal pneumonia
Haemoptysis (coughing up blood)	- colour, amount & density (clots, watery, dark, fresh, etc.) - ascertain that definitely due to coughing & not due to vomit - causes: infection (TB, pneumonia, bronchiectasis), bronchial carcinoma, PE (usually following a DVT), trauma, warfarin medication
Chest pain	- SOCRATES (see 'CV History' section for explanation) types: 1. non-central pleuritic pain (worse on breathing): pneumonia, PE, TB, pneumothorax, malignancy 2. non-central chest wall: rib fracture, metastatic bones 3. retrosternal: cardiovascualar, oesophageal, mediastinitis, tracheitis - NB. irritation of diaphragm refers to shoulder
SOB	- onset (at rest, exercising, variability during whole day, sleep disturbance/apnoea), duration, exercise tolerance (how far on flat/hill/stairs), what makes it worse/better (e.g. number of pillows patient sleeps on)
Noises	- wheeze: signifies lower respiratory tract problem (e.g. asthma or COPD), due to airflow through narrowed bronchi, usually during expiration - stridor: upper respiratory tract disease/narrowing/blockage, usually during inspiration (e.g foreign body, anaphylaxis, epiglottitis, trauma)
Weight loss	- how much & over what time period - usually due to: malignancy or the extra effort required to breath in chronic airflow obstruction
Fever or night sweats	- infection (if severe think TB)
PE risk factors (see 'Respiratory Revision' section)	- ask about the following if PE/DVT is a possibility: calf pain/swelling (DVT), COCP (oral contraceptive pill), long distance travel, inactivity, recent surgery, pregnancy, PMH/FH of PE/DVT

PMH	- list PMH + ask DEAR J SMITH *(see 'CV History' section for explanation)* + history of DVT/PE, pneumonia, chronic bronchitis/COPD
Medications, allergies, SMOKING & alcohol	- if ex smoker ask smoking history - NB. long term effects of steroids = thinning/bruising of skin, 'cushing-like' symptoms, ↑BP, acne, ↑weight
FH	- are parents/brothers/sisters alive, if so do they suffer from any diseases, if they have passed away (say "sorry to hear that") ask age & reason of death
Social/occupational history	- expand on occupation: working with asbestos & mouldy hay - keeping pets, birds, etc. - who is at home & how does this condition effect your life

Respiratory Exam

Introduction	- wash your hands - approach politely and introduce yourself - patient's name & DOB - explain to patient what you are going to do & obtain verbal consent - expose patient after asking - position at 45°
Inspection	- comment on patient & surroundings - O_2 mask, sputum pot, inhalers, etc. - does the patient look unwell: hypoxic, SOB (dyspnoea), etc. - noises: stridor (large airway obstruction noise), wheeze, cough - use of intercostal muscles on inspiration - powerful expirations = asthma or chronic bronchitis - puffing through pursed lips = stops bronchial wall collapse in severe airway obstruction/empysema (keeps lung pressure high) - coal dust tattoos
Respiratory rate	- 15/min = normal, ↑RR (is a good sign that something is wrong, e.g. fever, severe lung disease, hyperventilation), ↓RR (sedation) - N.B. changes in RR are a good measure of disease progression
Hands	- clubbing (is found in chronic conditions): respiratory (cancer or long term infection/disease), CV (heart disease), GI (inflammatory bowel disease) & endocrine (hyperthyroid) - peripheral cyanosis (can ⇒ hand muscle wasting over time) - red, warm & clammy can be due to CO_2 retention (palmar erythema) - nicotine stained fingers
Radial pulse	- assess rate & rhythm - if tachycardic think hypoxia (e.g. severe asthma or COPD) or infection
CO_2 retention flap	- hold both arms out straight with wrists bent back for 10seconds - due to ↑CO_2 - signifies type II respiratory failure *(see 'Respiratory Revision' section)*
Eyes	- anaemia - horner's syndrome (small pupil + ptosis = drooping of the upper eyelid) can be due to a pancostal lung tumour compressing the sympathetic nerve
Mouth	- central cyanosis (e.g. blue lips) - usually = unused (deoxygenated) Hb > 5g/dl or O_2 SATS < 85%
JVP	- if increased think right heart failure which can be due to chronic lung disease
Tracheal tug	- tell patient this maybe uncomfortable - put finger in suprasternal notch, if deviated check position of apex beat - causes for deviation: pnemothorax (pushes trachea to the opposite side), collapsed lung (pulls trachea towards problem), mass (cancer), ↑thyroid, etc.
Cervical & scalene lymph nodes	- palpate the scalene node maybe painful as situated deep behind clavicle - NB. subcutaneous emphysema (air under skin due to lung perforation/pnemothorax) ⇒crackling on palpation, found in clavicular region &/or near perforation site

Inspect chest & apex beat	- say what you see: scars, deformities, skin changes, etc. - kyphosis & scoliosis can restrict chest movement chest deformities: 1. pigeon chest (prominence of sternum + indrawing of ribs) = childhood asthma or rickets 2. funnel chest (depression at lower edge of sternum) = congenital/asymptomatic 3. barrel chest ($\uparrow$A-P diameter) = emphysema/COPD
COMPARE THE LEFT SIDE WITH THE RIGHT FOR EACH OF THE FOLLOWING STAGES	
Chest wall expansion	- place one hand on either side of chest, watch that both move equally on inspiration, if unequal = $\downarrow$air entry on the side not moving
Vocal fremitus (99)	- vibration felt on the patient's chest during vocalization - tell patient to "say 99 each time your hand touches their skin" - $\uparrow$vibrations = consolidation - $\downarrow$vibrations = collapse or pleural thickening - no vibrations = large pleural effusion
Percussion	- this diagram shows you approximately all the positions on the chest you need to percuss, always compare left with right as you ascend/descend the chest types of sound: - normal = resonant - dull = pleural fluid, pulmonary consolidation or lung collapse - stony dull = large pleural effusion (fluid in pleural cavity) - hyperresonant = $\uparrow$air space e.g. emphysema, bronchitis or pneumothorax

Ascultate lungs (listen with stethoscope)	- tell patient to "take a deep breath in & out each time stethoscope touches their skin" - ↓ air entry = infection (mucus build up), bronchial obstruction, emphysema, pneumothorax or pleural effusion/thickening - pleural rub = creaking as visceral pleura moves over the parietal pleura (these surfaces are usually smooth but in this case are infected/inflamed) - wheeze = air passing through narrowed bronchi e.g. asthma (during expiration) or bronchitis (inspiration & expiration) - crackles = excess secretions in small airways (pulmonary oedema) or reopening of airways occluded by mucus - NB. R lung = 3 lobes, L lung = 2, you must auscultate each lobe, listen in almost as many places as you percuss, as with percussion compare left with right as you ascend/descend the chest RUL · LUL · Front · RML · RLL · LLL · Front
Vocal resonance (99 – using stethoscope)	- tell patient to "say 99 each time stethoscope touches skin" - ↑noise = solid - ↓noise = liquid/air
Ask patient to sit forward and repeat above steps on their back	
Sacral & ankle oedema	- looking for heart failure
Common respiratory investigations	- peak flow, bloods, ABGs, sputum/blood culture, CXR, pulmonary function/spirometry, bronchoscopy, ventilation/perfusion (V/Q) scan, pleural aspiration, CT & biopsy

	Pleural effusion	Pneumonia (consolidation)	Collapse	Pneumothorax
Chest expansion	↓	↓	↓	↓
Percussion note	stony dull	dull	Dull	hyperresonant
Breath sounds	absent/↓	bronchial	absent/↓	absent/↓
Added sounds	none	crackles	None	none
Vocal resonance	absent/↓	↑	absent/↓	↓
Vocal fremitus	absent/↓	↑	absent/↓	absent/↓
Trachea & heart apex	trachea + apex beat displaced away from effusion		trachea + apex beat displaced towards collapse	trachea + apex beat displaced away from pneumothorax

Type I Respiratory Failure ($\downarrow pO_2$)	- failure of O_2 transfer in the lung - "pink puffer" appearance: $\downarrow pO_2$ & normal/$\downarrow pCO_2$ (can $\Rightarrow$respiratory alkalosis), central cyanosis, cool/sweaty, $\uparrow RR$ & $\uparrow HR$ - causes: ventilation/perfusion (V/Q) mismatch (e.g. COPD, PE, pneumonia), shunting (e.g. pulmonary oedema), altitude hypoxia ($\downarrow O_2$ density), diffusion impairment (e.g. pulmonary fibrosis) - treatment: O_2 + treat underlying cause - N.B. respiratory failure = $\downarrow pO_2$, type I = just $\downarrow pO_2$, type II =$\downarrow pO_2$ + $\uparrow pCO_2$
Type II Respiratory Failure ($\downarrow pO_2$ + $\uparrow pCO_2$)	- failure to remove CO_2 - "blue bloater" appearance: $\downarrow pO_2$ & $\uparrow pCO_2$ $\Rightarrow \uparrow H^+$ (respiratory acidosis) $\Rightarrow \uparrow$bicarbonate (−'ve ion/alkali retained by kidney to compensate for the respiratory acidosis, *see 'ABG Interpretation' in appendix*), central cyanosis, sleepy/confused, metabolic flap, warm/vasodilated peripheries, bounding pulse, $\uparrow RR$ & $\uparrow HR$ - causes: COPD, severe asthma, muscle weakness (guillian-barre), drug overdose (hypoventilation) - treatment: O_2 (keep an eye on their ABGs), treat underlying cause, reverse sedative drugs, CPAP (continuous +'ve airway pressure via intubation or tight mask), PEEP (+'ve end expiratory pressure = re-expand unventilated areas $\Rightarrow$ $\downarrow$shunts & $\uparrow pO_2$) - N.B. COPD can $\Rightarrow pCO_2$ driven ventilation, in this case ABGs would show type II respiratory failure but normal pH because the body has compensated over time by $\uparrow$bicarbonate production, this hypoxic drive may be disabled by infection, flare up of COPD, too much O_2, etc.
Respiratory acidosis ($\downarrow pO_2$ + $\uparrow pCO_2$ + $\downarrow pH$)	- usually due to a type II respiratory failure picture, CO_2 is acidic in the blood - causes: same as those above for type II respiratory failure - acute conditions $\Rightarrow \downarrow pH$ because the body does not have time to compensate, in chronic conditions pH can be normal due to metabolic compensation ($\uparrow$alkali/bicarbonate in the blood) - tests: ABGs, bloods, CXR etc. - treatment: O_2 (watch ABGs) + treat underlying cause
Respiratory alkalosis ($\downarrow pCO_2$ + $\uparrow pH$)	- patient literally blows off their bodies CO_2 reserves $\Rightarrow \downarrow$acid in blood $\Rightarrow \uparrow pH$ - causes: $\uparrow RR$ due to tissue hypoxia, panic attacks, artificial ventilation, respiratory drugs - tests: ABGs, bloods, CXR etc. - treat underlying cause
Noises	- the type of noise & whether it is during inspiration or expiration gives you an anatomical idea where the problem is - inspiration $\Rightarrow$ -'ve pressure in airways $\Rightarrow \uparrow$bronchioles (lower respiratory tract) diameter & $\downarrow$trachea (upper respiratory tract) diameter, therefore upper respiratory tract blockage/disease/infection $\Rightarrow$inspiratory noise - expiration: opposite to inspiration = $\downarrow$bronchioles diameter & $\uparrow$trachea diameter, therefore a lower respiratory tract disease/infection $\Rightarrow$expiratory noises (e.g. wheezing in asthma) - stridor: upper airway/trachea/larynx obstruction on inspiration, louder & more low pitched than wheeze, N.B. think foreign body in a child - bronchial breathing = consolidation (infection) - vocal resonance: $\downarrow$ = fluid & lung collapse, $\uparrow$ = consolidation

Respiratory Tract Infections	Upper (URTI): - flu = influenza A or B - sinusitis - common cold = rhinovirus - laryngitis - epiglottitis = influenza type B *(see 'Paediatrics' section)* lower (LRTI): - bronchitis = infection of the bronchial tree, can be viral (RSV =respiratory syncytial virus) or bacterial - pneumonia = infection of lung parenchyma - *N.B. more info can be found in the 'Paediatrics' section*
Pneumonia	- infection that disrupts gaseous exchange in the lungs - general presentation: cough, purulent/blood stained sputum, pleuritic pain, confusion & fever - investigations: bloods (signs of infection/inflammation), ABGs (looking for respiratory failure), culture pleural fluid/sputum/blood & CXR (shows radiological shadowing) - treat: resus (O_2, fluids, etc.), antibiotics (type depends on severity & culture results) +/- ITU admission - to assess severity in community acquired pneumonia the CURB 65 protocol (one point for each +'ve) is used =<u>C</u>onfusion, <u>U</u>rea (>7 mmol/l), <u>R</u>espiratory rate(≥30 breaths per minute), <u>B</u>lood pressure (<90mmHg systolic or <60mmHg diastolic), <u>65</u> yrs old or greater community acquired: - strep pneumoniae: is a gram +'ve diplococcus, creates α haemolytic draughtsman colonies, rapid onset, high fever, rust coloured sputum - mycoplasma pneumoniae: gram -'ve, can ⇒myocarditis, meninigo-encephalitis, rash, haemolytic anaemia - haemophilus influenza: bronchopneumonia hospital acquired: - staph aureus: high mortality, cavitations (lung abscesses ⇒large amount of purulent sputum)
Asthma	- is a reversible airway disorder - caused by bronchial airway narrowing due to: ↑secretions & constriction of smooth muscle - ⇒ SOB, wheeze & recurrent cough (biurnal = worse in morning & evening) - tests: ↓peak flow rate (↓FEV_1), bloods + cultures (rule out infection), ABGs, CXR (may show hyperinflation + rule out infection), spirometry (shows obstructive defect, ↓FEV_1/FVC, ↑residual volume) - general treatment: education, avoid provoking factors (e.g. smoking, dust, pets, etc.), check inhaler technique/compliance (*often used as station in OSCE exams, in children use a spacer device to help inhalation of drugs*), self monitoring (peak flow measurements twice daily) - N.B. causes of exacerbation (BASIC) = <u>B</u>ronchial hypersensitivity (smoke, fumes, etc.), <u>A</u>llergens, <u>S</u>tress, <u>I</u>nfection, <u>C</u>old temp/<u>C</u>ompliance to medication - medications: salbutamol (short acting bronchodilators/β_2 agonists, side effects =↑HR), salmeterol (long acting bronchodilators/β_2 agonists), fluticasone (inhaled steroid ⇒↓inflammation), prednisolone (oral steroid), hydrocortisone (IV steroid), ipratropium bromide (blocks muscarinic receptors in the lung

	inhibiting bronchoconstriction & mucus secretion) treatment steps: - step 1: salbutamol - step 2: salbutamol + fluticasone - step 3: salbutamol + ↑fluticasone - step 4: salmeterol + ↑fluticasone - step 5: salmeterol + prednisolone - give antibiotics if infective exacerbation - NB. patient needs to be educated to use a peak flow device & alter medication to a certain degree depending on results acute attack: - severe signs = too breathless to speak, RR>50, HR>140, peak flow <50% predicted, cyanosis, silent chest & LOC - acute management = high flow O_2, salbutamol nebulizer (add ipratropium bromide if required), oral prednisolone (or IV hydrocortisone if required) +/- antibiotics
COPD	- is an irreversible airway obstruction (in reality may have some degree of reversibility) - combination of bronchitis & emphysema - usually due to smoking which ⇒bronchial mucus gland hypertrophy ⇒↑mucus ⇒productive cough ⇒chronic bronchitis - emphysema = destruction of lung tissue/alveoli walls ⇒↓elastic recoil, gas trapping & hyperinflation ⇒V/Q mismatch ($↓pO_2$) + loss of diffusing surface ($↑pCO_2$) - ⇒respiratory failure & over time can ⇒cor polmonale (R heart failure due to chronic pulmonary hypertension ⇒↑JVP, oedema, etc.) - symptoms: SOB, cough, sputum, prolonged expiratory phase, wheeze, hyperinflated chest (hyperresonant to percussion) - tests: bloods (signs of infection + polycythaemia =↑Hb raised as part of bodies coping mechanism), ↑RR, accessory muscle use, lung function (spirometry = $↓FEV_1$ & $↓FEV_1/FVC$), ABGs (see respiratory failure above), sputum cultures, assess degree of reversibility (steroids & $β_2$ agonists as in asthma), CXR (hyperinflated lungs + large pulmonary vessels, exclude other causes e.g. infection), CT scan - treatment: education (e.g. SMOKING cessation), bronchodilators & steroids (may help), long term O_2 therapy, antibiotics (for infective exacerbation), pulmonary rehabilitation, lung volume reduction surgery
Bronchiectasis	- chronic infection ⇒bronchial wall damage & dilation ⇒retention of bronchial secretions ⇒ lung infections not properly cleared ⇒colonization - causes: localized (pneumonia, foreign body, tumour) or general (cystic fibrosis, autoimmune) - symptoms: chronic cough + lots of purulent sputum, haemoptysis, cyanosis, coarse crackles, chronic illness anaemia/polycythaemia, finger clubbing & cor pulmonale - can ⇒respiratory failure, brain abscess (if infection gets into blood) or renal failure (amyloid produced due to chronic inflammation effects kidney glomerulus/filtering system) - investigations: bloods (signs of infection/inflammation), cultures (blood & sputum), CXR, broncoscopy, cillary function tests + test for cystic fibrosis - treatment: O_2, physio, bronchodilators, high dose antibiotics, surgery

TB	- caused by mycobacterium tuberculosis
	- always suspect TB in an ill patient from a 3rd world country
	- primary infection: usually in childhood (droplet spread) ⇒lung lesion usually in upper lobe (ghon focus) + effects lymph supplying the surrounding area (ghon complex), usually asymptomatic but can ⇒fever, cough, night sweats, etc.
	- reactivation: any form of immunocompromise ⇒enlargement & fibrosis of initial lesion
	- pulmonary TB symptoms: cough, sputum, haemoptysis, night sweats & weight loss
	- reactivated TB can spread throughout the body infecting other regions, e.g. meningeal, bone, skin, pericardial, peritoneal, genitourinary
	- tests: bloods (signs of infection), culture everything, biopsy (shows caseating granulomas = lesions with necrosis in the centre) & CXR (consolidation, cavitation, fibrosis, pleural effusion & calcification all around ghon focus)
	- microbiology: uses a ziehl-nielsen stain on lowenstein-jensen medium incubated for up to 12 weeks (therefore treatment needs to be started beforehand on clinical findings)
	treatment (educate about medication compliance & monitor LFTs regularly due to liver toxicity):
	  1. Rifampicin 16 weeks (effects warfarin + turns urine reddish)
	  2. Isoniazid 16 weeks (⇒peripheral neuropathy)
	  3. Pyrazinamide 8 weeks
	  4. Ethambutol 16 weeks, only give if possible antibiotic resistance (⇒optic neuropathy)
	- centre for disease control (CDC) must be informed & contact tracing arranged + consider HIV in anyone with TB
	- NB. TB = caseating granulomas (i.e. necrosis in the centre) whereas sarcoidosis = non-caseating lesions

Sarcoidosis	- multi system non-caseating granulomas (no central necrosis), initial infection ⇒macrophage recruitment ⇒granulomas - symptoms: SOB, non-productive cough, fever & weight loss - no cure but treat flare ups with NSAIDs &/or steroids - N.B. as well as the respiratory tract this disease can affect virtually any other organ ⇒peripheral neuropathies, cardiomyopathy, cor pulmonale, hypopituitary, joint pain, hepatosplenomegaly, renal stones & lymphadenopathy
Extrinsic allergic alveolitis	- immune granulomatous reaction (immune response ⇒accumulation of macrophages ⇒granuloma) to organic dusts (animal proteins e.g. birds) & microbial spores - known as farmers lung - can ⇒ fibrosis - acute (4-8hrs after exposure) & chronic (constant low level exposure) - treat with steroids

Fibrosing alveolitis (Pulmonary fibrosis)	- immune inflammatory response ⇒alveolar wall thickening (due to fibroblasts creating scar tissue) ⇒contraction of lung tissue + honeycombing - symptoms: non productive cough, clubbing & fine 'velcro-like' end inspiratory crackles - ⇒↓lung volume, ↓diffusion & respiratory failure + ↑risk of lung cancer - tests: bloods (for signs of infection &/or inflammation), ABGs (show ↓pO_2), CXR (ground glass/honeycombing appearance), pulmonary function tests (show restrictive effect), CT & biopsy - treat with steroids - NB. associated with autoimmune conditions e.g. RA, SLE, IBD, systemic sclerosis
Pulmonary eosiophilia	- ↑eosinophils (immune system granulocytes) in blood can ⇒CXR abnormalities
Goodpasture's syndrome	- autoimmune attack of lung & kidney glomerular basement membrane - ⇒pulmonary haemorrhage ⇒anaemia, haemoptysis & respiratory failure - tests: anti-GBM antibodies found in blood, check kidney function (U&Es) & CXR - treatment: immunosuppression (e.g. steroids) & plasma exchange
Fungal infections	- develop mainly in the immunocompromised & in chronic lung diseases - asthma can ⇒allergic bronchiopulmonary aspergillosis (ABPA) =hypersensitivity response to the fungus Aspergillus ⇒eosinophilic infiltration, can ⇒bronchiectasis - symptoms: purulent sputum, fever & transient infiltrates on CXR, ↑eosinophilis, ↑↑IgE & a +'ve aspergillus skin test - treat with steroids, physio & anti-fungal medications - aspergilloma (fungus ball): starts off asymptomatic, can ⇒haemoptysis (can be massive), CXR (dense opacity + halo)
Asbestosis	- exposure to blue asbestos fibres, once in the lungs these fibres are engulfed by macrophages that release cytokines ⇒inflammation ⇒fibrosis in lower lobes + pleural plaques/thickening & effusions - symptoms: SOB, cough, end-inspiratory crackles & clubbing - ⇒restrictive lung defect ⇒type I respiratory failure - CXR = bilateral shadowing, honeycomb appearance & pleural plaques - ↑lung cancer risk therefore investigate any haemoptysis - can ⇒malignant mesothelioma (tumour arising in pleura) & pneumoconiosis (disorders due to dust inhalation)
Coal worker's pneumoconiosis	- coal dust particles are toxic to macrophages which die in the lungs, releasing their enzymes ⇒lung tissue damage ⇒fibrosis & nodules in lungs
Acute respiratory distress syndrome (ARDS)	- due to direct lung injury or complications of systemic illness (e.g. sepsis) - ⇒diffuse lung injury, damaged pulmonary vasculature & pulmonary oedema - can ⇒fibrosis - medical emergency, move to ITU, remove cause, support gas exchange & other failing organs, minimise pulmonary oedema, has a very high mortality

Pulmonary Embolism (PE)	- usually due to emboli dislodged from DVTs (therefore when performing an history or exam investigate for possible DVT)
	- symptoms: ↑RR, SOB, ↑HR, sudden onset pleuritic chest pain (usually easier when lying down) & haemoptysis
	- tests: ABGs ($\downarrow pO_2$ + $\downarrow pCO_2$), CXR (exclude pneumonia, pneumothorax, pulmonary oedema), ECG (rule out MI), ↑D-dimer (a fibrin breakdown product), V/Q scan & CT pulmonary angiogram
	- treatment: O_2, analgesia, thrombolytics (streptokinase dissolves clot if used in first 24hrs), anticoagulate immediately with IV heparin (quick acting) then oral warfarin (slow acting) for 6 months keeping INR between 2-3 + wear ted stockings
	DVTs are due to one or more of virchow's triad of factors:
	  1. venous stasis = recent long journey, immobility & prolonged pressure
	  2. vessel damage = surgery & trauma
	  3. ↑coagulation = thromboembolic disease, COCP & pregnancy
	- N.B. if recurrent DVT/PE patients are put on life long warfarin

Primary lung tumours	- causes: SMOKING, asbestos, radiation, etc.
	- general symptoms: dry cough, haemoptysis, SOB & weight loss
	- can metastasize to brain, bone & liver
	- tests: bloods, sputum/blood culture, CXR, lung function tests, bronchoscopy, biopsy, chest/brain/spinal/pelvis staging CT, isotope bone scan
	- staging: T 0-4 (degree of local invasion), N 0-3 (nodal involvement), M (metastases, 0=no, 1=yes)
	- treatment: radio/chemo therapy, surgery, palliative care
	types:
	  1. squamous cell carcinoma: large airways involved, slow growth, late metastasis, can release parathyroid hormone related peptide (PTHrP) ⇒↑osteoclast activity ⇒↑calcium in blood
	- symptoms of ↑calcium: can induce nephrogenic diabetes insipidus, renal stones, stomach pain, thirst and ↓consciousness (remember as stomach <u>groans</u>, psychic <u>moans</u>, <u>bones</u> & <u>stones</u>)
	- NB. bone mets can also ⇒↑Ca, treat with bisphosphonates
	  2. small cell carcinoma: rapid growth, early metastasis, can release anti-diuretic hormone (ADH) & adrenocorticotrophic hormone (ACTH)
	- syndrome of inappropriate ADH secretion ⇒↑water retention⇒↓Na concentration
	- ectopic adrenocorticotrophic hormone ⇒↑cortisol ⇒cushing's symptoms (e.g. hirsutism, acne, ↓K, ↑weight)
	affected area:
	- pancoast tumour = tumour lung's apex that has invaded the brachial plexus ⇒pain that radiates down arm & due to sympathetic nerve compression ⇒horner's syndrome (eye lid ptosis & small pupil)
	- mediastinum invasion ⇒recurrent laryngeal nerve palsy (hoarse voice), superior vena cava obstruction, phrenic nerve palsy (supplies diaphragm ⇒SOB) & oesophageal compression (⇒dysphagia)

Pneumothorax	- air in the pleural space
	- absent breath sounds on specific side, hyperresonant percussion, absent vocal fremitus/resonace, trachea deviated/pushed away from pneumothorax
	- CXR shows a black area devoid of any lung markings
	types:
	1. simple: closed wound, usually heals itself
	2. open: open wound, lung cannot re-expand
	3. tension: open wound with one way valve $\Rightarrow$ pneumothorax gradually increases in size deflating whole lung & pushing mediastinum over to opposite side
	- treat depending on severity, if asymptomatic it may heal by itself, if severe perform thoracocentesis (drain air via needle or chest drain into 2nd intercostal space mid clavicular line)
	- NB. a collapsed lung is the opposite to a pneumothorax, because it will pull the mediastinum over, all examined sounds $\downarrow$, CXR = double heart boarder
Pleural effusion	- fluid in pleural space, if infection = empyema (pus), if blood = haemothorax
	- symptoms: SOB, $\downarrow$lung expansion, stony dull to percussion, $\downarrow$sounds/resonance, CXR (blunting of costophrenic angle + noticeable fluid level in lung film)
	types of effusion:
	1. transudate ($\downarrow$protein) = $\uparrow$venous pressure (e.g. heart failure, constrictive pericarditis, fluid overload) or $\downarrow$blood protein (e.g. cirrhosis, nephrotic syndrome)
	2. exudate ($\uparrow$protein) = infection, malignancy or inflammation (e.g. pneumonia, TB, RA, SLE)
	- treat by aspiration (send samples to microbiology, cytology & biochemistry) + treat cause, in this case any chest drain should be inserted at base of lungs (due to gravity fluid will then drain out)
	- aspiration results: blood (malignancy or trauma), $\downarrow$glucose (infection), $\uparrow$neutrophils (inflammation &/or infection)

Gastroenterology History

Introduction	- approach politely and introduce yourself - patient's name, DOB & occupation

Oral pain	- SOCRATES *(see 'Cardiovascular History' section for definition)* - causes: infection (candidasis, dental sepsis, herpes simplex virus 1, etc.), systemic (crohn's, coeliac, $\downarrow$iron/folate/vitamin B_{12}, etc.)
Difficulty swallowing (dysphagia)	- painful mouth/throat, onset/progression, solid &/or liquids, where does it stick, is it brought back up - causes: neurological (difficulty with fluids, bulbar/pseudobulbar palsy), obstruction (difficulty with solids progressing onto liquids = oesophageal carcinoma or stricture), achalasia (oesophageal motility disorder)
Nausea & Vomiting	- pain/dyspepsia (does vomiting relieve symptoms), time of day (related to meals), frequency, taste/smell/colour, any blood - causes: metabolic, infection/inflammation, medication, neurological, obstruction, malignancy
Haematemesis (vomiting blood)	- colour (fresh or coffee ground), preceded by strenuous retching (mallory weiss tear) - coffee ground vomit = blood that has been oxidised by the acid in the stomach - cause: peptic ulcer, liver disease (related to alcohol excess $\Rightarrow$liver disease $\Rightarrow$portal hypertension $\Rightarrow$oesophageal varices), medication (steroids/NSAIDs)
Abdominal pain	- SOCRATES - colicky pain = waves of muscular contractions due to obstruction in a muscle lined tube (e.g. bile duct =gallstones, intestine =obstruction/constipation/strictures, ureter =renal stone, etc.) - pain usually begins generally over abdomen then as the specific organ/diseased area inflames more $\Rightarrow$parietal peritoneum irritation $\Rightarrow$localised pain - N.B. mesenteric atherosclerosis $\Rightarrow$angina type pain in the abdomen after eating or during exercise
Heart burn (dyspepsia)	- SOCRATES - causes: reflux oesophagitis, gastritis, or can be atypical pain associated with MI/angina
Jaundice	- $\uparrow$bilirubin in blood $\Rightarrow$change in skin colour, yellow eye sclerae, itching (pruritis)
Abdominal distension	- the 5fs: fat, flatus, faeces, fluid, fetus
Altered bowel habit	- diarrhoea (onset, timing, consistency, blood/mucus, recent travel abroad) - constipation (onset, timing, straining, pain, bleeding) - colour: melaena (tarry black =upper GI haemorrhage, blood gets oxidised by stomach acid), bloody (ulcerative colitis, diverticulitis, colorectal tumours campylobacter, salmonella & shigella), steatorrhoea (pale =fat malabsorption due to disease/blockage effecting pancreatic enzyme release)
Rectal bleeding	- bright red = from rectum/anus (e.g. haemorrhoids, anal fissure, polyps) but could also be due to problems with the end of the colon (e.g. ulcerative colitis, diverticulitis, colorectal tumours) - dark & mixed with stool = comes from intestines, ileum (e.g. crohn's), colon (e.g. ulcerative colitis, diverticulitis, colorectal tumours) - melaena = upper GI/stomach bleeding, e.g. peptic ulcer
Anorexia/weight loss	- how much weight & over what time scale - are they trying to diet - think malignancy or malabsorption

PMH	-	list PMH + ask DEAR J SMITH *(see 'Cardiovascular History' section for definition)*
Medications, allergies, smoking & alcohol	-	if ex-smoker ask smoking history
FH	-	are parents/brothers/sisters alive, if so do they suffer from any diseases, if they have passed away (say "sorry to hear that") ask age & reason of death
Social/occupational history	-	who is at home & how does this condition effect your life

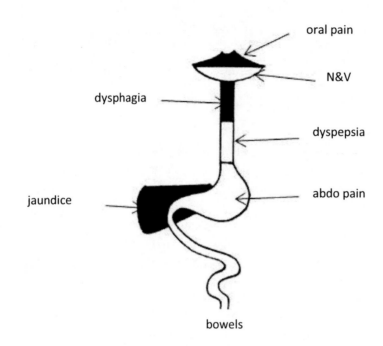

Gastroenterology Exam

Introduction	- wash your hands - approach politely and introduce yourself - patient's name & DOB - explain to patient what you are going to do & obtain verbal consent - expose patient after asking - lie flat
General Inspection	- comment on patient & surroundings - general health, SOB, obvious pain, surrounding apparatus/medications (vomit bowel, IV drip, O_2 mask, etc.)
Hands	nail signs: - spoon shape nails (koilonychia) = iron deficiency anaemia - white nails (leuconychia) = malabsorption - opaque nail bed = hypoalbuminaemia finger signs: - clubbing = due to chronic disease (e.g. chronic liver disease, liver cirrhosis, inflammatory bowel disease, primary biliary cirrhosis) palm signs: - palmar erythema - dupuytren's contraction = thickening & contraction of palmar fascia $\Rightarrow$ flexion usually of ring finger (can be caused by alcohol XS) - bruising = clotting abnormalities - scratches (due to pruritis) = jaundice - warmth of hands (crude indicator of perfusion)
Radial pulse	- tachycardia suggests infection or hypovolaemia (e.g. GI bleed) - N.B. AF can $\Rightarrow$ emboli in mesenteric arteries giving bowel ischaemia
Hepatic flap	- fine tremor in fingers (less coarse than a hypercapnic/$\uparrow CO_2$ flap) - associated with liver failure
Blood pressure	- gives an idea of perfusion & general health
Eyes	- pale conjunctivae = anaemia - yellow eye sclera = jaundice - pale green rings (kayser-fleischer rings) = copper deposits suggestive of wilson's disease
Mouth	- reddish brown cracks radiating from corners of mouth (angular stomatitis) = $\downarrow$ vitamin B, folate &/or iron - smooth & red tongue = $\downarrow$ vitamin B/folate (painful) or $\downarrow$ iron (painless) - pigmentation around mouth (peutz-jeugers syndrome) = small bowel polyposis (number of polyps in bowel lining) - ulcers = crohn's - sweet smelling breath = hepatocellular disease - faecal breath = obstruction $\Rightarrow$ faecal vomit - candidiasis = white creamy patches in mouth
Lymphadenopathy in neck & supraclavicular fossa	- enlarged node in left supraclavicular fossa (virchow's node) is related to stomach cancer (troisier's sign)
Inspect chest	- look for spider naevi (>5 on upper chest suggestive of liver disease - check for $\uparrow$ RR

Inspect abdomen	- scars, stomas (usually ileostomy = right iliac fossa, colonostomy = left iliac fossa, loop colostomy = transverse colon) - distension (5Fs = fat, flatus, fetus, faeces, fluid) - striae (cushing's syndrome + past/present pregnancy or obesity) - visible veins (caput medusa) = portal hypertension or obstructed inferior vena cava - sister mary joseph sign (nodule bulging into the umbilicus due to metastasis of a malignant cancer in the pelvis or abdomen) - campbell de morgan spots (haemangiomas), can be normal in elderly - obvious masses - rigid/board-like abdomen without respiratory movements due to severe pain
Palpate abdomen light then deep 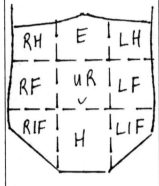	- ask if any pain then starting away from the painful area palpate all 9 sections in turn, observe patient's face, palpate all sections lightly first then start again only this time palpating deeper - severe pain, general rigidity, decreased bowel sounds & no movement on breathing usually indicates peritonitis - test for guarding = muscular tension on palpation - test rebound tenderness = ask "is it worse when I press in or when I let go", is +'ve if worse on release, suggests peritonitis - mcburney's point tenderness (1/3 of the way from anterior superior iliac spine to umbilicus) is suggestive of appendicitis - don't forget women can have ovarian pathology that present as abdominal pain (including ectopic pregnancy, so do a pregnancy test!) sections of abdomen & corresponding disease when tender (just think what anatomy is beneath where you are palpating): - R hypochondrium = gall stones, liver disease & pancreatic head Ca - epigastrium = gastritis, pancreatitis, AAA, gastric Ca & pancreatic body/tail Ca - L hypochondrium = spleen, pancreatic tail Ca & colon Ca - R flank = pyelonephritis, renal stones or UTI - umbilical region = AAA or pancreatic body/tail Ca - L flank = pyelonephritis, renal stones or UTI - R iliac fossa = appendicitis, ovarian disease/Ca, caecal Ca or Crohn's disease - hypogastrium = UTI or urinary retention - L iliac fossa = constipation, diverticular disease, ovarian disease/Ca & colon Ca - N.B. a mass in R/LIF could be a transplanted kidney (check for scars)

An acute abdomen is defined as a short-onset, severe, generalised abdominal pain
The classic way to test for peritonitis is via rebound tenderness, but this is currently viewed as being cruel, and percussion tenderness (percuss abdomen over all 9 sections) is now the preferred test
In the event of an acute abdomen, i.e. patient in excruciating pain, do not continue palpating the abdomen just say to the examiner that you would call for a senior opinion straight away, then mention you would follow the ABCs, start the patient on fluids/O_2 if required & order the following tests whilst waiting for your senior (bloods, urine analysis, pregnancy test, chest & abdo X-ray + organise further imaging e.g. abdo USS if required)

Palpate liver	- start in the RIF (hand should be at same angle as the ribs = approx. 2 o'clock angle), tell patient to breath in & hold, then push hand inwards & up using the edge of your index finger to feel, then redo a few centimetres up, continue till you feel the liver edge or reach the ribs - describe liver if palpable: distance below ribs it can be felt, is the liver sharp-edged, smooth, irregular, any obvious masses - causes of enlarged liver include congestive heart failure, alcoholic liver disease (fatty infiltration), hepatitis, malignancy

	- to palpate gallbladder ask patient to take a deep breath & feel under the liver, if causes pain =murphy's sign suggesting acute cholecystitis - percuss borders of liver from above (liver will be dull to percussion) - NB. courvoisier's law =jaundice & palpable gall bladder is due to malignancy not gallstones (because gallstones ⇒inflammation ⇒scar tissue ⇒gall bladder contracts)
Palpate spleen	- same as for liver but work diagonally across abdomen starting in RIF - common causes of enlarged spleen: portal hypertension, haemolytic anaemia, leukaemia, RA/SLE or malaria
Palpate kidneys	- technique is known as bimanual blotting (one hand on abdomen & one around patient's back, push the kidney forwards towards the abdomen to feel), if area is tender can sit patient forward & softly thump the renal angles (these will be tender in pyelonephritis) - assess size & surface if palpable - usually enlarged due to cancer, polycystic, etc.
Palpate bladder	- work down the centre of the abdomen trying to 'cup' the upper surface of the bladder - percuss from above to confirm border & presence of fluid (is dull to percussion) - enlarged due to urinary retention (acute retention is painful, chronic may not be)
AAA (abdominal aortic aneurysm)	- place index fingers of each hand either side of the abdominal aorta & feel for movement, if AAA present there will be an expansile pulsation (your fingers will be pushed up & outwards) - comment on width of AAA - surgery if > 5.5cm (exact size is difficult to assess so in an exam say small ones are sometimes safe to monitor, others need surgery) - N.B. don't press too hard!
Fluid/ascites	- shifting dullness test: percuss from centre of abdomen towards flank until percussion note goes dull, mark this point, roll patient on side, wait 10 seconds then percuss again, percussion notes should now have a different distribution (fluid has moved due to gravity) - fluid thrill tests: perform if large volume ascites present, place patient's hand in middle of their abdomen, flick one flank whilst feeling the other for thrills
Listen for bowel sounds	- listen in more than one region - no sound = paralytic ileus, peritonitis - ↑sound = bowel obstruction, infection, etc.
Stoma examination	- a stoma (greek for mouth) is an artificial opening of the bowel onto the abdominal skin surface - many different kinds most common are ileostomy (ileum to skin) or colostomy (colon to skin), and these types may be either loop stomas or single stomas - remove bag prior to examination, wear gloves & apron - inspection: comment on the position of stoma & suggest type (ileostomies are spouted with liquid chime being outputted, colostomies are flush to the skin & produce faeces), any abnormal swellings or erythema around stoma, any discolouration of the stoma mucosa (e.g. white =candida infection, dusky =ischaemic) - palpate around the stoma edge with the patient coughing for parastomal hernia (attempt to reduce any masses felt), if there was a large irreducible mass next to the stoma you could auscultate over it to hear for bowel sounds - pass your lubricated little finger into the stoma to assess the lumen for stenosis - wipe the patients abdominal wall clean & assist the placement of a new bag

In an OSCE situation say, "I would complete this examination by carrying out:
- *a groin examination looking for hernia*
- *a testicular or vaginal (PV) examination*
- *a rectal examination"*
then cover + thank the patient & turn to the examiner to await further questions

Hernias	- inspect inguinal & femoral canals (both sides) + scrotum whilst patient is preferably standing (can be done lying first) if there is a hernia: - ascertain whether the hernia has a cough response - reduce hernia (if possible), then occlude the internal inguinal ring & ask patient to cough again, if hernia reappears this is suggestive of a direct hernia, if not then it is probably an indirect hernia - if cannot reduce it & does not have a cough impulse could a be strangulated hernia - always check the both sides types of hernia 1. direct inguinal hernias (25%) push through weaknesses in the posterior wall of the inguinal canal (mainly found in the obese & in those who do heavy physical exercise) 2. indirect inguinal hernias (75%) travel along the inguinal canal, typically discovered when they descend into the scrotum 3. femoral hernias are seen as a lump below the inguinal ligament 4. umbilical hernia 5. incisional hernia = hernia at site of previous operation (due to abdo muscle weakness at incision point e.g. parastomal hernia) anatomy recap: - inguinal canal: runs from pubic tubercle to ant. sup. iliac spine (deep ring = mid-inguinal point, external ring = pubic tubercle), it contains the vas deferens + testicular vessels in men & the round ligament in women - femoral canal: below inguinal ligament (below & lat. to pubic tubercle)

Testicular exam	- inspect penis & scrotum, looking for scars, swelling & erythema
	- ask if the patient has any tenderness either side
	if there is an obvious scrotal swelling:
	- decide if the testicle is separate from the swelling
	- if you cannot get above the swelling & the testicle is separate, then it is likely to be an inguino-scrotal hernia
	- if you can get above it, and it is continuous with or involving the testicle, then it is confined to the scrotum & could be a hydrocoele, varicocoele, testicular or epididymal swelling
	- hydrocoele swellings will illuminate when a torch is shined at them (due to accumulation of fluid in tunica vaginalis)
	- describe any mass you feel *(see 'Lump Examination' in appendix)*
	if there is no obvious swelling on either side, but tenderness one side:
	- begin on the non-tender side
	- palpate testes, epididymis & spermatic cords for any swellings, masses, pulsations, etc. + check that the lie of the testicle is in correct anatomical orientation

Digital rectal exam	- say "this will be uncomfortable, but not painful, just relax"
	- position patient on their side with knees drawn up to their chest
	- inspect for external lesions, haemorrhoids or fistulae
	- lubricate the glove
	- insert finger & assess whether the patient is experiencing an unexpected amount of pain, if so stop
	- if sphincter spasms can use some anaesthetic jelly to relax it
	- twist the arm to feel the prostate or cervix
	- if pelvic mass detected can do bimanual exam (one hand on abdomen)
	- ask patient to squeeze your finger (checks sphincter tone)
	- on removal check your finger/glove for blood/faeces
	- should be performed for GI/GU problems + backache, lumbosacral nerve root pain, bone pain, iron def anaemia & unexplained weight loss

Investigations	- bloods *(see 'Blood Results' section in appendix)*
	- MSU & stool culture
	- CXR, abdominal X-ray (ask for KUB if suspected renal stone), CT (with contrast = outlines bowel)
	- barium: swallow (outlines oesophagus, e.g. dysphagia, dyspepsia), meal (outlines stomach & duodenum), follow-through (outlines small bowel, e.g. strictures, Ca), enema (outlines colon, e.g. diverticular disease, cancer)
	- upper abdominal/pelvic/urinary tract ultrasound
	- upper endoscopy (OGD) & lower endoscopy (flexible sigmoidoscopy or colonoscopy)
	- ERCP = direct imaging of biliary tree with camera +/- removal of stones
	- MRCP = MRI scan of biliary tree
	- renal angiography (test for renal artery stenosis)
	- laparoscopy = direct visualization of bowels via key hole/fibre optic camera insertion into abdomen

Gastroenterology Revision

Gastroenteritis (food poisoning)	onset: - 2-6hrs: caused by toxin release, staph aureus & bacillus cereus = D&V + abdominal pain - 12-48hrs: salmonella, campylobacter (bloody diarrhoea), e coli (bloody diarrhoea + haemolytic uraemic syndrome=RBC destruction ⇒blockage of renal arteries ⇒blood in urine), botulism (D&V + toxins ⇒paralysis of muscles + visual problems) - > 1 week: giardiasis (D&V, abdo pain, malaise) can ⇒chronic infection - amoebiasis:, bloody diarrhoea & ulcers, recent travel/antibiotic use - clostridium difficile: can follow recent antibiotic treatment, symptoms =diarrhoea, white plaques in intestinal mucosa & toxins which ⇒gut symptoms (e.g. intestinal dilatation), can ⇒death in immunosuppressed patients - tests: general bloods (check for infective & inflammatory markers), stool/urine/blood cultures, abdo X-ray, sigmoidoscopy & rectal biopsy - treatment: fluids & antiemetics + treat cause if severe
Ascites	- fluid in abdominal cavity - usually due to liver disease/cirrhosis/malignancy diagnosed by peritoneal tap, send results for microscopy, culture & cytology: 1. transudate = <30g/l protein (due to liver disease/cirrhosis, R heart failure, nephrotic syndrome & malnutrition) 2. exudates = >30g/l protein (due to malignancy & infection) - treatment: drain if severe + treat cause
Hiatus hernia	- hernia of proximal stomach into chest due to lower oesophageal sphincter weakness caused by congenital &/or acquired (lifestyle) factors - there are 2 types: sliding (80%) & rolling (20%) - symptoms: usually asymptomatic but can worsen ongoing heartburn (dysphagia) due to gastro-oesophageal reflux &/or inflammation to the distal third of the oesophagus (reflux oesophagitis), a strangulated rolling hernia can ⇒perforation - tests: endoscopy (OGD) & barium swallow - if assessing sphincter weakness can do oesophageal pH studies, oesophageal manometry (measure of intra-luminal & sphincter pressures) - treatment: lifestyle changes (↓weight + avoid alcohol, smoking, spicy foods & large meals), antacids, proton pump inhibitors (e.g. omeprazole), surgery (as a last resort =nissen fundoplication) - NB. reflux can ⇒oesophageal metaplasia (barrett's = pre-malignant change from squamous to columnar epithelium) ⇒adenocarcinoma *(see below)*
Duodenal ulcer (peptic ulcer)	- causes: helicobacter pylori is the main cause, NSAIDs (non-steroidal anti-inflammatory drugs e.g. ibuprofen or diclofenac) & lifestyle - symptoms: ↑acid, abdo pain (worse at night, relieved by food), haematemesis (coffee ground vomiting) & can ⇒perforation (surgical emergency) - tests: endoscopy (OGD) + h. pylori breath test - treatment: lifestyle changes, h. pylori triple therapy (proton pump inhibitor + 2 different antibiotics) + avoid NSAIDs - N.B. duodenal ulcers don't usually ⇒malignancy

Gastric ulcer (peptic ulcer)	- helicobacter pylori is main cause, NSAIDs & lifestyle - can be the first presentation of gastric malignancy - symptoms: abdo pain usually after eating (this is the opposite to duodenal ulcer), can get haematemesis & perforation - investigate & treat as duodenal ulcer + repeat OGD to check healing & to rule out malignancy
Coeliac's disease	- disorder of small bowel where sensitivity to gluten causes villous atrophy & malabsorption - symptoms: malabsorption, abdo cramps, diarrhoea (steatorrhoea =↑fat in faeces due to malabsorption), N&V, bloating & Fe deficiency anaemia - investigations: duodenal biopsy & check for endomysial antibodies (EMA) - treat with education =gluten free diet + vitamin & iron replacement - N.B. long term complications = anaemia & osteoporosis (due to malnutrition) + ↑risk of small bowel lymphoma
Ulcerative colitis (inflammatory bowel disease, IBD)	- inflammation limited to the mucosa of the bowel, is always present in rectum & can extend into the proximal colon (spreads in a continuous path, i.e. no skip lesions as in crohn's) - has a relapsing & remitting course - causes: unknown but there are some genetic factors & smoking seems to protects against UC - symptoms: malnutrition, pain, diarrhoea (also nocturnal diarrhoea which is important because it means it is unlikely to be functional + the frequency of diarrhoea is linked to disease severity), rectal mucus/bleeding & weight loss - in acute conditions can ⇒perforation, haemorrhage, toxic megacolon - associated with other autoimmune conditions, it can therefore ⇒extra-intestinal features e.g. joints (arthritis), skin (pyoderma gangrenosum = large skin ulcers, erythema nodosum = inflammation of fat layer) & the eyes (uveitis) - ↑risk of colon cancer - diagnosis: bloods (inflammatory markers ESR/CRP + FBC etc.), stool culture (to exclude infections like shigella, c diff, salmonella, campylobacter, e coli, etc.), abdo imaging, camera up the rectum (sigmoidoscopy/colonoscopy), barium studies + rectal biopsy - treat with nutritional advice, steroids/immunosuppression, antibiotics +/- surgery (usually needed by ~20% of patients at some point) - NB. more common than crohn's
Crohn's disease (inflammatory bowel disease, IBD)	- chronic transmural (effects all layers) granulomatous inflammatory disease affecting anywhere in the bowel (mouth to anus) with fistula, deep ulceration, strictures, abscesses & skip lesions (areas of abnormal mucosa that are not continuous) - symptoms: diarrhoea, abdominal pain, weight loss/malnutrition, fever & can ⇒bowel strictures, fistulae & abscesses - in acute conditions can ⇒perforation, haemorrhage, toxic megacolon - extra-intestinal features are the same as for UC + hepatitis & primary sclerosing cholangitis, also associated with other autoimmune conditions - investigate & treat as UC - >50% will need surgery at sometime - NB. generally worse than ulcerative colitis as more aggressive & effects mouth to anus

Diverticular disease	- a diverticulum is an outpouching of the colon (95% occurs in the sigmoid, but can be along the whole length) complications: 1. diverticulitis (inflammation of diverticulae) 2. diverticular abscess (abdo pain, spiking fever & abdominal mass) 3. fistulae (hole eaten through structure, if into bladder =colovesical, into vaginal vault =colovaginal, into small bowel =coloenteric, into another part of colon =colocolonic) 4. colonic stricture (due to repeated inflammation ⇒scar tissue ⇒narrowing/contraction of lumen ⇒obstruction) 5. colonic bleeding = bright red blood (when diverticulae form where blood vessels are situated in the colon wall) - symptoms include nausea, flatulence, altered bowel habit & left sided abdo pain/colic generally eased with defecation, can ⇒perforation - diagnosis: bloods (for anaemia, infection & inflammation), barium enema, colonoscopy + abdominal & pelvic CT - treat with high fibre diet + depending on cause antibiotics & surgery as a last resort
Liver function tests	- aspartate transaminase (AST) & alanine transaminase (ALT) both leak from hepatocytes when damaged, therefore both usually increase in the blood during liver disease (e.g. hepatitis) - bilirubin: raised in various liver diseases (e.g. hepatitis & gall stones) or due to haematological causes, if raised 2-3 times above the normal range then patient is classed as jaundiced, N.B. if no accompanying liver damage think haemolysis or gilbert's syndrome - alkaline phosphatase (found in the biliary tract wall) is raised in obstructive conditions, e.g. gallstone obstruction of the common bile duct or pancreatic head carcinoma - the liver produces albumin & clotting factors, chronic & severe liver disease can ⇒↓liver synthetic function ⇒↑prothrombin time (due to ↓clotting factors production) + ↓albumin (⇒ascites) - γGT: raised in obstructive liver disease & large volume alcohol consumption - amylase is produced by the pancreas, usually increased due to pancreatic disease or obstruction to the pancreas' drainage system (the common bile duct)
Jaundice	- biochemical diagnosis if serum bilirubin is raised 2-3 times above the normal range - clinical diagnosis made if discolouration of eye sclera & skin +/- itching - bilirubin is a breakdown product of the haem group in red blood cells, it is transported in blood to liver as unconjugated bilirubin, the liver then conjugates it (makes it water soluble) so can be excreted via bile into the GI system (makes stools brown), some is reabsorbed & can later be excreted by the kidneys into the urine - because bilirubin is conjugated by the liver if problem is pre-liver ⇒↑unconjugated bilirubin, whereas if the problem is based within or post liver ⇒↑conjugated bilirubin types: 1. pre-hepatic: due to any disease that ⇒↑haemolysis (e.g. haemolytic anaemia, malaria) ⇒↑unconjugated bilirubin, N.B. gilberts syndrome = failure to conjugate bilirubin so will also ⇒↑unconjugated bilirubin

	2. hepatic/hepatocellular: ↓ability of hepatocytes to metabolise & excrete bilirubin ⇒↑conjugated bilirubin, due to hepatitis/liver disease, alcohol excess, medications or sclerosing cholangitis 3. post-hepatic/obstructive (interruption of bile drainage): because bilirubin is conjugated in the liver but is not able to drain into the intestines ⇒dark urine (↑bilirubin in urine via kidneys) & pale stools (↓bilirubin due to blockage), caused by gall stones, pancreatic head Ca, biliary atresia (in infants, *see 'Paediatric' section*), ductal Ca, etc. - treat underlying cause - N.B. courvoisier's law = jaundice & a palpable gall bladder is not caused by gallstones, need to rule out malignancy
Gallstone disease 	- more common in fat, fair, females in their forties! types of stones (only 10% show on X-ray): a. pigmented (due to haemolysis = small, irregular, radiolucent) b. cholesterol (large & radiolucent) c. calcium (radiopaque, the only ones you can see on X-ray) stones blocking: 1. gallbladder/cystic duct ⇒RUQ pain (worse after fatty foods due to ↑bile production), biliary colic (intermittent regular pain), can ⇒acute cholecystitis (inflammation of gallbladder), check for murphy's sign *(see 'Gastroenterology Examination' above)* 2. common bile duct ⇒obstructive jaundice (⇒pale stools & dark urine), RUQ pain, and if ascending cholangitis (bile duct infection, usually due to e coli) develops, then charcot's triad can occur (fever, rigors & jaundice) 3. pancreatic duct (via ampulla of vater) ⇒acute pancreatitis - tests: bloods (LFTs + infective/inflammatory signs), abdo USS, abdo X-ray, ERCP (imaging of bile ducts + removal of stone), MRCP (MRI of bile ducts) - treatment: analgesia, antibiotics, fluids, removal of gall stones (via ERCP), removal of gallbladder (cholecystectomy, usually done laparoscopically) - N.B. colic pain comes in waves & signifies a blockage to a muscular tube (e.g. gallstones, kidney stones & constipation)
Primary biliary cirrhosis	- granulomatous inflammation of small interlobular bile ducts ⇒fibrosis which then obstructs bile from reaching the intestine - associated with autoimmune diseases - symptoms: jaundice, steatorrhoea, pruritis (itching), fatigue & eventually cirrhosis - diagnosis: bloods (e.g. LFTs =↑alkaline phosphatase), anti mitochondrial antibody studies (these are antibodies formed against mitochondria, primarily the mitochondria in liver cells =autoimmune process), imaging & biopsy - treatment: immunosuppressants & in severe cases may need a liver transplant
Appendicitis	- inflammation of the appendix - is a surgical emergency as can ⇒perforation ⇒peritonitis & abdominal sepsis - typical symptoms: generalized abdo pain for a few days which then localizes in the RIF as the inflammation worsens + fever, anorexia, N&V - diagnose is made clinically on symptoms & bloods (raised infection & inflammatory markers), sometimes imagining is performed to rule out other causes (USS or CT) + CXR (check for air under the diaphragm =perforation) - rovsing's sign =deep palpation in the LIF ⇒pain in the RIF - treatment: surgical removal (appendicectomy, can be done laparoscopically nowadays) +/- antibiotics

Acute pancreatitis	- inflammation of pancreas, as pancreatic cells are destroyed they release their enzymes ⇒self digestion - has high mortality ~10% - quick onset ⇒triad of symptoms: severe epigastric pain radiating to back, vomiting & jaundice - differential diagnosis = aortic dissection/rupture, peptic ulcer or cholecystitis - other symptoms: fever & steatorrhoea (↑fat in faeces due to it not being broken down by amylase which is produced by the pancreas) - investigations: bloods (↑amylase + infection/inflammatory signs), ↑glucose (due to ↓insulin production by islets of langerhans in pancreas), abdo X-ray + CXR (check for air under the diaphragm = perforation), USS, CT & ERCP - if also ↑AST & ↑bilirubin suggests liver involvement, e.g. stones in common bile duct blocking bile + amylase - treatment: resus, analgesia, aggressive fluids, digestive enzymes (replace those the pancreas usually makes), insulin & alcohol advice +/- surgery (removal of gall stones) - causes (GET SMASHED): <u>G</u>all stones, <u>E</u>thanol, <u>T</u>rauma, <u>S</u>teroids, <u>M</u>umps, <u>A</u>utoimmune, <u>S</u>corpion bite, <u>H</u>yperlipidaemia, <u>E</u>RCP, <u>D</u>rugs - N.B. pancreatitis patients must be scored using the ranson's score, glasgow score or modified APACHE score to tailor treatment to their clinical condition - glasgow score: you don't need to remember this, I just want to show you how severity is assessed, severe = 3 or more of factors below, remember neumonic PANCREAS = <u>P</u>O2 <8kPa, <u>A</u>ge >55 years, <u>N</u>eutrophils (=WCC >15 x10^9/l), <u>C</u>alcium <2mmol/l, <u>R</u>enal function (=urea >16mmol/l), <u>E</u>nzymes (ALT >200 units), <u>A</u>lbumin <32g/l, <u>S</u>ugar (=glucose >10mmol/l)
Chronic pancreatitis	- mainly due to alcohol XS & is common in cystic fibrosis patients - acute flare-ups can cause pain (epigastric→back), steatorrhoea & weight loss - can cause diabetes (due to disruption of insulin produced in pancreas) and pancreatic insufficiency (↓digestive enzyme production) - treatment: lifestyle advice, diabetic control, analgesia, digestive enzymes

Pancreatic cancer	- 95% are adenocarcinomas (cancer of columnar cells = production/gland cells)
	- usually presents late + very poor survival figures
	- check for tumour marker Ca19-9 (also found in colon Ca)
	types & symptoms:
	  1. pancreatic tail (15%): anorexia, fatigue & high risk of metastases
	  2. body (25%): diabetes, steatorrhoea, weight loss & ↑pain (because near celiac nerves)
	  3. head (60%) ⇒obstructive jaundice (due to obstruction of common bile duct)

Acute Hepatitis (liver disease)	- self limiting liver inflammation, lasts < 6months - symptoms: abdo pain, general malaise +/- jaundice - tests: bloods (↑LFTs, ↑INR + normal/↓albumin, FBCs & inflammatory markers), viral studies & imaging - causes: hep A/B & drug reactions (e.g. paracetamol, use n-acetylcysteine to counteract in overdose patients)
Chronic Hepatitis (liver disease)	- continual liver damage/inflammation ⇒liver fibrosis ⇒less active liver cells & portal hypertension - can progress to cirrhosis then liver failure - symptoms: general malaise, jaundice + varices (oesophagus due to portal hypertension), hepatosplenomegaly (due to portal hypertension), ascites (due to ↓albumin/protein normally produced by the liver), clubbing, spider naevi,

	- ↓muscle mass, bruising (↓coagulation factors ⇒↑INR/clotting time) & oedema - tests: bloods (LFTs, FBC, CRP, clotting, etc.), iron studies (checking for haemochromatosis) & copper studies (wilson's disease), viral studies, imaging + biopsy
Pathology of alcoholic liver disease	stages: 1. early fatty change is reversible (bloods = deranged LFTs) 2. alcoholic hepatitis (inflammatory change + hepatocyte necrosis) 3. mallory's hyaline (pink bodies in hepatocytes) 4. central hyaline sclerosis (fibrosis around central veins) 5. cirrhosis: deranged LFTs/haematology +/- encephalopathy (altered consciousness +/- metabolic flap), ↑γGT, pathology (=micro→macro nodular), other symptoms (jaundice, ascites, splenomegaly, spider naevi, bruising, rash, skin pigmentation, dupuytren's contracture) - treatment: treat underlying cause, alcohol & lifestyle advice, nutritional support (thiamine, vitamin B_{12} + multivitamins)
Fulminant liver failure	- liver failure + encephalopathy (altered consciousness +/- hepatic flap) - high risk of haemorrhage due to oesophageal variceal bleed & coagulopathy (↑prothombin time due to ↓coagulation factor production ⇒↑risk of haemorrhage) - causes: hepatitis B/C, drug reactions (e.g. alcohol, paracetamol) - treatment: resus, treat encephalopathy (lots of laxatives + stop any drugs that ⇒drowsiness) - NB. N-acetylcysteine counteracts paracetamol in overdose patients
Oesophageal varices	- caused by portal hypertension due to liver failure - symptoms: most are asymptomatic but can ⇒vomiting fresh blood + hypovolaemic shock - differential diagnosis: oesophagitis, mallory-weiss tear (due to retching), peptic ulcer - tests: bloods (check Hb + clotting), if unsure of diagnosis perform an OGD - treatment: ABCs + fluid resus (replace lost blood volume with blood/fluids) +/- surgery
Hepatitis A (acute)	- due to a RNA virus - faeco-oral transmission with 2-6 weeks incubation - symptoms: jaundice +/- abdo pain, deranged LFTs (↑AST/ALT) & immunology shows ↑IgM (IgG is detectable for life after acute infection has passed) - usually self-limiting, just symptom control
Hepatitis B (acute)	- due to a double stranded DNA virus - transmission route = bloodborne (IV drugs/transfusion, sex, neonatal-maternal) - incubation = approximately 1 month - diagnosis: bloods (deranged LFTs + ↑infection/inflammatory markers), imaging + viral studies (immunology) - immunology: HBsAg (= ongoing infection), HBeAg (= marker of viral replication), anti HBs + anti HBc (if HBsAg not present = previous infection), if only anti HBs (= has been immunized or overcome an infection), they all take 1-6 months to peak, *see 'Viral Hepatitis Serology' section in appendix* - symptoms: jaundice +/- abdo pain - will usually settle itself, just symptom control - vaccinate people at risk - can cause chronic hepatitis &/or hepatocellular carcinoma, therefore needs regular screening for cancer

Hepatitis C (chronic)	- RNA virus, high mutation rate - transmission route: bloodborne - patient could be an asymptomatic carrier - is a major cause of chronic liver disease & can cause hepatocellular carcinoma - diagnosis: bloods (deranged LFTs + ↑infection/inflammatory markers), immunology (↑anti HCV antibody), imaging & biopsy - treatment: anti viral therapy (α-interferon & ribavirin) - needs regular screening for hepatic cancer
Autoimmune hepatitis	- caused when antinuclear antibodies (ANA) attack hepatoctyes - type I: ANA &/or anti-smooth muscle antibodies - type II: children only, anti liver/kidney/muscle antibodies (LKM1) - presents as acute or chronic liver failure *(see above)* - associated with other autoimmune diseases (e.g. pernicious anaemia, autoimmune thyroid disease, SLE, RA, etc.) - treat with steroids
Haemochromatosis	- iron overload, due to autosomal recessive C282Y mutation of HFE gene chromosome 6 ⇒↑GI iron absorption which is then deposited in liver (⇒hepatitis), pancreas (⇒diabetes), joints (⇒arthropathy) & heart - can cause liver fibrosis & can ⇒hepatoma - symptoms: skin has bronzed appearance, diabetes, cardiomyopathy, pericarditis, joint problems, erectile dysfunction - test: bloods (FBC, glucose, clotting, LFTs), iron studies (↑Fe, ↑ferritin, ↓TIBC), liver biopsy, US liver/pancreas - treatment: ↓iron intake, regular venesection, checks for hepatoma & genetic counselling
Wilson's disease	- autosomal recessive disorder (gene on chromosome 13) ⇒inability to excrete copper via bile - copper builds up in most organs, but mainly in the liver & nervous system - symptoms: kayser-fleischer rings, hepatitis, neurological signs + psychiatric problems - tests: bloods (LFTs, clotting, ↑Cu level), ↑conc. of Cu in urine, liver biopsy - treatment: penicillamine mops up copper, ↓Cu in diet, liver transplant if severe, genetic counselling
Oesophageal carcinoma	- squamous cell carcinoma (~50%) is more common in upper 2/3 of oesophagus, mainly due to smoking - adenocarcinoma (45%) more common in the lower 1/3, due to gastro-oesophageal reflux & the transition zone (oesophagus = squamous cell, stomach = columnar) ⇒barrett's (premalignant transition of oesophageal epithelia from squamous→columnar) - symptoms: gradual dysphagia (first to solids then fluids) + ↓weight - has poor prognosis: approx. 10% 5yr survival (after surgery) - tests: barium swallow, endoscopy, CT, biopsy - treatment: radio/chemotherapy + surgery or palliative (stenting, laser ablation) - NB. columnar cells are 'producing' cells & are found wherever secretions are produced (i.e. glands), transition zones = ↑risk of malignancy

Gastric carcinoma	- mainly due to peptic ulcer disease *(see above)*, smoking, diet & family history - symptoms: usually a late presentation, abdo pain, dyspepsia, anaemia (GI bleed), anorexia, ↓weight, vomiting, enlarged virchow's node, metastases (e.g. hepatomegaly) - tests: general bloods, endoscopy (OGD), staging CT (thorax, abdo & pelvis) + biopsy - treatment: radio/chemotherapy + surgery or palliative - NB. virchow's node (enlarged left supraclavicular fossa node) is suggestive of upper GI cancer

Colorectal cancer	- predisposing factors: colon polyps, ulcerative colitis/crohn's, low fibre diet & FH
	- symptoms: change in bowel habit, weight loss, anaemia, rectal bleeding & metastases (↑lymph nodes, liver dysfunction, etc.)
	- diagnosis: general bloods (may show anaemia), carcinoembryonic antigen (CEA tumour marker), Ca19-9 tumour marker, barium enema, colonoscopy & look for metastases
	- treatment: radio/chemotherapy & surgery or palliative
	duke's staging:
	  A. limited to bowel wall (confined beneath the muscularis mucosa)
	  B. penetrates bowel wall (extension through the muscularis mucosa + no metastases)
	  C. regional lymph node metastases
	  D. distant metastases (e.g. liver)
	- N.B. the 5yr survival drops from 90% with duke's A, to <10% in patients with duke's D

Mesenteric angina	- pain 10-15mins after eating & passing motions which are usually diarrhoea - diagnosed by angiography - the gut has rich collateral network so large number of vessels must be stenosed before symptoms occur, patient will usually already suffer from peripheral vascular disease - acute mesenteric ischaemia is a surgical emergency =severe abdominal pain, shock, bloody diarrhoea & metabolic acidosis - diet is important = small regular meals (≡angina of gut so think of small meal as a short walk and large meal as a long walk)

Haemorrhoids	- swelling & inflammation of anal vascular cushion
	- risks factors = low fibre diet, pregnancy & straining when passing motions
	- symptoms: pain & bleeding (bright red blood found on toilet paper)
	- a full abdominal assessment must be performed to anyone with rectal bleeding, including a sigmoidoscopy
	- treatment: lifestyle changes (high fibre diet), sclerosant injections (these encourage the growth of new collagen fibres with the effected tissues ⇒gradually destroy the vessels involved) or surgery (either remove or use rubber band ligation, depending on size of haemorrhoids)
	types:
	  1. 1st degree = confined to rectum
	  2. 2nd degree = prolapses when passing motions then reduces afterwards
	  3. 3rd degree = needs to be reduced by hand
	  4. 4th degree = remains constantly prolapsed

Gentiourinary History

Introduction	- approach politely & introduce yourself - patient's name, DOB & occupation

Dysuria (pain on urination), **frequency & urgency**	- SOCRATES *(see 'CV History' for explanation)* - usually due to UTI = inflammation/infection of bladder (cystitis), can also effect the kidneys (pyelonephritis), prostate (prostatitis) or urethra (urethritis) - can also be due to cancer of the renal tract
Colour of urine	- orange/brown = concentrated urine, conjugated bilirubin (water soluble form of bilirubin, is conjugated by the liver) & rhubarb - red/brown = blood, medication (e.g. rifampicin) & beetroot - brown/black = bilirubin & medication (e.g. L-dopa)
Haematuria (blood in urine)	- painless = UTI, renal/bladder/prostate tumour, glomerulonephritis, renal vascular disease, ↑BP - painful = renal stones, UTI, reflux nephropathy, acute renal vascular disease (e.g. due to an emboli)
Polyuria (↑urination)	- causes: diabetes, diabetes insipidus (nephrogenic =↓ADH sensitivity in kidneys, cranial =↓ADH secretion) or medication (e.g. diuretics)
Nocturia (↑urination at night)	- usually due to prostatic obstruction or diabetes
Oliguia (↓urination)	- normal = 0.5mls/kg/hr - causes: obstruction, dehydration, severe burns, severe infection (⇒sepsis), syndrome of inappropriate ADH release (=↑ADH, may cause oliguia without renal failure, but can ⇒renal failure, *see 'Endocrine Revision' section*), & renal failure
↓stream, hesitancy & dribbling	- prostate enlargement or urethral stricture
Incontinence	types: 1. stress incontinence: due to ↓bladder sphincter function, brought on when ↑bladder pressure (cough, laugh, etc.), can be caused by old age, spinal cord trauma/compression, multiple sclerosis, pelvic floor damage after childbirth, prostate problems, or vaginal degeneration (e.g. post menopausal) 2. urge incontinence: due to detrusor instability (i.e. an overactive bladder muscle) ⇒sudden urge to urinate, usually comes out before patient can get to toilet
Abdo pain	- SOCRATES
Sexual	- number of sexual partners in last 12 months, male/female, casual/relationship - condom use (unprotected sex) - history of STDs - male problems with: sex drive, erections, ejaculation, orgasm - female problems with: sex drive, pain during intercourse
Menstrual & Obstetric	- you may need to perform a quick obstetrics & gynaecology history if you suspect this is related to the presenting complaint, *see 'Obstetrics & Gynaecology' section*

PMH	- list PMH + ask DEAR J SMITH *(see 'CV History' for explanation)*
Medications, allergies, smoking & alcohol	- if ex smoker ask smoking history
FH	- are parents/brothers/sisters alive, if so do they suffer from any diseases, if they have passed away (say "sorry to hear that") ask age & reason of death
Social/occupational history	- who is at home & how does this condition effect your life - expand on occupation

The kidney	- each kidney has about one million nephrons, each of which has a glomerulus (in the renal cortex), which filters products out of the blood into the renal tubes (proximal tube →loop of henle →distal tube→collecting ducts→ureters) - juxtaglomerular apparatus (attached to the ascending loop of henle) secrete renin which regulates glomerular blood flow & filtration rate - water excretion is adjusted in the collecting ducts by antidiuretic hormone ADH (vasopressin) which is released by the pituitary gland
Glomerular filtration rate (GFR)	- measured via creatinine clearance (creatinine = end product of skeletal muscle metabolism, is an inert molecule) - creatinine clearance per hour (GFR) $= \dfrac{[Urine_{Cr}]}{[Plamsa_{Cr}]} \times UrineVolume$ per hour - relationship looks like 1/x graph - N.B. renal failure =↓waste removal, therefore blood =↑urea & creatinine
Hypokalaemia (↓K)	- usually due to diuretics, but also GI losses (e.g. diarrhoea & vomiting), acute illness, insulin treatment (insulin pulls both blood sugar & potassium from the blood into cells), ↑mineralocorticoids (these effect water/salt balance e.g. aldosterone, they can be effected by pituitary tumours, steroid medication & ectopic ACTH from small cell lung cancer) - symptoms: weakness, arrhythmias & ECG changes (T wave flattening + U wave, *see diagram on left*) - treat underlying cause + give IV or oral potassium
Hyperkalaemia (↑K)	- mainly due to renal failure (impaired excretion), ↓mineralocorticoid (e.g. addison's disease), ACE inhibitors, K sparing diuretics & cell destruction (haemolysis liberates K into the blood stream) - symptoms: weakness, arrhythmias & ECG changes (peaked T waves + widened QRS + loss of P waves, *see diagram on left*) - treat acutely with IV calcium gluconate (stabilises cardiac myocardium) + IV insulin with glucose (insulin pulls both glucose & K from the blood into cells) + treat underlying cause

Hyponatraemia (↓Na)	- sodium is linked to water balance, i.e. ↑water ≡↓sodium concentration & vice versa
	- symptoms: headache, N&V, lethargy, irritability, depression, muscle weakness/cramp & in late stages confusion, convulsions & coma
	- treat depending on cause/type: IV fluid (containing Na), ↓fluid intake, diuretics
	3 types of ↓Na concentration (depends on changes to water volume in the body):
	  1. hypovolaemia (↓ in both Na & water): renal loss (diuretics, addison's disease, rapid steroid withdrawal), extrarenal loss (vomiting, diarrhoea, burns, sweating)
	  2. normovolaemia (normal or slightly↑water): ↑fluids, hypothyroid, syndrome of inappropriate ADH section (due to small cell lung malignancy)
	  3. hypervolaemia (↑Na & ↑↑water): renal/heart/hepatic failure, nephritic syndrome, ↑fluids
	- N.B. both hyper & hyponatraemia should be treated slowly, rapid rehydration can ⇒cerebral oedema

Hypernatraemia ($\uparrow$Na)	- symptoms: thirst, $\downarrow$consciousness, confusion & coma
	- treat depending on cause/type: IV fluids, diuretics, etc.
	3 types of $\uparrow$Na conc. (depend on changes to water volume in the body):
	  1. hypovolaemia ($\downarrow$Na & $\downarrow\downarrow$water): renal loss (diuretics), extrarenal (diarrhoea, burns, sweating)
	  2. normovolaemia (normal or slightly $\downarrow$water): diabetes insipdus ($\downarrow$ADH secretion), fluid deprivation
	  3. hypervolaemia ($\uparrow\uparrow$Na, $\uparrow$water): cushing's, hyperaldosteronism

Metabolic acidosis	- most common causes = diabetic ketoacidosis (DKA), lactic acidosis & renal failure
	general causes:
	  1. ingestion of acid
	  2. accumulation of acid in tissue: lactic acid (in muscle use/breakdown), ketones (in DKA) or general cell destruction (e.g. sepsis)
	  3. failure to excrete acid (renal failure)
	  4. loss of alkali (e.g. diarrhoea)
	  5. can also happen to compensate for respiratory acidosis
	- symptoms: $\uparrow$RR (kussmaul's respiration = body tries to blow off CO_2 to counteract acidosis by creating a respiratory alkalosis) & shock
	- tests: ABGs (arterial blood gas), bloods (for infection, $\uparrow$glucose, etc.)
	- treat cause, give fluids (+ insulin in DKA) +/- IV bicarbonate
	- N.B. anion gap = difference between cations (Na) & anions (chloride & bicarbonate), $\uparrow$anion gap = addition of anions, $\downarrow$anion gap =loss of anions

Metabolic alkalosis	causes:
	  1. $\uparrow$ intake of alkali
	  2. failure to excrete bicarbonate
	  3. loss of acid (e.g. vomiting)
	  4. can also happen to compensate for a respiratory acidosis
	- assess with ABGs + treat cause
	- N.B. both metabolic acidosis & alkalosis if the primary cause will $\Rightarrow$the opposite condition within the respiratory system to compensate

Acute renal failure	- rapid $\downarrow$GFR $\Rightarrow\downarrow$urine output (depending on the cause can $\Rightarrow\uparrow$BP, $\uparrow$JVP, pulmonary/peripheral oedema, accumulation of nitrogenous waste), metabolic acidosis, $\uparrow$K, & can $\Rightarrow$anaemia ($\downarrow$production of erythropoietin by kidneys)
	causes:
	  1. pre-renal (above kidneys): $\downarrow$blood supply $\Rightarrow\downarrow$glomerular perfusion $\Rightarrow$kidney failure & tubular necrosis, causes =hypovolaemia (haemorrhage, diarrhoea & vomiting), cardiogenic shock, sepsis, burns, severe liver disease & renal artery stenosis (made worse by ACE inhibitors)
	  2. renal (within kidney): glomerulonephritis, vasculitis, myeloma, etc.
	  3. post renal (below kidneys): urinary tract obstruction (prostate enlargement, stones, tumours)
	- tests: bloods (abnormal U&Es +/- $\uparrow$infection/inflammatory markers), MSU + dipstick, check for bence-jones protein in urine (=myeloma), ECG (due to $\uparrow$K), imaging (abdomen X-ray, USS) & renal biopsy
	- treatment: resus (inc. fluids + catheterise) + treat cause & any electrolyte imbalance (e.g. hyperkalaemia which can $\Rightarrow$cardiac dysrhythmias), if severe may need dialysis
	- blood results: if $\uparrow$urea is relatively greater than $\uparrow$Cr when compared with

	- normal values it usually points towards a pre renal cause - NB. ↑K treatment = IV Ca gluconate (stabilizes myocardium) then IV insulin + glucose (insulin drives K out of blood & into cells)
Chronic renal failure	- slow ↓GFR - causes (almost the same as above but on a slower scale): diabetes, glomerulonephritis, tubular nephritis, reflux nephropathy, polycystic kidney, obstructed urine - ⇒↓urine output (⇒↑BP, ↑JVP, pulmonary/peripheral oedema, accumulation of nitrogenous waste), metabolic acidosis, hyperkalaemia, anaemia (↓production of erythropoietin by kidneys), confusion, infection & bone disease (↓renal excretion of vitamin D ⇒↓Ca absorption by gut ⇒↑parathyroid hormone release ⇒↑osteoclast activity ⇒↓bone density) - treatment: control BP & anaemia (oral iron supplements, blood transfusion, or erythropoietin), lifestyle factors (diet =↓K/Na/sugars/cholesterol)
Drugs in renal failure	- some drug that are usually excreted may accumulate in renal failure: digoxin, lithium, morphine & antibiotics - frusemide needs to be increased to have the same effect - potassium sparing diuretics ⇒hyperkalaemia - corticosteroids ⇒↑urate - penicillin, NSAIDs & gold, all ⇒renal toxicity - ACE ⇒↓renal function (especially in renal artery stenosis)
Urinary tract infection (UTI)	- introduction of bacterial via the urethra into the bladder, can ⇒pyelonephritis (bacterial kidney infection) - usually E coli (gram –'ve) - increased risk in: STDs, pregnancy, incomplete bladder emptying (e.g. MS, spinal cord injury), urinary stones, diabetes, structural abnormalities (e.g. reflux) & catheterization - symptoms: dysuria, ↑frequency, urgency, discomfort, loin pain, fever, haematuria, offensive smell, confusion (in elderly), can ⇒sepsis - tests: bloods (infection/inflammatory signs), urine dipstick, mid stream urine (MSU) culture, image renal tract for abnormalities in men & children with recurrent infection - treat with antibiotics (trimethoprim or nitrofurantoin) + ↑fluid intake - NB. infection of bladder =cystitis, prostate =prostatitis & kidney =pyelonephritis
Renal calculi/stones	- associated with ↑calcium & ↑uric acid in the blood - symptoms: haematuria, pain (severe sudden onset colicky loin to groin pain), N&V, renal failure (post renal = due to obstruction), can ⇒UTI & pyelonephritis - tests: full bloods (check renal function + for signs of infection), MSU (culture + dipstick =blood usually present), KUB abdominal X-ray (a small % of stones are visible on X-ray), renal CT &/or IV urogram (radioactive die into urinal tract) - treatment: analgesia, ↑fluid intake, antibiotics, ultrasonic stone break up or surgery (removal &/or insertion of stent into ureter) - long-term management: prophylactic diuretics (⇒↓Ca) & allopurinol (⇒↓urate) - N.B. colicky pain = waves of muscular contractions due to obstruction of a muscle lined tube (e.g. bile duct =gallstones, intestine =obstruction/constipation/strictures, ureter =renal stone)

Proteinuria	- the kidneys glomerular basement membrane is basically a filter, so the more damaged it is the larger the protein molecules it allows through into the urine types: 1. microalbuminuria (small sized proteins) = first signs of damage, e.g. early stages of diabetic nephropathy 2. proteinuria (large sized proteins) = caused by later stage renal disease, e.g. glomerulonephritis, myeloma, diabetes, vasculitis or SLE - investigations: bloods (U&Es, glucose, infection, autoimmune antibodies), MSU (urine dip + microbiology) + diabetic screen *(see 'Endocrine Revision' section)* - NB. urine dipsticks only detect albumin not pathological proteins (e.g. bence-jones proteins found in myeloma)
Nephrotic syndrome	- has a triad of symptoms: proteinuria (protein in urine) $\Rightarrow$hypoalbuminaemia ($\downarrow$protein in blood) $\Rightarrow$oedema - causes: glomerular disease (glomerulonephritis), diabetes, amyloid plaques (primarily or associated with myeloma or RA/SLE) & drugs (e.g. those used in rheumatology), basically anything that damages the kidneys filtering system (glomerular basement membrane) - complications are mainly due to $\downarrow$albumin $\Rightarrow$oedema & hyperviscosity ($\uparrow$risk of blood clot) - tests: bloods (inc. U&Es, albumin & glucose), check for anti-glomerular BM antibodies (goodpasture's syndrome), renal function (creatinine & protein clearance over 24hrs), urine (microscopy/culture & dipstick), renal ultrasound, renal biopsy & throat swab for streptococcal (=nephritic syndrome, *see below*) - treat with lifestyle, diuretics ($\downarrow$oedema), $\downarrow$salt, steroids +/- anticoagulation
Nephritic syndrome	- is an acute condition usually following a streptococcal throat infection symptoms (as nephrotic syndrome but acute + with blood in the urine): 1. haematuria 2. mild proteinuria 3. inability of kidney to excrete fluids $\Rightarrow\downarrow$GFR $\Rightarrow$oedema & $\uparrow$BP - investigations: same as nephrotic syndrome above - treat symptoms + antibiotics against strep (penicillin)
Glomerulonephritis	- affects both kidneys symmetrically $\Rightarrow$proteinuria, haematuria & urinary casts (dead material detected in the urine) - may be primary, or secondary to autoimmune diseases (e.g. SLE & vasculitis) - tests: bloods (inc. U&Es & albumin), kidney biopsy (establishes disease type), test for infection (e.g. strep & immunology) & imaging disease types: 1. vasculitic conditions: acute onset $\Rightarrow$crescentic cells in bowman's capsule $\Rightarrow$thickening of the glomerular basement membrane (BM) 2. goodpasture's syndrome: acute renal failure + pulmonary haemorrhage due to anti-glomerular BM antibodies (usually occurs post strep infection) 3. berger's disease: IgA antibodies, haematuria + upper respiratory tract infection 4. chronic glomerulonephritis: small kidneys with fibrotic changes on biopsy - treat cause + steroids/immunosuppression & BP medications +/- antibiotics
Amyloidosis	- deposition of protein fibrils in organs - associated with myeloma/lymphoma ($\Rightarrow$bence-jones light chain proteins in urine + lytic lesions in bones) or secondary to chronic infection/inflammation - $\Rightarrow$ similar symptoms to nephrotic syndrome & $\uparrow$BP

Polyarteritis nodosa	- vasculitis (auto immune disease) affecting large blood vessels - $\Rightarrow$micro aneurysms, arterial narrowing, $\uparrow$BP & vasculitic rash - associated with hepatitis B - tests: bloods (inc. $\uparrow$inflammatory markers) +/- biopsy - treat with immunosuppression (e.g. steroids)
Wegner's granulomatosis	- vasculitis which $\Rightarrow$ granulomatous disease of upper airway + renal impairment due to necrotizing glomerulonephritis
Renal artery stenosis	- presents with $\uparrow$BP, renal impairment, oedema (fluid overload) & small asymmetrical kidneys - tests: bloods, MSU & imaging of renal arteries (e.g. USS, angiography =dye into vessels & MRI) - treatment: balloon angioplasty/stenting of renal artery - N.B. do not give ACE inhibitors to $\downarrow$BP as can $\Rightarrow\downarrow$renal perfusion
Polycystic kidneys	- autosomal dominantly inherited via chromosome 16 (the autosomal recessive mutation usually effects kids) - as the cysts enlarge $\Rightarrow\downarrow$renal function - symptoms: haematuria, loin pain, infection, blottable kidneys, UTIs, $\uparrow$BP - associated with berry aneurysms which can $\Rightarrow$subarachnoid haemorrhages - tests: bloods (inc. U&Es & creatinine clearance), MSU & imaging (USS) - treat by controlling BP & genetic counselling (family may need screening) - NB. can also get polycystic liver disease
Nephritis	- inflammation of kidney tubules $\Rightarrow$damage/disease $\Rightarrow\downarrow$kidney function - symptoms: renal impairment ($\Rightarrow$electrolyte imbalance), proteinuria & haematuria - acute condition: caused by antibiotics, NSAIDs or autoimmune disease - chronic condition: caused by urinary reflux/obstruction or secondary to renal disease (e.g. glomerularnephitis, sarcoidosis, ischaemia, myeloma) - tests: MSU + dip urine, bloods (check renal function + for infection/inflammation), USS of kidneys & renal tract - treat depending on cause - NB. if due to a bacterial infection called pyelonephritis
Reflux nephropathy	- vesicoureteric junction incompetence $\Rightarrow$urine reflux/backflow from bladder into ureters & then to kidneys $\Rightarrow$chronic nephritis $\Rightarrow$scarred shrunken kidneys - usually presents in children as UTI - specific tests: MCUG scan (inject radioactive dye into bladder via catheter shows actual reflux) + DMSA (isotope injection into blood shows any kidney scaring) - treatment: prophylactic antibiotics, repeat scans, counselling, treat any $\uparrow$BP
Renal bone dystrophy	- renal failure can results in $\downarrow$vitamin D ($\Rightarrow\downarrow$calcium) & $\uparrow$phosphate (due to reduced excretion by kidneys) - $\downarrow$vitamin D $\Rightarrow\downarrow$Ca absorption/uptake by gut $\Rightarrow\uparrow$parathyroid hormone release which stimulates osteoclasts to breakdown bone releasing calcium into the bloodstream ($\Rightarrow\downarrow$bone density) & an enlarged parathyroid gland - symptoms: bone pain, easy bone fractures +/- parathyroid gland swelling - tests: bloods ($\downarrow$calcium, $\uparrow$parathyroid hormone &$\uparrow$alkaline phosphatase a bone breakdown product), X-rays show looser's zones/pseudofractures (horizontal areas of radiolucency =$\downarrow$bone density) - treat renal failure & give vitamin D supplements

Stress incontinence	- due to bladder sphincter weakness, brought on when ↑bladder pressure (cough, laugh, sneeze, etc.) - causes: old age, spinal cord trauma/compression, MS, pelvic floor damage after childbirth, prostate problems, vaginal degeneration (post menopause due to ↓oestrogen) - tests: rule out UTI + perform urodynamic studies - treatment: lifestyle (↓weight etc.), pelvic floor muscle training/exercise, HRT & surgery
Urge incontinence	- due to detrusor instability (i.e. overactive bladder muscle) ⇒sudden urge to urinate which usually happens before patient can get to the toilet - tests: rule out UTI + urodynamic studies - treatment: behavioural/bladder training, antimuscarinic drugs (⇒↓bladder muscle innervation) & surgery (to disrupt nerves to bladder)
Fournier's gangrene	- necrotising fasciitis of male genitalia & surrounding area (a surgical emergency) - common organisms: clostridium, pseudomonas, β haemolytic strep, e coli - usually effects elderly or diabetics after urological surgery - symptoms: cellulitis of external genitalia (swelling & erythema), black spots (areas of necrosis), crepitus (crackling/popping sounds under the skin due to pockets of gas produced by the bacteria), rapid progression, usually ⇒sepsis - treatment: minutes matter, contact a senior urologist immediately (for early surgical debridement), then whilst waiting start broad spectrum antibiotics, IV fluids & prepare for theatre (e.g. bloods, ECG etc.)
Testicular torsion	- testicle twists about its cord structures ⇒venous congestion ⇒infarction - usually seen in teenagers/young men & is a surgical emergency - symptoms: sudden onset painful/tender testicle with radiation to groin & sometimes loin (embryological origin of testicle), patient may have had previous episodes (intermittent torsion), 'bell clapper' appearance (high riding & horizontal lying testicle), irreversible ischaemia can occur within 6 hours - treatment: needs surgical exploration (orchidopexy = untwist & fix, if still looks ischaemic & dusky orchidectomy = removal of testicle)
Phimosis	- narrowing of the foreskin (preputial) orifice - due to: scarring from forcible retraction, chronic foreskin inflammation (balanitis), or can be congenital - symptoms: poor urinary stream & ballooning of foreskin - treatment: circumcision (surgical removal of foreskin)
Paraphimosis	- foreskin (prepuce) is retracted over the penis head/glans ⇒a band like constriction preventing venous return ⇒a painful swollen glans - is common after an erection or at time of urethral catheterisation where the retracted foreskin is not replaced to its normal resting position - symptoms: non reducible foreskin, swollen painful glans - N.B. due to increasing swelling it becomes harder to reduce with time - treatment: ice & compress manually to reduce oedema then attempt foreskin reduction (under local penile block if necessary), if this fails a slit can be made in the foreskin to ↓compression, consider circumcision (to avoid recurrence)
Balanitis	- inflammation of the foreskin and glans usually due to a staph or strep infection - can be acute or chronic (can ⇒scarring & phimosis) - investigations: MSU + swabs, bloods (inc. sugar to rule out diabetes) - treat with antibiotics, in chronic cases consider circumcision

Epididymal cyst	- may contain clear or milky fluid (spermatocoele) - symptoms: painful scrotal swelling, translucent on examination & palpable as separate from the testis (*see 'Gastroenterology Examination' section*) - treatment: surgical resection if symptomatic
Hydrocoele	- serous fluid filled sacs within the layers surrounding the testicle (the tunica vaginalis or processus vaginalis), will also illuminate with torch examination there are 4 types: 1. vaginal hydrocoele: most common, fluid fills the tunica vaginalis & surrounds the testicle but does not extend into the cord & does not communicate with the peritoneal cavity, the testis will be difficult to palpate 2. congenital hydrocoele: basically a hernial sac is present but it is filled with fluid as opposed to bowel, it communicates with the peritoneal cavity, it should partially empty if elevated 3. infantile hydrocoele: similar to congenital, but the sac is closed off proximally at the internal ring so the fluid can surround the cord but does not communicate with the peritoneal cavity 4. hydrocoele of the cord: rare, fluid is confined to a sac that bulges out along the cord, it is separate from the testes below & the peritoneal cavity above, it should descend with the testicle on traction - treatment: can resolve spontaneously, may need simple aspiration or surgery - N.B. a hydrocoele may be secondary to underlying pathology (e.g. tumour or inflammation), perform an USS if suspicious
Varicocele	- enlargement of the veins that drain the scrotum & testicles - mainly occurs on the left, because the left testicular vein drains at right angles into the left renal vein, also this junction is often absent of valves making flow backwards far more likely - symptoms: scrotal mass that expands on standing, looking like a 'bag of worms' - N.B. varicoceles may be secondary to other pathology blocking testicular venous drainage, e.g. a renal tumour causing renal vein occlusion - treatment: if asymptomatic reassure the patient, if causing pain use scrotal support, in severe cases perform embolization or surgical tying of testicular vein
Epididymo-orchitis	- inflammation of the epididymis (epididymitis) &/or the testicle (orchitis) - epididymitis: is more common, usually bacterial (in old men = e coli, in young men think STD e.g. gonorrhoeae or chlamydia) - orchitis: less common, usually viral (e.g. the mumps) - symptoms: testicular pain & swelling, can also have UTI type symptoms - tests: bloods, MSU, USS (rule out abscess), STD swabs - treatment: analgesia & scrotal support +/- antibiotics - N.B. testicular torsion is a differential, if in doubt always explore
Benign prostatic hypertrophy (BPH)	- presents with bladder outflow obstruction $\Rightarrow$poor stream, terminal dribbling, hesitancy, $\uparrow$frequency, nocturia, overflow incontinence & dysuria - can $\Rightarrow$urinary retention & renal failure - is highly dependent on androgens (testosterone) - tests: bloods for kidney function (U&Es) & prostate specific antigen (PSA), urodynamics, image renal tract, transrectal USS & biopsy - treatment: α-adrenergic blockers (relax smooth muscle in the prostate & bladder neck), medication to block testosterone conversion to its active form (e.g. finasteride) & surgery (transurethral resection of prostate, TURP, can $\Rightarrow$impotency)

Prostatic cancer	- because the prostate is a gland & made up of columnar cells this is usually due to an adenocarcinoma (metastasizes to bone & lymph) - usually not aggressive $\Rightarrow$approx. 10 yr life expectancy - is also highly dependant on androgens - treatment: medication to block testosterone, radio/brachy/chemo therapy, surgery (remove prostate +/- bilateral testicular removal)
Bladder & urinary tract malignancy	- transitional cell carcinoma (TCC) is most common, 95% of tumours affect the bladder, 5% affect the upper urinary tract - bladder TCC is the 2nd most common urological cancer (1st = renal cell) - risk factors: smoking, rubber & dye industrial agents, chronic inflammation (e.g. recurrent infections & long term catheters) - symptoms: painless haematuria, ~5% present with metastatic disease - diagnosis is made with cystoscopy (camera inserted into urethra) + multiple biopsies, may need imaging (to rule out metastatic disease) - treatment: in simple cases surgery = transurethral resection of bladder tumour (TURBT), in more severe cases large areas may need surgical removal (neo bladders = a new bladder is fashioned using small bowel), radio/chemotherapy - N.B. in the over 50's haematuria must always be investigated
Penile cancer	- squamous cell carcinoma - rare in circumcised (uncircumcised can $\Rightarrow$poor hygiene & retained smegma) - symptoms: erythematous patch, ulcer +/- bloody discharge $\Rightarrow$erosion through prepuce, local spreading to proximal shaft & to inguinal lymph nodes - treatment: depending on severity radiotherapy +/- surgical amputation & inguinal nodal resection (patient may need a permanent urostomy $\equiv$ stoma)
Testicular cancer	- common in young men - a previously undescended testicle $\Rightarrow$10 fold increase in risk - 95% have germ cell pathology = seminomas or non seminomatous germ cell tumours (NSGCT) - tumour markers: α feta protein (raised only in teratomas = NSGCT), βHCG (raised by all NSGCT & in smaller quantities by seminomas) - treatment: in these cases a biopsy is usually not performed (risk of cancer cell seeding), instead an orcidectomy is performed (cure in 80% + pathological diagnosis), if metastatic disease present use radio/chemotherapy
Renal investigations	- urine dipstick checks for blood, protein, glucose, ketones, nitrites, bilirubin & leucocytes - MSU send to microbiology for culture - bloods (FBC, U&Es, LFTs, CRP, etc.) - imaging: ultrasound or CT scan - IV urogram = radioactive dye injected & X-rays taken at set times afterwards - renal angiography diagnoses renal artery stenosis, stenting & blood clots - renal biopsy

Neurology History

Introduction	- approach politely and introduce yourself - patient's name, DOB & occupation

Headache	- SOCRATES (<u>A</u>ssociated symptoms: most are covered below + neck stiffness, N&V & fever)

Fits, Faints & Funny turns (3Fs)	- what happened before, during & after the event (eye witness account if possible)
	- associated with: most are covered below + incontinence, tongue biting, any injures, palpitations
	types:
	  1. syncope (due to insufficient oxygen in the brain or ↓BP): vasovagal (faints), postural, exertional, arrhythmias (stokes-adams attack)
	  2. epilepsy: partial or generalized, simple (no LOC) or complex (LOC), myoclonic (involuntary twitching of a muscle or a group of muscles) or tonic-clonic (muscles contract & relax rapidly causing convulsions), can also have absence seizures (patient may appear to be staring into space)
	  3. vertigo: includes hearing problems (deafness, tinnitus, etc.)
	  4. falls/drop attacks: usually in the elderly

Vision	- photophobia, diplopia, visual flashes, blurred vision, visual field loss (e.g. hemianopia & quadrantanopia, *see 'Visual Field Defects' section in appendix*)
Hearing	- ask about hearing problems, dizziness & balance
Smell	- any obvious changes
Swallowing problems	- if so does it affect solids &/or liquids

Speech or language disturbances	- dysphasia = lesion in speech centres ⇒disorder in speech comprehension or production
	- dysarthria (disorder in articulation): defective movement of lips, tongue or palate e.g. cerebellar disease (= staccato speech) or alcohol intoxication
	- dysphonia (disorder in vocalisation): vocal cord lesion giving impaired sound production
	areas of brain involved:
	  1. broca's (motor area for word production): patient understands but cannot answer appropriately ⇒motor dysphasia
	  2. wernicke's (temporal area for language comprehension): patient does not understand what is being said to them ⇒fluent disorganised speech = sensory dysphasia

Weakness & ↓Sensation	- SOCRATES *(versions of this can be used for a number of situations as well as pain)* - associated with: most covered in this history + muscle wasting - risk factors for stroke (are covered in PMH/FH) & haemorrhage (covered in medication)
Tremors/involuntary movements	- choreiform/involuntary movements = huntington's chorea tremor types: - resting = parkinson's (5Hz frequency, pill rolling) - intension = cerebellar (5Hz) - action = hyperthyroid/anxiety (10Hz)
Sphincter control	- faecal &/or urinary incontinence
Mental health	- depression, elation, agitation, sleep disturbances, etc.

PMH	- list PMH + ask DEAR J SMITH
Medications, allergies, smoking & alcohol	- if ex smoker ask smoking history
FH	- are parents/brothers/sisters alive, if so do they suffer from any diseases, if they have passed away (say "sorry to hear that") ask age & reason of death
Social/occupational history	- who is at home & how does this condition effect your life - expand on occupation

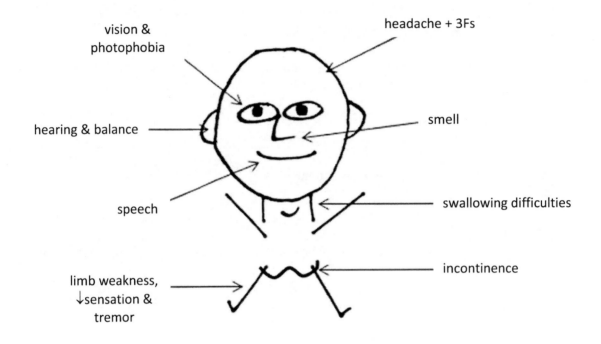

Neurological Limb Exam

Introduction	- wash your hands - approach politely and introduce yourself - patient's name & DOB - explain to patient what you are going to do & obtain verbal consent - expose patient after asking

Examination steps: Inspection, Tone, Power, Reflexes, Sensation, Vibration, Proprioception & Coordination

Lower Limb

Inspection	say what you see: - comment on any deformity, scars, colour changes - muscle wasting (↓use, muscle disease or denervation), muscle hypertrophy (duchenne's muscular dystrophy = doughy feel due to fat infiltration) - fasciculations (small contractions in muscle + wasting = LMN) - choreiform/involuntary movements (huntington's chorea) - dystonic movements (repetitive muscle contractions due to extrapyramidal dysfunction usually basal ganglia) tremors: - resting = parkinson's (5Hz frequency, pill rolling) - intension = cerebellar (5Hz) - action = hyperthyroid/anxiety (10Hz)
Tone	- tell patient to go floppy/relax - flex & extend each joint in turn + internally & externally rotate the hip - briskly raise knee off bed & observe if ankle also raises off bed =↑tone - ankle clonus: quickly flex foot upwards & hold, continued beating =↑tone (can also do a knee clonus by pushing the patella towards the foot) - spasticity = ↑tone at start of joint movement which then gives way - rigidity = ↑tone sustained throughout joint movement, if jerky = cogwheel rigidity
Hip power	- flexion (iliacus & psoas muscle = L1,2 spinal innervation), perform against gravity first = straight leg raise off bed, then "stop me pushing leg down" - extension (gluteus maximus L5, S1,2) "push leg into bed & squash my hand" - N.B. if patient cannot perform any of the 'power' movements against gravity they can be tested without gravity by converting the movement into an horizontal motion instead of a vertical one, e.g. turn on their side to perform hip fexion
Knee power	- flexion (hamstrings L5, S1,2) "pull your foot towards your bum, stop me straightening your knee" - extension (quadriceps L2,3,4) "resist me bending your knee, straighten your leg"
Ankle power	- dorsiflexion (tibialis ant. L4,5) "resist me plantar flexing your ankle" - plantar flexion (gastrocnemius & soleus S1,2) "resist me dorsiflexing your ankle"
Power scoring system	0. paralysis 1. flicker of contraction 2. movement when gravity eliminated 3. movement against gravity 4. reduced against resistance 5. normal

Reflexes absent + hyporeflex ++ normal +++ hyperreflex	- always look at the muscle proximal to the tendon being struck 1. knee L3,4 (support knee whilst performing) 2. ankle S1,2 (put under tension i.e. dorsiflex foot) 3. plantar L5, S1,2 (stroke sole of foot around lateral edge, babinski sign = +'ve if big toe goes up = UMN lesion) - if no reflex ask patient to clench teeth or interlock fingers & pull - NB. if it takes time for muscle to relax consider hypothyroidism

Sensation
(superficial & deep)
 	
L2
      L3
   ( )
L5
      L4
S1
	- with cotton wool (tests light touch sensation) then with pin/neuro tip (tests pain sensation)
	- first test/show what it feels like on patient's chest
	- upper outer thigh = L2
	- inner thigh/ant. knee = L3
	- inner calf = L4
	- outer calf = L5
	- lat. foot = S1
	- N.B. can also test temperature sensation using hot & cold substances (it is unlikely this will come up in an exam)
	spinal tracts:
	- dorsal column carries innervation to light touch, proprioception & vibration
	- spinothalamic carries innervation to pain & temp receptors

Vibration	- start at boney prominence of distal interpharangeal (DIP) joint of big toe - use a 128Hz tuning fork (place on chest first so patient knows the feeling) - ask patient to close their eyes & tell you when the vibrations stop (stop vibrations when you are ready) - continue up leg if deficit is detected - N.B. this sense is 1st to be affected in patients with diabetes
Proprioception (joint position)	- fix DIP joint of big toe by holding it either side with one hand whilst you move it with the other, "which way am I moving your big toe, up or down" - continue up leg if needed testing progressively larger joints to measure height of deficit - N.B. this sense is 2nd to be affected in patients with diabetes
Coordination	- close eyes, run each heel in turn up & down opposite shin
Romberg's test	- stand feet together eyes closed (you stand close by in case they start to fall) - +'ve test = patient starts to sway/fall - assesses damage to nerves from the dorsal columns of the spinal cord, which are essential for joint position sense (proprioception) & vibration
Gait	tests: - walk heel-to-toe (cerebellar = wide gait 'drunken walk') - walk on tiptoes, looks for S1 lesion - walk on heels, looks for foot drop = L4,5 lesion

Upper Limb

Inspection	*(as above)*
Tone	- hold out hands with palms facing up, eyes closed (UMN =downwards/medial drift due to weakness, cerebellar disease =upwards drift, loss of proprioception =drifts in number of directions) - tell patient to go floppy/relax - flex & extend each joint in turn (test wrist, elbow & shoulder) - spasticity = ↑tone at start of movement which then gives way - rigidity = ↑tone sustained throughout movement, if jerky = cogwheel rigidity
Shoulder power	- chicken wings position - "don't let me push arms down" (deltoid muscle =C5,6 spinal innervation) - "resist me raising your arms" (latissimus dorsi C6,7,8)
Elbow power	- flex elbows to 90°, 'boxing guard' position - flexion (biceps C5,6) "don't let me straighten your arms" - extension (triceps C7) "don't let me bend your arms further"
Wrist power	- flexion (flexor muscles C6,7,8) "don't let me extend your wrist" - extension (extensor muscles C7,8) "don't let me bend your wrist"
Finger power	- squeeze my hand (most finger movements = C7,8) - straighten fingers, "don't let me bend them" - DAB (Dorsal interossei muscles ABduct) = spread fingers apart, "don't let me close them" use your 1st & little fingers push against their 1st & little fingers (should always test like-for-like when performing examinations) - PAD (Palmar ADducts) = hold fingers together, slide piece of paper between, "stop me pulling the paper out"
Reflexes	- biceps C5,6 (hit your finger which you place on the biceps tendon) - triceps C7,8 - supinator C5,6 (hit your finger) - N.B. hoffmann's reflex =quickly move patient's pointing finger tip up & down, look for movement in thumb (=brisk reflexes ≡babinski sign)
Sensation (superficial & deep)	- with cotton wool then with pin/neuro tip (first test/show how they feel on patient's chest) - outer upper arm = C5 - lat. forearm & thumb = C6 - middle fingers = C7 - little finger = C8 - medial upper arm = T1 C5 T1 C6 C8 C7
Vibration	- start at boney prominence of DIP joint of thumb - use a 128Hz tuning fork, place on chest first so they know the feeling - ask patient to close their eyes & tell you when the vibrations stop (stop vibrations when you are ready) - continue up arm if deficit is detected

Proprioception	- use DIP of thumb - fix joint by holding it either side with one hand whilst you move it with the other, "which way am I moving your finger, up or down" - continue up arm if needed testing progressively larger joints to measure height of deficit
Coordination	- finger-nose test (cerebellar disease =intention tremor & past pointing), move your finger between each repetition - hand-palm test: show them what to do + ask them to speed up if possible (cerebellar disease ⇒dysdiadochokinesis =inability to execute rapidly alternating movements)

	UMN lesion	LMN lesion
Tone	↑	↓
Power	↓(in some)	↓
Reflexes	↑	↓
Plantar	+'ve	normal/absent

Cranial Nerve Exam

Introduction	- wash your hands - approach politely and introduce yourself - patient's name & DOB - explain to patient what you are going to do & obtain verbal consent
Inspection	- comment on patients general health & surrounding apparatus/medications - scars, deformity, facial asymmetry, obvious ptosis, inequality of pupils, etc.
Olfactory (1)	- sense of smell (test in each nostril separately) - may have a cold, check nose for blockage - this is rarely performed in an OSCE exam
Optic (2)	there are a number of tests that need to be performed on the eyes: 1. visual acuity: using snellen chart (perform with glasses if usually worn) assess 2 & 3 using the confrontation method =compare your vision with the patient's, positioning & explanation are important, sit so you can test vision half way between you & the patient 2. visual inattention: both eyes open, "is my finger moving on one or both sides simultaneously", test in upper & lower quadrants, inattention =cannot see both sides move simultaneously, e.g. stroke 3. visual field defects: patient covers eye not being tested, you cover your apposing eye, bring finger in diagonally from upper then lower quadrants & L then R sides, "tell me when you can see my finger" *(see 'Visual Field Defects' in appendix)* 4. direct & consensual pupil light responses: ask patient to look into the distance & bring torch in from the lateral side, firstly looking for a direct reflex (in the eye you are shining the touch into) then again looking for a consensual reflex (in the eye the torch is not being shone into), then repeat in other eye, an afferent papillary defect = no direct response but still a consensual one, efferent papillary defect = fixed & dilated but other pupil responds consensually 5. accommodation (both eyes at same time): focus on distant point then on examiners finger, eyes converge + pupils constrict 6. ophthalmoscopy: examine each eye using the ophthalmoscope, *see 'Ophthalmology' section for more details*
Oculomotor (3) **Trochlear** (4) **Abducens** (6)	- eye movements, test both eyes at same time - "keep your head still & follow my finger with your eyes", trace out an 'H' shape then 'I' shape down centre - look for nystagmus: ask patient to look to their extreme L and hold $\Rightarrow$slow drift to R then fast correction to L (=L horizontal nystagmus), repeat in other direction, NB. the nystagmus is the fast correction - ask about double vision - the oculomotor (3rd nerve) controls all eye muscles apart from superior oblique (supplied by 4th nerve, moves eye inwards + down) & lateral rectus (6th nerve, moves eye outwards), mnemonic = $O_3 SO_4 LR_6$ - oculomotor also supplies the muscles that open the eye lid & constrict the pupil - NB. $\uparrow$ICP can $\Rightarrow$6th nerve palsy $\Rightarrow$eye cannot move down or outwards/laterally $\Rightarrow$double vision

Trigeminal (5)	divisions:
	  1. ophthalmic
	  2. maxillary
	  3. mandibular
	sensation:
	- superficial trigeminal: close eyes & touch each division with cotton wool
	- deep trigeminal: close eyes & touch each division with pin/neuro tip
	- corneal reflex: approach from side, lightly touch the cornea with a damp cotton wool = both eyes blink (the sensory nerve for this reflex is the ophthalmic division of the trigeminal whilst the blink movement is via the facial nerve), N.B. you will probably not be asked to perform this in an exam situation
	motor:
	- muscles of mastication: clench teeth & feel the masseter muscle, "stop me from opening your mouth"
	- jaw-jerk reflex (brisk =UMN lesion), usually not be asked to perform in OSCE exam

Facial (7)	- motor: muscles of facial expression, ask patient to screw up eyes, raise eyebrows, blow out cheeks, purse lips/whistle & smile to show teeth - sensation: taste for anterior 2/3 of tongue - responsible for producing tears & saliva - bell's palsy = 7th nerve LMN palsy, effects muscles & sensation supplied by the facial nerve, caused by inflammation of the nerve (can be due to herpes simplex virus), treat with steroids +/- antivirals - NB. LMN lesion = all muscles affected on one side (ipsilateral), UMN lesion =ipsilateral except forehead because fontalis muscle has bilateral innervations (is innervated by both sides of the brain) - *neumonic to remember facial nerves (temporal, zygomatic, buccal, mandibular & cervical): Two Z B My Cats, I'll leave you to fill in the blanks!*
Vestibulocochlear (8)	- "repeat what I say", whisper into each ear in turn - rinne's test = 256 or 512 Hz tuning fork placed on the mastoid process (assesses bone conduction) then next to ear (air conduction), ask "which is louder" (determines whether bone or air conduction is best, it should normally be air) - weber's test = tuning fork placed on centre of forehead, "which side can you hear it loudest", normal =central - examine tympanic membrane using an auroscope - *see 'ENT' section for more detail*
Glossopharyngeal (9) =sensory innervation for pharynx, tonsils & post. 1/3 of tongue **Vagus** (10) =motor innervation for pharynx & larynx	- say 'aah' - inspect palate - assess for difficulty swallowing (can ask them to drink some water) - gag reflex (will not be tested in an OSCE exam) - do they have a hoarse voice
Accessory (11)	- inspect trapezius muscle from behind - shrug shoulders, "stop me pushing your shoulders down" - "turn your head against my hand", feel opposite sternomastoid as head turned
Hypoglossal (12)	- stick out tongue - LMN lesion = wasting & tongue deviates to effected side

Mnemonic to remember the cranial nerves: <u>O</u>h <u>O</u>h <u>O</u>h <u>T</u>o <u>T</u>ouch <u>A</u>nd <u>F</u>eel <u>V</u> Girls <u>V</u> And <u>H</u>

Sorry I cannot publish all the mnemonic as it gets a bit graphic, use your imagination to fill in the gaps

Neurology Revision

Glasgow coma scale (out of 15)	eye opening: 1. none 2. to pain 3. to voice 4. spontaneous	motor response 1. none 2. extension to pain 3. flexion to pain 4. localising pain 5. moves to command 6. spontaneous	verbal response 1. none 2. unrecognisable sound 3. inappropriate words 4. confused conversation 5. normal speech
Stroke			

Stroke

- disruption/blockage of blood supply to the brain ⇒neurological deficit lasting more than 24hrs
- symptoms: initial contralateral (opposite side to lesion) paralysis, then after several days ⇒ contralateral UMN lesion symptoms (↑tone, hyper reflexes, ↓power, up going plantar & clonus = involuntary muscular contractions due to sudden stretching of the muscle, *see examination above*)

causes:
1. emboli (blood clot, fat emboli or detached segment of thrombus) ⇒ischaemia, ↑risk if suffer from: AF, heart valve disease, prosthetic valve in-situ, recent MI
2. thrombosis (due to polycythaemia/hyperviscocity, ↑alcohol, oral contraceptive pill, thrombophilia, vasculitis e.g. SLE) ⇒ischaemia
3. intra-cranial bleed (ruptured blood vessel due to ↑BP, anticoagulation or trauma)

- ischaemic stroke usually only effect the area supplied by the blocked artery whereas haemorrhage results in more global symptoms due to the ↑intracranial pressure (ICP)
- tests: bloods, ECG, CXR, CT head, carotid doppler, angiography (X-ray of blood vessels after contrast injected)

specific treatment:
- emboli = immediate antiplatelet +/- anticoag therapy (e.g. aspirin & heparin/warfarin)
- thrombosis = thromboylsis (breaks down thrombotic clots e.g. spironolactone, do not give if bleed is suspected) +/- aspirin & heparin/warfarin
- bleed = surgery to clip bleeding vessel
- general treatment (except for bleed): rehab (physio, speech therapy, etc.), lifestyle advice, lifelong aspirin +/- warfarin, surgery (heart valve replacement, carotid artery stenting, etc.)

specific area of stroke + symptoms:
1. internal carotid artery blockage ⇒ocular features (loss of vision in ipsilateral eye, amaurosis fugax = curtain coming across vision for few minutes due to transient occlusion of the retinal artery, or permanent monocular blindness = retinal infarction) & hemispheric features (↓power/sensation to contralateral arm/leg +/- dysphasia)
2. vertebrobasilar artery blockage =dizziness, collapse, transient/complete blindness in both eyes
3. brainstem strokes will result in cranial nerve abnormalities
4. cerebral cortex strokes will effect memory (temporal lobe), speech (broca's area =expressive symptoms, wernicke's =receptive symptoms), vision (occipital lobe) & confusion (frontal lobe)
5. cerebellum stoke = ataxia & ↓coordination

Transient ischaemic attack (TIA)	- a stroke that lasts <24hrs, sometimes just a few minutes - usually due to emboli - 80% originate from carotid/vertebral artery thrombi & 20% from heart valves - diagnose & treat as stroke
Subarachnoid haemorrhage	- bleeding into subarachnoid space surrounding the brain - usually due to a ruptured berry aneurysm (associated with polycystic kidney disease) + ↑BP - symptoms: specific thunderclap headache, ↑ICP, meningism signs (stiff neck, photophobia, N&V, etc.) +/- papilloedema (optic disc swelling due to ↑ICP) - tests: bloods (inc. clotting & infection markers), CT, LP (after 8-12hrs due to chance of coning, look for xanthochromia ≡ bilirubin a red blood cell breakdown product), angiography (X-ray of blood vessels with injected contrast) - treatment: surgical clipping, analgesia, stool softeners, control BP, bed rest & nurse in quiet room - NB. blood in CSF can ⇒ cerebral artery spasm (↓ by giving nimodipine)
Subdural haemorrhage	- venous bleed between inner arachnoid membrane and the dura mater, acts as a space occupying lesion ⇒↑ICP ⇒slow focal neurological signs - causes: vein rupture (due to minor trauma, common in boxers) or brain atrophy (due to age, dementia or alcohol) - diagnosed with CT - treat by surgical evacuation
Extradural haemorrhage	- bleed into the potential space between the dura and the skull - usually due to a fractured temporal/parietal bone ⇒laceration of middle meningeal artery & vein - ↑ICP ⇒gradual LOC &/or UMN signs - treat by surgical evacuation
Headache	types: 1. migraine: unilateral throbbing pain ⇒general headache, preceded by visual aura, photophobia or N&V, usually resolves over hours, risk factors =menstruation, cheese, red wine, oral contraceptive pill, etc. 2. cluster: repetitive headaches over weeks, severe, unilateral (around one eye), usually at the same time each day, risk factors = men & alcohol 3. ophthalmic/trigeminal neuralgia: effects 5th cranial nerve ⇒intense unilateral pain usually lasting only a few seconds in the mandibular/maxillary region, can be secondary to MS, tumours or herpes zoster (shingles) 4. tension: tight band around head 5. temporal arteritis: typically patients complain of pain putting on glasses, due to vasculitis (giant cell arteritis) =autoimmune disease, check bloods for inflammatory response (e.g. ↑CRP/ESR), treat with steroids - acute causes = subarachnoid haemorrhage, meningitis & glaucoma - progressive causes: tumours, benign intracranial hypertension (usually young overweight women) & hydrocephalus - progressive ↑ICP symptoms: worse on coughing/sneezing/bending over, worse in morning, visual disturbance (papilloedema), N&V - treat depending on cause: simple analgesia, antiemetics (to reduce N&V), steroids (for arteritis), CT head, etc.
Dizziness/vertigo	- think inner ear problems (e.g. infection or trauma), meniere's disease *(see 'ENT' section)* & cranial nerve damage or lesions

Blackout	causes: 1. vasovagal syncope: due to standing for too long or emotional distress, both ⇒reflex bradycardia & peripheral vasodilation, preceded by nausea, sweating & closing of visual fields 2. situation syncope: exercise or rapid change in position ⇒changes in vascular tone 3. epilepsy: fitting, incontinence, tongue biting, aura, etc. 4. transient arrhythmias: tachycardia, bradycardia or irregular rhythms (stoke-adams attacks), basically any heart problem that ⇒↓cardiac output 5. hypoglycaemia (always check a patient's blood sugar)
Epilepsy	first establish the type of seizure (general or partial) then whether it was complex or not: 1. generalized seizures effect both hemispheres & can present as tonic-clonic, myoclonic jerks or with absence attacks (patient may seem awake but are unresponsive) 2. partial seizures effect only one part of the brain, they can present as motor or somatosensory irregularities, can ⇒generalized seizure 3. simple seizure = no LOC, complex seizure = LOC - history: ask patient & eye witness about timeline of events (pre seizure, during & post) + predisposing factors (trauma, infection, flashing lights) - ask about tongue biting, incontinence, injury during seizure, etc. - investigations: bloods (inc. infection/inflammatory markers & glucose =hypoglycaemic fit), ECG, EEG +/- CT/MRI brain - general treatment education: involve family/school/work, provoking factors, preventing injury (e.g. recovery position + maintain airway) - specific treatment: if have 2 or more generalized seizures give sodium valproate (side effects =↑weight, hair loss, tremor & vomit/diarrhoea), if 2 or more partial seizures give carbamazepine (side effects =rashes, diplopia, ataxia & will effect oral contraceptives) - N.B. inform DVLA as patient cannot drive until 1 year free from seizures
Status epilepticus	- seizure for >30mins or several in a row without gaining consciousness - if patient not a known epileptic consider an intracranial mass, haemorrhage, infection or metabolic causes - treatment: resus (ABCs + O$_2$), correct any hypoglycaemia, if due to alcohol/malnutrition give IV thiamine & vitamin B$_{12}$ + do a toxicology screen, bloods (for infective/inflammatory markers), ECG & CT brain - to stop seizure: IV lorazepam or diazepam slowly, if no IV access give PR diazepam - N.B. if patient pregnant could be due to eclampsia *(see 'Obstetric' section)*
Multiple sclerosis (MS)	- autoimmune inflammatory condition ⇒demyelination of nerves ⇒↓nerve impulse conduction velocity condition types: 1. relapsing remitting = gradual decline with recovery periods between episodes 2. relapsing progressive = no recovery between episodes 3. primary progressive = a continual aggressive disease - symptoms: fatigue, optic neuritis/atrophy (central visual field defect), nystagmus (damage to nerves supplying eye muscles), motor weakness, UMN signs (spasticity), sensory loss & cerebellar ataxia (↓coordination & balance) - tests: MRI, lumbar puncture (=oligoclonal bands of IgG) & nerve conduction

	velocity studies (e.g. retina→occipital lobe)
	- there is no cure but treat flare-ups with high dose steroids, β interferon (immunosuppression) + symptom control (catheter, viagra, antidepressants, etc.) + physio/speech therapy etc.
Meningitis	- inflammation/infection of the meninges by bacteria (e.g. neisseria meningiditis, strep pneumoniae) or less severely by a virus (enterovirus)
	- is an emergency as patient can quickly go septic
	- symptoms of meningitis: fever, headache, photophobia, neck stiffness, kernig's sign (lower back pain if try to raise legs whilst lying down), brudzinski's sign (hips flex on bending head forward), signs of ↑ICP (N&V, fits, drowsiness, bulging fontanelle in infants, papilloedema, etc.)
	- once a non blanching purpuric rash is visible shows patient has meningococcal septicaemia
	- tests: bloods (↑infection & inflammatory markers), culture everything & lumbar puncture (send for CSF analysis + culture, do not perform if signs of ↑ICP get CT head instead)
	- treat with immediate antibiotics (in general practice setting if not allergic give children IM benzylpenicillin straight away) + fluid resuscitation if septic
	lumbar puncture CSF analysis:
	- bacteria in CSF ⇒↑pressure, ↑protein, ↑neutrophils, ↓glucose
	- virus in CSF ⇒ ↑lymphocytes, all others normal
	- bacteria can be seen in CSF under microscope using a ziehl-nielsen stain
Encephalitis	- acute inflammation of the brain, commonly caused by a viral infection, but can result from a bacterial infection (e.g. bacterial meningitis)
	- symptoms: headache, confusion, drowsiness, seizures & general fever/malaise
	- tests: bloods, LP, brain CT/MRI (shows focal inflammation)
	- treat by resus + acyclovir (antiviral) &/or antibiotics
Cerebral/brain abscess	- collection of infected material within the brain tissue, arising from a local (ear, dental, etc.) or remote (lung, heart, kidney etc.) infective source
	- symptoms: fever (spiking temp), headache & focal neurological signs
	- tests: bloods (inc. HIV test & cultures), CT/MRI, do not perform a LP due to high risk of coning
	- treatment: IV antibiotics + surgical drainage
	- NB. an abscess is an infection that has been 'walled in' by the body to stop it spreading, the abscess wall/capsule not only stops it spreading by also stops immune cells from attacking the bacteria, most abscesses ⇒characteristic spikes in temperature & need surgical drainage (the wound is then packed so the area does not 'wall off' again but heals from the bottom up)
CNS tumours	- 50% usually metastasize from the body resulting in secondary tumours
	primary tumours:
	1. astrocytoma: rapid growth, common in elderly
	2. oligodendroglioma: slow growth, common in young
	3. lymphoma: common in HIV patients, ebstin barr virus (EBV) drives tumour growth, is sensitive to steroids
	- symptoms: signs of ↑ICP, papilloedema + focal deficits depending on area of growth, can ⇒epilepsy
	- investigations: bloods (inc. tumour markers), CT/MRI + biopsy, do not perform a LP due to high risk of coning
	- treatment: dexamethasone (⇒↓brain oedema ⇒↓focal signs), chemo/radiotherapy, surgical removal +/- palliative care

Spinal tracts	- dorsal column tracts carry nerve innervation for light touch, proprioception & vibration
	- spinothalomic tracts carry innervation for pain & temp receptors
Spinal cord compression	- symptoms: LMN signs at level of compression and UMN below, pain radiating down legs, urinary incontinence & sensory loss below compression
	- causes: tumours (from breast, prostate & lung), prolapsed disc, trauma, etc.
	- tests: bloods (for tumour markers), X-ray, CT/MRI spine
	- treat by surgical decompression
Degeneration of cord	- vitamin B_{12} deficiency $\Rightarrow$impaired DNA replication $\Rightarrow$corticospinal tract damage $\Rightarrow$limb weakness + peripheral neuropathy (e.g. absent ankle jerks)
	- associated with alcoholism & pernicious anaemia *(see 'Haematology Revision' section)*
	- symptoms: UMN signs in legs (e.g. positive babinski sign) & $\downarrow$sensation in the peripheries, reflexes usually are absent
	- treat by giving vitamin B_{12} injections
Cervical spondylitis	- degenerative changes + osteophytes (bony spurs) in the vertebra (can be seen on X-ray) $\Rightarrow$constriction of cervical spinal cord, therefore when head moves $\Rightarrow$damage to cord
	- symptoms: neck pain/crepitus, muscle wasting/weakness, sensory loss + LMN signs at level of compression and UMN below
	- treat with analgesia +/- surgery
Motor neuron disease	- degeneration of upper & lower motor neurons
	- $\Rightarrow$both UMN & LMN signs with no associated sensory deficit (this differentiates it from multiple sclerosis), it also never effects the muscles for eye movement (this differentiates it from myasthenia gravis)
	- can present with progressive weakness &/or bulbar palsy (=LMN signs in tongue & muscles of chewing/swallowing)
	- tests: muscle biopsy, MRI of spine, LP & electromyography (shows $\downarrow$muscular activity)
	- there is no cure, discuss prognosis & counsel family, speech/swallowing/physio therapist, nutrition support & palliative care
	- NB. pseudobulbar palsy $\Rightarrow$UMN signs in tongue & muscles of chewing/swallowing
Myasthenia gravis	- autoimmune antibodies attack acetylcholine (ACh) receptors at neuromuscular junction
	- symptoms: proximal muscle weakness $\Rightarrow$quick fatigue, extraocular (eye movement) muscles involved ($\Rightarrow$diplopia & ptosis) & bulbar palsy
	- is associated with thymic tumours + autoimmune diseases (e.g. hyperthyroid, RA & SLE)
	- tests: bloods (inc. ACh autoantibodies & inflammatory markers), CT of thymus gland & tensilon test (IV tensilon blocks the breakdown of acetylcholine by cholinesterase $\Rightarrow\uparrow$ACh at the neuromuscular junction $\Rightarrow\uparrow$muscle strength in patients with myasthenia gravis)
	- treat with: anticholinesterase (a cholinesterase inhibitor =$\downarrow$ACh breakdown), immunosuppression (steroids) +/- thymectomy

Myotonic muscular dystrophy	- autosomal dominant mutation in gene that codes for the myotonin protein - gets worse through generations ⇒disease shows at an earlier age in successive generations - is a multi system disorder ⇒distal muscle weakness & wasting, myotonia (slow relaxation of the muscles after contraction), male pattern baldness, diabetes & cataracts - tests: bloods =↑creatine kinase (CK, a muscle breakdown product), ECG abnormalities, genetic testing + tests for diabetes *(see 'Endocrine Revision' section)* - treatment: no cure, membrane stabilisers can reduce myotonia + treat symptoms & genetic counselling
Guillain barre syndrome	- polyneuropathy due to an autoimmune demyelination response following a recent infection (e.g. campylobacter, EBV & mycoplasm) - symptoms: ascending paralysis, normal/↓ sensation, patients have LMN signs (hypotonia, ↓reflexes, ↓power, normal/absent plantars), as paralysis ascends can ⇒respiratory failure - tests: bloods (inc. infection/inflammatory markers) & nerve condition studies (=↓conduction velocity) - treatment: γ globulin (donor antibodies = boosts a patient's immunity against disease) + steroids, & supportive treatment (treat infection, ventilate, etc.)
Polyneuropathies	- neurological symptoms effecting more than one limb causes: 1. metabolic: diabetes (predominantly sensory, vibration goes first, 'glove & stocking' distribution), vitamin deficiencies (B_{12} & folate), chronic renal failure & hyperthyroid 2. toxic: alcohol, lithium, etc. 3. malignancies
Mononeuropathy	- neurological symptoms effecting a single limb carpal tunnel syndrome: - median nerve compression ⇒pain, tingling & wasting of affected thumb, index & middle finger - clinically = +'ve phalen's & tinel's tests *(see 'Musculoskeletal Examination' section)* - associated with pregnancy, RA, diabetes, hypothyroid & trauma - treat with NSAIDs +/- surgical release ulnar nerve: - compression/injury at elbow ⇒pain & tingling of the ring & little fingers + ulnar border of hand
Alzheimer's disease	- degeneration of cerebral cortex ⇒↓brain size, neurofibillary tangles, amyloid protein plaques & granulovacuolar bodies - symptoms: gradual onset, short term memory loss, personality change & ↓general intellect ⇒↓cortical function - symptoms can be slightly reduced with: acetylcholinesterase inhibitors & treat depression/anxiety

Parkinson's disease
 	
Tremor
Rigidity
Akinesia
Micrographia
Po face
Shuffling gait/slow speech
	- extrapyramidal disease resulting in ↓dopamine production by the substantia niagra (section of basal ganglia) ⟹↑ACh (dopamine inhibits ACh)
	symptoms:
	  1. resting tremor (4-7Hz, pill rolling)
	  2. rigidity (lead pipe, cog wheel, clasp knife)
	  3. akinesia (slow movement + difficulty initiating movement)
	  4. micrographia (small handwriting)
	  5. no expression on face
	  6. slow speech
	  7. shuffling gait with poor arm swing
	- treatment: multidisciplinary = nurses, occupational health, physio, speech therapy, dieticians, etc.
	- medical treatment: start with monoamine oxidase inhibitor MAOI (stops dopamine breakdown), later on add in L-dopa (dopamine precursor) + peripheral decarboxylase inhibitor (decreases dopamine's effects on body) + anticholinergic drug (reduces ACh levels)
	- NB. parkinsonian symptoms can be induced by: drugs (some antipsychotic mental health drugs ⟹↓dopamine), heavy metal poisoning, CO poisoning & cerebral ischaemia

Huntington's disease	- autosomal dominant condition (full penetrance on chromosome 4) ⟹50% chance of middle age onset - ⟹degeneration of basal ganglia ⟹↓GABA & ↓ACh but normal dopamine levels - symptoms: chorea (involuntary movements can ⟹altered posture), ataxia & dementia - no cure, treat with genetic counselling & social support
Cerebellar damage	symptoms: - **D**ysdiadochokinesis (use hand-palm test) - **A**taxia (staggering gait + use romberg's test) - **N**ystagmus - **I**ntention tremor (use finger-nose test) - **S**taccato speech - **H**ypotonia
Tremors	- types: benign essential, anxiety, thyrotoxicosis, action (cerebellar disease), resting (parkinson's, wilson's disease, syphilis)
Eyes Horner's 3rd nerve	- horner's syndrome: loss of sympathetic nerve supply ⟹ptosis & small pupil, causes = brainstem lesion, base of neck trauma, stroke, pancoast tumour, etc. - 3rd nerve palsy: loss of parasympathetic nerve supply ⟹ptosis, large pupil & eye pulled laterally - bilateral large pupils: fear, death, intoxication, cannabis - bilateral small pupils: opiates, cholinesterase inhibitors

Anaemia	- $\downarrow$haemoglobin (Hb) in blood
	categorised by the associated mean corpuscular volume (MCV) of RBCs:
	  1. microcytic = $\downarrow$MCV (usually due to iron deficiency or thalassaemia)
	  2. normocytic = normal MCV (usually due to chronic disease)
	  3. macrocytic = $\uparrow$MCV, this is further split into megaloblastic (large immature/dysfunctional RBCs e.g. vitamin B_{12} & folate deficiency) & non-megaloblastic (alcoholism & haemolytic)
	- symptoms: general tiredness, lethargy, pallor & can $\Rightarrow$tachycardia & SOB
	- treatment: see below for specifics, if patient is experiencing end stage symptoms &/or has heart disease consider a blood transfusion
	- NB. this is a serious problem in patients with heart disease as the heart's oxygen requirements become harder to maintain

Iron deficiency anaemia *microcytic, hypochromic* *(small RBCs with $\downarrow$Hb)*	- as well as $\downarrow$Hb & $\downarrow$MCV, blood can also have $\downarrow$iron (Fe), $\downarrow$ferritin & $\uparrow$transferrin/TIBC ($\equiv$body's total iron-binding capacity which is high because there is less iron to bind so more unbound transferrin is free) - causes: Fe deficiency, GI bleed, chronic disease (e.g. crohn's $\Rightarrow$malabsorption), thalassaemia trait & lead poisoning - symptoms: tiredness, lethargy, pallor, koilonychia (spoon shaped nails), angular stomatitis (cracked corners of mouth) & can $\Rightarrow$ tachycardia & SOB - tests: bloods (inc. iron studies) + investigate blood loss everywhere (especially GI tract, with endoscopy of stomach & colon), Hb electrophoresis (looking for thalassaemia) & bone marrow biopsy - treat underlying cause, iron supplements +/- blood transfusion (depending on symptoms & Hb level, usually transfuse if Hb <80g/dL) - NB. ferritin is an acute phase protein, therefore it will also be raised during an inflammatory response
Anaemia of chronic disease *normocytic*	- chronic disease $\Rightarrow\downarrow$RBC lifespan, $\downarrow$Fe stores & $\downarrow$erythropoietin (hormone produced by kidney that normally $\Rightarrow\uparrow$RBC production) - due to: malignancy, chronic disease infection/inflammation - tests: bloods ($\downarrow$Fe, $\downarrow$TIBC, $\uparrow$ferritin & check for signs of infection/inflammation e.g.$\uparrow$WBC & $\uparrow$CRP/ESR) - treat cause + iron supplements +/- transfusion
Folate def anaemia *macrocytic, megaloblastic*	- $\downarrow$folate $\Rightarrow$impaired DNA synthesis $\Rightarrow$ megaloblastic bone marrow - can $\Rightarrow$pancytopenia (=triad of symptoms):$\downarrow$RBCs (anaemia), $\downarrow$WBCs (neutropenia) & $\downarrow$platelets (thrombocytopenia) - causes: nutritional (e.g. starvation, alcoholism), malabsorption (e.g. crohn's, celiac, etc.), excess utilisation (e.g. pregnancy, malignancy) or medication related (e.g. methotrexate) - give oral folic acid
Vitamin B_{12} def anaemia *macrocytic, megaloblastic*	- can be due to pernicious anaemia *(see below)* or malabsorption (e.g. crohn's, celiac disease, post gastrectomy surgery) - treat with: B_{12} injections

Pernicious anaemia *macrocytic, megaloblastic*	- vit B_{12} absorption from the gut requires intrinsic factor (made by parietal cells), an autoimmune response against these cells $\Rightarrow\downarrow$intrinsic factor $\Rightarrow\downarrow$intracellular vit $B_{12}\Rightarrow$impaired DNA synthesis - can also $\Rightarrow$pancytopenia & peripheral neuropathy ($\downarrow$DNA synthesis effects neurones) - tests: bloods (inc. $\downarrow$Hb, $\uparrow$MCV, $\downarrow$vit B_{12}), intrinsic factor antibodies, schilling's test (part 1 = patient drinks radiolabelled vitamin B_{12}, normally >10% is excreted in the urine over 24hrs, if this is impaired perform part 2 = repeat above step giving oral intrinsic factor, if patient has pernicious anaemia excretion will now be normal) - associated with other autoimmune disease e.g. addisons & thyroid *(see 'Endocrine Revision' section)* - treatment: IV vitamin B_{12}

Haemolytic anaemia
macrocytic, non-megaloblastic
	- damage to RBC $\Rightarrow\downarrow$RBC lifespan $\Rightarrow\uparrow$unconjugated bilirubin (a Hb breakdown product) & $\uparrow$LDH (lactate dehyrogenase due to damaged RBC)
	- symptoms: anaemia, jaundice, splenomegaly & gallstones
	- blood film microscopy shows fragments of RBCs (schistocytes), small round RBC (spherocytes) & $\uparrow$reticulocytes (young RBCs)
	- treatment: if autoimmune give steroids, otherwise treat cause +/- Fe & folic acid supplements
	genetic diseases that $\Rightarrow$ haemolytic anaemia:
	  1. hereditary spherocytosis = abnormalities in the RBC membrane (autosomal dominant + spherocyte cells seen on blood film)
	  2. sickle cell & thalassaemia = abnormalities in the Hb molecule *(see below)*
	  3. disorders of G6PD enzyme (X linked + Heinz bodies seen on blood film) & pyruvate kinase enzyme (autosomal recessive + prickle cells on blood film)
	acquired haemolytic anaemia:
	  1. due to immune response: haemolytic disease of newborn (ABO or Rh, *see 'Paediatrics' section*) or blood transfusion reactions
	  2. due to autoimmune response: warm (IgG antibodies on RBC surface) & cold (IgM), coomb's test identifies antibodies on RBC surface, it would be +'ve in both immune & autoimmune causes (1 & 2)
	  3. due to trauma: e.g. cardiac haemolysis (prosthetic heart valve) $\Rightarrow$ RBC fragments in blood $\Rightarrow$platelet aggregation which can $\Rightarrow$clots
	  4. due to infection: malaria & general sepsis

Thalassaemia
RBC disorder
	- due to genetic disorder causing reduced production of the globin chains in the Hb molecule (normal adult Hb = 2β + 2α globin chains, fetal = 2α + 2γ chains)
	- can affect α-chains (α-thalassaemia) or β chains (β-thalassaemia)
	- $\Rightarrow$haemolytic anaemia + $\downarrow$MCV
	- diagnosed by electrophoresis
	- disease severity depends whether an individual is homozygous or heterozygous
	- N.B. β-thalassaemia is most common in mediterranean & asian people
	1. trait/minor (heterozygous):
	  - β = one normal + one abnormal β Hb chain
	  - α = one normal + one abnormal α Hb chain
	  - can be asymptomatic or cause a slight microcytic anaemia
	  - afflicted individuals are carriers
	2. major (homozygous):

	- β = hepatosplenomegaly, skull bossing (symptoms develop during 1st year of life as Hb switches from foetal to adult) - α = fetal death (α chains are required for foetal Hb) - treat with blood transfusion & bone marrow transplant + genetic counselling
Sickle cell *RBC disorder*	- due to genetic disorder producing abnormal β globin chain - more common in afro-caribbean's as protects against malaria - diagnose with electrophoresis + blood film shows RBCs that are sickle shaped - as with thalassaemia there are 2 levels of severity 1. trait (heterozygous) = HbAS usually asymptomatic, patient is protected against malaria but is a carrier + can experience problems when they are put under anaesthetic 2. major (homozygous, person has disease) = HbSS $\Rightarrow\uparrow$RBC rigidity $\Rightarrow$obstructed blood flow (can $\Rightarrow$small vessel infarcts$\Rightarrow$ischaemia) & haemolysis - symptoms: anaemia, chronic leg ulcers, renal necrosis, pigmented gallstones, splenomegaly, avascular necrosis of femoral head - no cure so treat symptoms: analgesia, anticoagulation, genetic counselling
Bone marrow failure	- impairment of bone marrow $\Rightarrow$pancytopenia =$\downarrow$RBCs (anaemia), $\downarrow$WBCs ($\Rightarrow$bacterial infection) & $\downarrow$platelets ($\Rightarrow$purpuric rash + bleeding) - tests: FBC ($\downarrow$Hb & $\downarrow$WBC) + coagulation profile (shows $\uparrow$prothrombin time, i.e. clot takes longer to form) - can be due to sepsis, $\downarrow$vit B$_{12}$, myelodysplasia (bone marrow stem cell disorder), leukaemia, drug toxicity (radio/chemotherapy) or malignancy - treat depending on cause: antibiotics, immune suppression, bone marrow transplant, chemotherapy, etc.
Aplastic anaemia	- bone marrow failure ($\Rightarrow$pancytopenia) + hypocellular ($\downarrow$density) bone marrow - causes: autoimmune, leukaemia, malignancy, viral (e.g. HIV/hep C) & drugs (e.g. chemo, gold & antiepileptics/psychotics) - treat depending on cause: antibiotics, immune suppression, bone marrow transplant, chemotherapy, etc.
Acute lymphoblastic leukaemia **(ALL)** *cancer of WBC $\Rightarrow\uparrow$blasts*	- all leukaemias = cancer of blood or bone marrow, in this case it is specifically of the lymphocytes (WBCs) - $\Rightarrow\uparrow$production of WBCs but in their primitive 'blast cell' form, because they are young/immature these WBC that do not function properly $\Rightarrow\uparrow$risk of infection - usually affects kids, peak onset = 4 yrs old - has an insidious/fast progression - symptoms: weight loss, bone marrow failure/suppression (all energy goes into creating these cancerous blast cells $\Rightarrow$ pancytopenia =bruising/bleeding, anaemia & infection), bone pain, enlarged lymph nodes & hepato-splenomegaly - diagnose with bloods (=$\downarrow$Hb & $\downarrow$platelets) + lymph & bone biopsies (show $\uparrow$WBC blasts) - the philadelphia chromosome is sometimes present (in 5% of children & 25% adults) - all leukaemias are malignancies of bone marrow, treat all with chemotherapy & bone marrow transplant + blood transfusion, platelets & antibiotics as needed - N.B. if T cell ALL $\Rightarrow$mediastinal mass on CXR

Acute myeloid leukaemia (AML) *cancer of WBC $\Rightarrow \uparrow$ blasts*	- cancer of the myeloid line of blood cells (any leukocyte/WBC that is not a lymphocyte), as with ALL $\Rightarrow$ rapid growth of abnormal WBCs = 'blasts' - usually affects older patients - has an insidious/fast progression - diagnosed by the presence of auer rods in bone marrow & blasts in blood - symptoms & treatment similar to ALL above
Chronic lymphocytic leukaemia (CLL) *cancer of WBC $\Rightarrow \uparrow$ mature cells*	- cancer of β lymphocytes - cells look mature but do not function correctly - $\uparrow$ incidence with age - symptoms: in early stages asymptomatic, then as disease progresses $\Rightarrow$ pancytopenia ($\Rightarrow$ recurrent infections, bruising/bleeding & anaemia), bone pain, enlarged lymph nodes, hepatosplenomegaly - diagnosis: bloods (=$\uparrow\uparrow$ WCC) + lymph & bone biopsies show mature cells - treat as above - N.B. prognosis of chronic leukaemia is generally worse than that of acute, this is because in acute the malignant cells replicate fast & therefore take up more of the chemotherapy $\Rightarrow \uparrow$ malignant cell death
Chronic myeloid leukaemia (CML) *cancer of WBC $\Rightarrow \uparrow$ mature cells*	- cancer of the myeloid line of blood cells, in this case $\Rightarrow \uparrow$ mature granulocytes (neutrophils, eosinophils & basophils) - affects middle aged, caused by ionising radiation & benzene - blood tests & bone marrow biopsies show $\uparrow\uparrow$ WBCs & $\uparrow$ mature granulocytes - 90% have philadelphia chromosome present - symptoms: pancytopenia ($\Rightarrow$ recurrent infections, bruising/bleeding & anaemia), bone pain, enlarged lymph nodes & massive hepatosplenomegaly - treat as above
Hodgkin's lymphoma *cancer of β & T lymphocytes in lymph nodes*	- lymphoma = cancer of β & T lymphocytes (type of WBCs) $\Rightarrow$ abnormal proliferation, spreads from one lymph node group to another - usually effects young or elderly (not the middle aged) - general symptoms: lymph node lumps that usually start in neck & anaemia - B symptoms (=disease has progressed): fever, night sweats & weight loss - tests: blood (normocytic anaemia, $\uparrow$ CRP/ESR, later stages = liver involvement $\Rightarrow$ abnormal LFTs), staging CT, node biopsy (reed-sternberg cells present + epstein-barr virus found in 80% of biopsies) - ann arbor staging: 1 & 2 $\equiv$ number of nodes effected, 3 = disease has spread above and below the diaphragm, 4 = liver or bone involvement (add "B" after the number if B symptoms present) - treatment: early stage = radiotherapy, later stage = chemo & radiotherapy
Non-Hodgkin's lymphoma *cancer of β & T lymphocytes in lymph nodes*	- all lymphomas in which reed-Sternberg cells are not present - usually affects middle aged types: 1. low grade = slow dividing cells making it virtually incurable 2. high grade (e.g. burkitt's) = because the malignant cells undergo rapid division in this form of the disease there is a good chance it can be cured (i.e. fast dividing malignant cells take up more of the chemotherapy) - symptoms: weight loss, night sweats, lymph node lumps & pancytopenia - tests: blood (normocytic anaemia, $\uparrow$ CRP/ESR, later stages = liver involvement $\Rightarrow$ abnormal LFTs), staging CT, lymph node biopsy - treat as above

Myeloma *cancer of plasma cells*	-	malignancy of bone marrow plasma cells (usually produce antibodies) ⇒high production of a certain immunoglobulin (M band or paraprotein) ⇒↓production of other immunoglobulins ⇒↓immunity ⇒↑risk of bacterial infection
	-	one of these immunoglobulins is a bence-jones protein, increased production of this ⇒it being deposited in the kidneys filtering mechanism ⇒kidney failure
	-	hypercalcaemia (↑Ca in blood) results because myeloma cells release cytokines ⇒↑osteoclast activity ⇒lytic bone lesions (visible on X-ray) ⇒osteoporotic fractures
	-	symptoms mainly due to hypercalcaemia (⇒psychic <u>moans</u>, stomach <u>groans</u>, pain/fractures in <u>bones</u> & renal <u>stones</u>) + anaemia of chronic disease
	-	tests: blood (↓Hb & WBC, ↑inflammatory markers), bence-jones proteins in urine & ↑density of plasma cells in bone marrow
	-	death is usually due to renal failure or infection
	-	treat with chemo therapy & bisphosphonates (to ↓osteoclast activity ⇒↓Ca)
Myelofibrosis	-	bone marrow fibrosis
	-	⇒↓RBC production in bone marrow ⇒haemopoiesis (RBC production in spleen & liver) ⇒hepatosplenomegaly
	-	presents with bone marrow failure = pancytopenia
	-	signs: immature 'tear drop' RBCs and immature WBCs
	-	treat symptoms as there is no cure
Polycythaemia *↑RBCs*	-	bone marrow disorder ⇒↑RBCs
	types:	
	1.	primary: polycythaemia rubra vera *(see below)*
	2.	secondary: due to ↑erythropoeitin due to hypoxia (e.g. COPD, heavy smoking, cyanotic heart disease) or inappropriate erythropoietin secretion (e.g. renal cell tumours)
	3.	relative: due to reduced plasma volume (number of RBCs stay the same but their concentration increases)
	-	can ⇒hyperviscosity & haemorrhage (RBCs can interfere with clotting)
	-	symptoms: tiredness, gout & splenomegaly
	-	treat underlying cause +/- anticoagulation & venesection
Polycythaemia rubra vera *all components ↑*	-	bone marrow disorder ⇒↑RBCs, ↑WBCs & ↑platelets ⇒hyperviscosity
	-	symptoms: raynaud's, itching after hot bath, gout (due to ↑RBC turnover), ↑haemorrhage (due to platelets functioning abnormally), ↑risk of blood clots (due to ↑viscosity)
	-	treatment: cytotoxic treatment (chemicals that are toxic to the cells they are targeted at, e.g. chemotherapy) +/- anticoagulation & venesection
	-	NB. cythaemia ≡↑, cytopenia ≡↓
Essential thrombocythaemia *platelet disorder*	-	↑↑platelets with abnormal function
	-	⇒thrombosis + microvascular occlusion
	-	treat with aspirin

Thrombocytopenia *platelet disorder*	- ↓platelets - ⇒pupura (spontaneous bleeding into skin), easy bruising, ↑bleeding during trauma & a rash causes: 1. low platelet production e.g. bone marrow malignancies/infections, aplastic anaemia & certain medications 2. intravascular =↑breakdown of platelets in blood (e.g. disseminated intravascular coagulation *see below)* or drug induced (e.g. heparin) 3. extravascular =↑breakdown of platelets in liver or spleen e.g. idiopathic thrombocytopenic purpura (autoimmune antibodies against antigens on platelets surface, usually formed following a respiratory tract infection ⇒platelet destruction by reticuloendothelial cells in spleen, treat with steroids +/- spleen removal) - investigations: bloods (↓platelets), clotting = normal (because clotting factor pathway unaffected) + bone marrow biopsy - give platelets to stop bleeding
Physiology of haemostasis	when there is an injury to a blood vessel the following steps occur: 1. local vasoconstriction 2. adhesion & activation of platelets via von willebrand's factor (which has collagen & platelet binding sites), when platelets become activated they release agents (e.g. ADP) to recruit other platelets 3. activation of clotting cascade/factors to create fibrin clot 4. coagulation inhibitors restrict clotting to site of injury 5. breakdown of fibrin clot (fibrinolysis)
Haemophilia A *clotting factor disorder*	- genetic deficiency of factor VIII (8) - transmitted via an X linked recessive gene, therefore only effects men - ⇒prolonged bleeding + bleeding into muscles & joints (inflammation then destroys the joint ⇒disability) - treat by giving factor VIII - NB. in the past many haemophiliacs infected with hepatitis C & HIV via blood transfusions
Haemophilia B *clotting factor disorder*	- X linked deficiency of factor IX (9) - (as above)
von Willebrand's disease *clotting factor disorder*	- deficiency of von willebrand's factor - von willebrand's factor (vWF) is essential for normal platelet adhesion & for the transport of factor VIII - causes: mainly genetic (mildly autosomal dominant), but can also be acquired via some autoimmune diseases - symptoms: bruising & prolonged bleeding, in severe cases can ⇒bleeding into the joints (as above) - treat by giving factor VIII & DDAVP (↑vWF by inducing the release of stored vWF)
Liver disease	- coagulation factors are synthesised by the liver - liver failure ⇒clotting factor deficiency - treat underlying cause + if needed give FFP (fresh frozen plasma = the fluid portion of human blood that has been centrifuged, it contains almost all the clotting factors & is therefore used in the acute treatment of many bleeding disorders)

Vitamin K	- is needed as a coenzyme for coagulation factors to work properly - if deficient ⇒prolonged bleeding - N.B. warfarin works by antagonising vitamin K
Disseminated intravascular coagulation (DIC)	- massive activation of coagulation pathway in response to infection ⇒microvascular thrombosis (lots of small clots) ⇒end organ damage - once coagulation factors used up ⇒bleeding - example causes: septicaemia, malignancy & obstetric emergencies - treat underlying disorder + blood, platelet & FFP transfusions as required
Antiplatelet agents	- these are generally used for angina, MI, TIAs & strokes - aspirin = irreversible blockage of platelet activation sites, lasts for several days till new platelets produced - NSAIDs = reversible, work by preventing thromboxane synthesis in platelets ⇒↓platelet aggregation ⇒↓clot formation - clopidogrel inhibits platelet ADP receptor, it is also irreversible
Anticoagulants	- these are generally used for DVT, PE, AF & artificial heart valves - heparin is a natural anti-thrombin agent, has immediate onset & is short acting, is usually given subcuticularly (S/C) - warfarin is a vitamin K antagonist, it is slower working & longer lasting than heparin & is given orally (patient's INR must be monitored regularly to make sure they are not being over anticoagulated) - N.B. patient's are usually started on heparin as it is fast acting whilst a warfarin loading dose is given, once INR is in treatment range (usually 2-3, maybe higher in some cases e.g. recurrent PE) the heparin is stopped
Transfusions & blood products	- RBC: used regularly in hospital for anaemia & bleeding - fresh frozen plasma (FFP): contains all coagulation factors in clotting pathway - platelets: prevent bleeding e.g. in thrombocytopenia - albumin (protein): if deficient from blood ⇒oedema/ascities - immunoglobulins: used for patients susceptible to infection

Endocrine History

Introduction	- approach politely and introduce yourself - patient's name, DOB & occupation

Appetite & weight change	- amount of weight change & timescale - thyrotoxicosis & uncontrolled diabetes (both $\Rightarrow \uparrow$appetite, $\downarrow$weight), cushing's ($\uparrow$appetite, $\uparrow$weight), adrenal insufficiency ($\downarrow$appetite, $\downarrow$weight), hypothyroid ($\uparrow$weight)
$\uparrow$Urine/thirst	- diabetes, diabetes insipidus, hypercalcaemia
Lethargy	- hypothyroid, addison's, diabetes
Headache/visual disturbance	- $\uparrow$pituitary gland (usually due to tumour) $\Rightarrow$bitemporal hemianopia (loss of peripheral vision)
Hair change	- hirsutism & hair recession (polycystic ovarian syndrome, cushing's, acromegaly, obesity, androgen secreting tumour) - no facial hair in men (hypogonadism) - loss of axillary & pubic hair: in women (adrenal insufficiency), in men (hypopituitarism)
Neck lumps	- duration & rate of change/growth - associated symptoms: pain, difficulty swallowing/breathing
Altered bowel habit	- constipation (hypothyroid/calcaemia), diarrhoea (hyperthyroid)
Sweating	- hyperthyroid, hypoglycaemia, acromegaly, anxiety, infection
Skin changes	- dry (hypothyroid), pigmented growths in armpits (diabetes, cushing's, PCOS), skin atrophy/bruising/striae ($\uparrow$steroids, natural e.g. cortisol, or medication), pigmentation (hypoadrenalism $\Rightarrow$compensatory $\uparrow$ACTH)
Menstrual & obstetric (in women)	- date of first day of last period, frequency, duration, regularity, heavy/light/spotting/flooding - date of menarche & menopause (depending on patient's age) - contraceptive & HRT use - see 'Obstetrics & Gynaecology' sections
Impotence (in men)	- neuropathies due to diabetes, $\uparrow$BP, vascular disease, alcohol, medication (e.g. β-blockers)
Emotional feelings	- depression (diabetes, cushing's, hypothyroid, adrenocortical insufficiency), delirium (thyrotoxicosis), anxiety (hyperthyroid)

PMH	- list PMH + ask DEAR J SMITH
Medications, allergies, smoking & alcohol	- if ex smoker ask smoking history
FH	- are parents/brothers/sisters alive, if so do they suffer from any diseases, if they have passed away (say "sorry to hear that") ask age & reason of death
Social/occupational history	- who is at home & how does this condition effect your life - expand on occupation

See 'Hormones & Their Effects' section of appendix

Neck (Thyroid) Examination

Introduction	- wash your hands - approach politely and introduce yourself - patient's name & DOB - explain to patient what you are going to do & obtain verbal consent - expose patient after asking - position them sitting in a chair
Inspection	- comment on: scars, prominent veins, obvious swellings, protruding eyes (=exophthalmos, found in hyperthyroid along with lid retraction & lid lag)
Swallow water	- a goitre & thyroglossal cyst will move when patient swallows because they are attached to the larynx
Stick out tongue	- a thyroglossal cyst will move
Palpate radial pulse	- assess rate & rhythm - hyperthyroid can ⇒tachycardia & AF
Check for clubbing	- due to chronic conditions

Palpate neck	- this is ideally done whilst standing behind the patient
	- ask if tender anywhere
	assess any lump:
	  1. site: confined to one or in both lobes
	  2. size
	  3. shape: smooth/irregular, diffuse/nodular, can you feel upper & lower margins
	  4. consistency: soft, firm (simple goitre), hard (hashimoto's, carcinoma, calcified cyst)
	  5. mobility
	- *see 'Lump Examination' in appendix for further steps if interested*

Palpate cervical lymph nodes	- assess any lump
Palpate carotid pulses	- do one side at a time (or the patient may pass out) - these can be infiltrated by malignancy
Tracheal deviation	- tell patient this maybe uncomfortable - assess by putting finger in suprasternal notch
Percuss sternum	- need to do if cannot feel lower margin of mass as it may extend retrosternally
Auscultate thyroid lobes	- bruits are sometimes detectable in graves (make sure these are not carotid bruits you are hearing)
Tremor	- hold hands out (you can place a piece of paper on patient's hands to help you assess their tremor)
Reflexes	- hypothyroid = slow relaxing - hyperthyroid = brisk
Palpate tibia	- pre-tibial myxoederma = pain on palpating tibia, this is associated with graves disease (hyperthyroid)
Get up from chair (without using hands)	- ↓proximal muscle ⇒ weakness = hyperthyroid

Diabetic Foot Exam

Introduction	- wash your hands - approach politely and introduce yourself - patient's name & DOB - explain to patient what you are going to do & obtain verbal consent - expose patient after asking
Inspection	- legs: look for skin changes, hair loss & muscle wasting - feet: comment on deformity, signs of peripheral vascular disease (pale/dusky colouration), ulceration (arteriopatic on tips of toes & heels or neuropathic on pressure sights e.g. metatarsal heads), callus (run hand up sole to feel) & autonomic dysfunction (dry skin, oedema & distended veins) - N.B. look all over feet, make sure the examiner sees you look under & in-between the toes
Temperature	- run back of your hand down each leg to assess temp change - compare dorsum of each foot - N.B. should always use the back of your hand to assess temp as it is more sensitive
Pulses	- absent (peripheral vascular disease), bounding (neuropathic disease)
Reflexes + hyporeflex ++ normal +++ hyperreflex	- ankle jerk S1,2 (put joint under tension when performing), if absent move up to knee - knee L3,4 (support knee whilst doing this) - if no reflex ask patient to clench teeth or interlock fingers & pull - N.B. always look at muscle above/proximal to the tendon you are striking when checking for reflexes
Sensation/pinprick	- perform with cotton wool then with pin/neuro tip (show feeling on patient's chest first) - start distally & work up leg to assess level of neuropathy - inner calf = L4 - outer calf = L5 - lateral aspect of foot = S1
Vibration	- start at the distal interpharangeal (DIP) joint of the big toe, continue up leg if deficit is detected - use 128Hz tuning fork, place on patient's chest first so they know the feeling - ask patient to close their eyes & tell you when the vibrations stop (stop vibrations when you are ready) - N.B. this is the first sense to go in a diabetic foot
Proprioception (joint position)	- start at the DIP joint of the big toe - fix joint by holding it either side with one hand whilst you move it with the other, "which way am I moving your big toe, up or down" - continue up leg if needed, test progressively larger joints to measure height of deficit - N.B. this sense is 2nd to be affected in a patient with diabetic foot disease
Inspect gait	- for abnormalities
Inspect shoes	- for abnormal wear & tear

This examination has the same steps as the neurological limb exam with 2 slight changes (assess temp instead of tone & pulses instead of power)

Endocrine Revision

See 'Hormones & Their Effects' section of appendix

Diabetes (DM) type I	- insulin is produced by β cells in the islet of langerhans section of the pancreas, insulin $\Rightarrow\uparrow$glucose uptake from blood into cells - $\uparrow$glucose in the blood $\Rightarrow$damage to small vessels, e.g. those supplying nerves & the retina - DM I = autoimmune β cell destruction $\Rightarrow$insulin dependency - symptoms: $\uparrow$thirst, weight loss, polyuria (children may wet the bed), retinopathy + cataracts, nephropathy (microalbuminuria advancing to proteinuria), peripheral vascular disease, neuropathy (glove & stocking sensory loss $\Rightarrow$patient unaware of foot injury/disease) & recurrent infections - diagnosis: random (>11) or fasting blood glucose (>7), glycosuria + proteinuria, glucose tolerance test (glucose given & timed to see how quickly it is removed from the blood, this will decrease in diabetic patients), HbA1c (a rough measure of the average plasma glucose concentration over a prolonged period of time =diabetic control over last 2-3 months), eye examination (look for signs of diabetic retinopathy) - treatment: insulin, education (inc. technique + self monitoring) & regular checkups (eyes, feet, etc.) - N.B. diabetic retinopathy = micro aneurysms (dots) & micro haemorrhages (blots), cotton wool spots (areas of ischaemia), hard exudates (lipid deposition in retina due to vessel leakage) & proliferative retinopathy (due to new vessel formation $\Rightarrow\uparrow$immature vasculature $\Rightarrow$bleeding, can $\Rightarrow$retinal detachment)
Diabetes type II	- continual over eating $\Rightarrow$overuse of insulin $\Rightarrow$body becomes tolerant to insulin (gradually higher concentrations needed) until the amount needed exceeds that being produced - symptoms: as above - treatment: depends on the severity, start with education (lifestyle & diet), progressing onto metformin (increases body's sensitivity to insulin) + gliclazide (increases insulin release by direct action on pancreatic β cells) & finally onto insulin, all diabetics also get regular checkups
Diabetic Ketoacidosis (DKA)	- effects type I diabetics only, usually those who are not compliant with their treatment or those who have another underlying illness - no insulin $\Rightarrow$uncontrolled hyperglycaemia (glucose in the blood but not the cells where it is needed) $\Rightarrow$cells begin to burns ketones (alternative source of energy) $\Rightarrow\uparrow$ketone bodies $\Rightarrow$metabolic acidosis - symptoms: thirst, polyuria, dehydration, N&V, abdo pain, kussmaul respiration ($\uparrow$RR =body tries to blow off CO_2 reserves creating a respiratory alkalosis to counteract the metabolic acidosis) & $\downarrow$consciousness - diagnosis: bloods (hyperglycaemia), ketonuria ($\uparrow$ketones in urine) & metabolic acidosis ($\downarrow$pH, assessed by performing ABGs) - treatment: resus, fluids (too fast can $\Rightarrow$cerebral oedema), insulin (sliding scale =blood sugar checked hourly & insulin altered accordingly), potassium (because insulin also pulls available K into cells) + treat underlying cause (e.g. infection)

Hyperosmolar non ketotic coma (HONK)	- effects type II diabetics only, usually those who are not compliant with their treatment or those who have another underlying illness - ⇒hyperglycaemia but no ketoacidosis (enough sugars in the cells that ketones need not be burnt) - symptoms: thirst, polyuria, hyperviscosity (↑risk of DVT, stroke, PE) & ↓consciousness - treatment: same as DKA but less insulin needed +/- anticoagulate
Hyperprolactinaemia *↑prolactin*	- prolactin is a pituitary hormone that ⇒↓GnRH ⇒↓sex hormones (oestrogen in women, testosterone in men), N.B. prolactin production is inhibited by dopamine from the hypothalamus - symptoms in women: menstrual disturbance, infertility, ↑milk production - symptoms in men: breast growth, impotence & infertility, together these symptoms are known as galactorrhoea - causes: renal failure, pituitary tumour (usually an adenoma, can present as bitemporal hemianopia +/- headache), hypothyroid (↓thyroxine ⇒↑TSH ⇒↑prolactin, both produced by pituitary), polycystic ovarian syndrome (PCOS), pregnancy & mental health medication used to treat schizophrenia (e.g. haloperidol = dopamine antagonists ⇒↓dopamine ⇒↓prolactin inhibition) - tests: bloods & brain imaging - treat cause + can use dopamine agonists (⇒↑prolactin inhibition) +/- surgery
Acromegaly *↑GH*	- excessive growth hormone (GH) usually due to a pituitary tumour - symptoms: hand & foot enlargement, carpel tunnel syndrome, deep voice, large tongue, broadened nose + lips, enlarged mouth & frontal bossing - also can ⇒↑BP, diabetes & cardiac failure - diagnosis via glucose tolerance test (+'ve if ↑glucose does not ⇒↓GH), bloods & brain imaging - as in hyperprolactinaemia check vision for pituitary tumour (⇒bitemporal hemianopia) - treat with dopamine agonists, surgery &/or radiotherapy
Hypothyroid	- thyroid stimulating hormone (TSH) released by the pituitary ⇒thyroxine production by the thyroid gland types: 1. primary = disease of thyroid ⇒↓T_4 (thyroxine) + ↑TSH 2. secondary = pituitary disease ⇒↓TSH ⇒↓T_4 - causes: atrophic/autoimmune thyroiditis, hashimoto's thyroiditis (autoimmune ⇒goitre/lump), iodine deficiency (iodine is used by the body to produce thyroxine) & pituitary disease - symptoms: fatigue, weight gain, cold intolerance, dry skin/hair, ↓HR, constipation, aches in joints & slow relaxing reflexes, basically the bodies metabolism slows down - diagnosis: bloods (inc. TFTs), check for thyroid antibodies & for ↓cortisol (hypoadrenalism = addison's, also an autoimmune disease), CXR, USS of thyroid nodules, radioisotope scanning (in this case use radioactive iodine) & biopsy - treat cause + give thyroxine +/- thyroidectomy - acute form can ⇒myxoedematous coma, in this case treatment = resus + IV thyroxine bolus followed by oral thyroxine when stable

Hyperthyroid	- bloods = $\uparrow T_3/T_4 + \downarrow TSH$ - symptoms: protruding eyes (exophthalmos), $\uparrow HR$ (can $\Rightarrow AF$), proximal myopathy (muscle breakdown), brisk reflexes, amenorrhoea, tremor, sweating, papilloedema (optic disc damage due to $\uparrow ICP$, on examination = blurring of disc & loss of venous pulsation $\Rightarrow\downarrow$vision) - diagnosis: bloods (inc. TFTs), check for thyroid antibodies, CXR, USS of thyroid nodules, radioisotope scanning & biopsy types: 1. graves disease (IgG): autoimmune (check for thyroid antibodies), associated with graves eye disease, proximal muscle weakness, pretibial myxoderma (shin pain), radioisotope imaging shows diffuse thyroid gland uptake, treat with carbimazole (works by decreasing thyroid hormone synthesis) 2. single/multinodular goitre: treat with oral radioactive iodine (I^{131} destroys sections of the thyroid, is known as radioactive thyroid ablation, N.B. it may also damage surrounding structures e.g. the parathyroid), carbimazole &/or surgery - N.B. surgery can $\Rightarrow$vocal cord problems (damage to laryngeal nerve), hypothyroid & hypocalcaemia (due to damage to the parathyroid gland $\Rightarrow\downarrow PTH$)
Hypercalcaemia *$\uparrow calcium$* (groans, moans, bones & stones)	- causes: hyperparathyroid ($\uparrow PTH \Rightarrow\uparrow$osteoclast activity =removes calcium from bones into the blood), thiazide diuretics ($\Rightarrow\downarrow$fluid within body $\Rightarrow\uparrow Ca$ concentration), bone diseases/malignancies (e.g. multiple myeloma), squamous cell carcinoma of lung ($\Rightarrow$ectopic PTHrP production resulting in symptoms $\equiv$hyperparathyroid + due to $-$'ve feedback $\downarrow PTH$) - symptoms: renal stones, stomach pain, thirst, $\downarrow$consciousness & $\downarrow Ca$ density in bones (if disease due to $\uparrow PTH$ or ectopic PTHrP, results in boney cyst formation + marrow fibrosis) + can induce nephrogenic diabetes insipidus *(see below)* - remember: stomach <u>groans</u>, psychic <u>moans</u>, <u>bones</u> & <u>stones</u> - tests: bloods (inc. calcium & PTH), ECG, CXR + bone imaging (inc. bone radioisotope scan & MRI) - treat cause: parathyroid hyperplasia/oedema (treat with surgery), bone malignancy (treat with chemo/radiotherapy & surgical removal or with palliative care + bisphosphonates/calcitonin $\Rightarrow\downarrow$osteoclast activity) - N.B. $\uparrow$pituitary $\Rightarrow$bitemporal hemianopia
Hypocalcaemia *$\downarrow calcium$*	- calcium levels are dependant on: vitamin D (promotes absorption of Ca from gut) & PTH (controls osteoclast activity, which if required transfers Ca from bone to blood), therefore problems with either mechanism can change Ca blood levels - in this case is mainly due to renal/liver failure $\Rightarrow$failure to convert vitamin D $\Rightarrow\downarrow Ca$ - can also happen following thyroid/parathyroid surgery or due to autoimmune causes (both $\Rightarrow\downarrow PTH$) - symptoms: tingling, tetany, seizures, trousseau's sign (tap facial nerve $\Rightarrow$muscle contraction) - tests: bloods & ECG - treat with Ca gluconate

Adrenal failure ↓*cortisol*	- ACTH released from the pituitary is converted to cortisol (a corticosteroid involved in response to stress & anxiety) by the adrenal gland - disease types: 1° = adrenal failure, 2° =↓ACTH 1. primary = addison's: due to autoimmune adrenal antibodies ⇒↓cortisol ⇒↑ACTH (adrenocorticotrophic hormone) ⇒hyperpigmentation of buccal mucosa, is associated with other autoimmune diseases (e.g., hypothyroid, type I DM, pernicious anaemia & ovarian failure) 2. secondary to steroid therapy withdrawal: steroids suppress ACTH (due to artificial steroids the body does not need to produce as many itself) ⇒adrenal cortex atrophy ⇒↓ACTH ⇒↓cortisol, therefore steroid withdrawal must be done very slowly - general symptoms: pigmentation (in primary adrenal failure due to ↑ACTH), weight loss, fatigue/muscle weakness, postural hypotension, GI disturbances, depression, joint pains, confusion - N.B. in its severe form this is known as an adrenal/addisonian crisis & is a medical emergency - tests: bloods (↑K, ↓Na, ↓glucose, ↓cortisol), abdominal X-ray diagnosis: 1. short synacthen test: give IV ACTH, if no cortisol created = adrenal failure 2. long synacthen test: give IV ACTH over 3days, if adrenal cortex not totally destroyed will ⇒some cortisol - treatment: steroid therapy (e.g. oral prednisolone or IV hydrocortisone)
Cushing's syndrome ↑*cortisol*	- due to prolonged ↑steroid, either naturally or via medication types: 1. ACTH dependant: pituitary adenoma (cushing's disease) & ectopic ACTH (small cell lung cancer) both ⇒↑ACTH ⇒↑production of cortisol by adrenal glands 2. ACTH independent: adrenal ademoma/carcinoma/hyperplasia, i.e. cortisol produced by diseased adrenal gland independently of ACTH ⇒↓ACTH (due to negative feedback mechanism) 3. steroid treatment - symptoms: moon face, acne, hirsutism, thin air/skin, depression, hypertension, obesity, striae, easy bruising, proximal myopathy (↑gluconeogenesis ⇒muscle wasting/weakness), impaired glucose tolerance (also due to ↑gluconeogenesis) - diagnosis: ↑24hr urine cortisol & salivary cortisol, suppression of serum cortisol with dexamethasone (⇒no change in cortisol levels if ectopic ACTH or adrenal tumour), CXR, CT abdo (to visualise adrenal glands) & brain MRI (looking for pituitary tumours) - treat cause: metyrapone (stops cortisol synthesis) &/or radio/chemotherapy + surgery (if pituitary, adrenal or lung cancer) - N.B. alcohol excess can mimic cushing's symptoms

Hyperaldosteronism
↑*aldosterone*
	- aldosterone (produced by the adrenal gland) works on the kidneys to increase reabsorption of Na & H_2O whilst increasing excretion of K via urine, therefore ↑aldosterone ⇒water retention
	causes:
	  1. primary = adrenal benign adenoma (conn's syndrome), bilateral adrenal hyperplasia or phaeochromocytoma (tumour of adrenal medulla)
	  2. secondary = due to activation of renin-angiotensin system (e.g. by diuretic therapy, congestive heart failure, nephrotic syndrome or renal artery stenosis)
	- symptoms: treatment resistant hypertension, tiredness, muscle weakness & ↓K, can ⇒heart failure
	- treat underlying cause, control ↑BP & ↓K +/- surgery (adrenalectomy)
	- N.B. the renin-angiotensin system: low blood volume ⇒renin secreted by the kidneys, renin stimulates the production of angiotensin (causes blood vessels to constrict ⇒↑BP), angiotensin also stimulates the secretion of aldosterone from the adrenal cortex which stimulates the kidney tubules to increase the reabsorption of sodium & water ⇒↑volume of fluid in the body ⇒↑BP

Diabetes insipidus (DI)	types:
	  1. cranial DI =↓ADH (vasopressin) secretion due to pituitary/hypothalamic lesion
	  2. nephrogenic DI = renal resistance or ↓responsiveness to ADH
	- causes: idiopathic, head injury, hypokalaemia, toxic drugs (e.g. lithium), genetic (nephrogenic DI can be X linked)
	- symptoms: polyuria, nocturia, polydipsia (↑thirst), bitemporal hemianopia (if due to pituitary lesion)
	- tests: bloods (inc. glucose, K & Ca) + test for other causes of ↑urination
	- water deprivation test: restrict water to patient then give desmopressin (≡ADH), if ⇒↑urine shows disease is due to a defect in ADH production (=cranial DI), if urine stays low is due to a defect in the kidneys response to ADH (=nephrogenic DI)
	- treat with desmopressin (synthetic form of ADH/vasopressin)
	- N.B. remember DI has similar mechanism to DM: type 1 = ↓insulin, type 2 = ↓cell responsiveness to insulin, whereas in this case cranial =↓ADH & renal =↓cell responsiveness to ADH

Syndrome of inappropriate ADH release (SIADH)	- ↑ADH ⇒↓urine - causes: small cell lung malignancy, pneumonia, meningitis & head trauma - symptoms = those of hyponatraemia (because of ↑↑H_2O retention): headache, N&V, lethargy, irritability, depression, personality change, muscle cramps & weakness, progressing onto confusion, convulsions & coma - diagnosis: ↓plasma osmolarity, ↑urine conc., ↑urinary Na, normal renal function - N.B. plasma osmolarity is a measure of the concentration of substances within the blood, the more concentrated the blood the greater it's osmolarity
Hormone secreting lung cancers	- squamous cell lung carcinoma can produce ectopic PTHrP (parathyroid hormone-related protein) ⇒↑osteoclast activity ⇒↑calcium in the blood & less in the bones - small cell lung carcinoma can ⇒SIADH (syndrome of inappropriate antidiuretic hormone ⇒↓urination) & ectopic ACTH
Hypogonadism	types: - primary = damage to testis/ovaries =↓testosterone/oestrogen ⇒↑LH/FSH (e.g. turner's syndrome XO chromosomes in women ⇒gonadal atrophy) - secondary = damage to pituitary: ↓LH/FSH ⇒↓testosterone/oestrogen - treatment: androgen replacement therapy + genetic counselling

Musculoskeletal Examination

Examination steps:
1. inspection: joints are 3-dimensional so examine each from the front, side & back
2. palpation
3. range of movement: assess movement both actively & passively, also some joints/muscles have special tests
4. neurological
5. function

Once you have examined the effected joint/area, say "to complete this exam I would....." (you may be asked to perform one of these steps):
- assess the joint above & below the effected region
- examine the opposite joint/area for comparison
- assess neurovascular status (if not already done)
- perform an X-ray of the area &/or suggest relevant further imaging *(see 'Orthopaedic X-rays' in appendix)*

Introduction	- wash your hands - approach politely and introduce yourself - patient's name & DOB - always ask for a chaperone if appropriate - explain to patient what you are going to do & obtain verbal consent - expose patient after asking

Hand & Wrist *(remember: look, feel, move)*

Inspect ('Look')	- expose patient's hands & wrists, examine preferably next to each other on a table, palms upwards then downwards - joints: swelling & deformity (infective/inflammatory conditions or trauma) - tremor: neurological disease (e.g. parkinson's = resting tremor), anxiety, thyrotoxicosis - skin: rash (psoriasis/eczema), bruising (side effect of steroid treatment or trauma), colour, scars (past surgery), tightness (chronic inflammatory disease) - nails: clubbing (raynaud's & chronic disease), onycholysis (separation/loosening of nail from bed = psoriasis), nail folds infarcts (vasculitis) - muscles: wasting due to ↓use or neuro/vascular conditions (e.g. carpel tunnel syndrome, check 1st web space =base of thumb, thenar & interossei muscles are usually affected) - tendons: flexor thickening (e.g. dupuytren's contracture) - lumps: rheumatoid nodules, tophi (uric acid deposits ⇒gout), calcinosis
Palpate ('Feel')	- joints: bimanually palpate all joints, squeeze across MCPs to check for tenderness & assess temp (with the back of your hand) - tendons (before & during movement): nodules, crepitus, trigger finger (=tendon not smooth enough to travel through sheath & therefore gets stuck), & tendon rupture (damage to tendons can ⇒partial or full thickness tear = gap sometimes palpable)
Range of movements ('Move')	1. prayer sign (fixed flexion disorder would = gap between palms) 2. flare: extend/spread fingers whilst in prayer 3. make a fist (look from the side, each finger joint should be at 90° to its neighbour) 4. tell patient to pinch each finger & thumb together in turn on same hand 5. wrist – assess flexion, extension, pronation & supination (N.B. for 'sup'ination think about holding a bowl of soup to remember position of the hand)

Neuro/special tests	median nerve power:
	- muscles supplied remember 'LOAF' = <u>L</u>umbricals, <u>O</u>pponens pollicis, <u>A</u>bductor pollicis brevis & <u>F</u>lexor pollicis brevis
	1. hold hand out, palm facing upwards & move thumb towards the sky against resistance
	2. touch thumb & little finger together (opposition)
	ulnar nerve power:
	- supplies small muscles of the hand (apart from those supplied by median nerve)
	1. patient spreads fingers out & you test power by pushing their index finger & little finger together (abduction)
	2. hold piece of paper between fingers (adduction)
	3. froment's sign: pinch paper between thumb and index finger, flexion at interphalangeal joint of the thumb suggests weakness of adductor pollicis =ulnar nerve palsy
sensation	radial nerve power:
	- extensors of the wrist and fingers, test finger & wrist extension against resistance
	sensation *(see diagram)*
	- median: thumb + first 2.5 fingers
	- ulnar: little finger + half of ring ringer
	- radial: small patch on hands dorsal aspect 1st web space
	carpal tunnel syndrome (due to median nerve compression)
	- tinel's sign: tap over medial nerve in wrist ⇒sensation changes
	- phalen's sign: hold prayer sign for 30-60secs (pushing base of hands together) ⇒sensation changes
Function	- assess writing or doing up clothing buttons

When assessing the following joints follow the above steps, i.e. always start with inspection & palpation before moving onto range of movement

Elbow

Inspection	- look for a fixed flexion deformity, skin changes, scars, swellings (especially of the olecranon bursa = a soft fluid filled area, can ⇒bursitis if inflamed) & nodules
Palpate	- assess temperature
	- palpate for tenderness
	- rheumatoid nodule = hard, in tendon, usually found on extensor surface
Range of movements	- extension & flexion of elbow (normal = 0-140°)
	- pronation & supination of hand with elbows tucked into side (normal = 90° in both directions)
Neuro/special tests	- golfer's elbow: tender medial epicondyle, resisting hand flexion ⇒pain on medial side
	- tennis elbow: tender lateral epicondyle, resisting hand extension ⇒pain on lateral side

Shoulder

Inspection	- patient should be standing: look for muscle wasting, skin changes, scars & swellings
Palpation	- start at sterno-clavicular joint (medial side of clavicle), move across clavicle to acromio-clavicular joint (prominence in this joint = dislocation or arthritis) then to scapula + palpate surrounding muscles for tenderness - assess joint temp - check axilla for effusion or lymphadenopathy
Movement	- flexion: arms straight up in front (normal = 0-170°) - extension: arms straight backwards (normal = 0-40°) - abduct arms from their side straight up, scapular does not move for first 90°, observe from behind (normal = 0-160°), pain during the arc (between 70-120°) suggests impingement syndrome. - external rotation: bend at elbow & turn arm outwards (normal = 0-70°), will be reduced in frozen shoulder (=connective tissue surrounding shoulder becomes inflamed ⇒adhesions ⇒restricted movement + pain) - internal rotation: bend at elbow and turn arm inwards (normal = 0-90°) - can also ask patient to: put hands behind head & elbows back (tests internal rotation & abduction of shoulder joint) or to get their thumb as high up their back as possible (also tests internal rotation of shoulder joint) - NB. if patient cannot perform movement actively, you do it for them passively until you reach a point of pain
Neuro/special tests	- sensation: the most common neurological deficit is axillary nerve palsy following a dislocation, therefore test sensation over the deltoid muscle ='badge patch' sign - motor: check for contraction of deltoid with abduction against resistance - apprehension test: gently externally rotate the shoulder whilst in the 90° abduction & 90° elbow flexion position, patient will becoming apprehensive = a sign of anterior instability, usually due to a previous anterior dislocation - copeland's test: abduct shoulder against resistance with arm in neutral then internally rotated, increased pain when internally rotated suggests impingement syndrome (=wear & tear of the shoulder's rotators cuff tendon)
Function	- assess whether patient has any difficulty dressing

The spine

For any spinal complaint:
- inspect for any obvious deformity (e.g. kyphosis & scoliosis), trauma, scars, muscle wasting, etc.
- palpate all spinal processes + joining muscles
- test range of movement *(see below)*
- perform (or say you would perform) a full neuro limb exam

N.B. if a cervical spine traumatic injury is suspected the patient should have their head & neck immobilised until assessment can take place (usually done in A&E), immobilisation = neck collar with head blocks either side & usually strapped to a spinal board

Cervical spine

Movement (3 planes)	1. chin on chest then upwards (flexion & extension) 2. ear on each shoulder (lateral flexion) 3. chin on each shoulder (rotation)

Thoracic spine

Movement (1 plane)	- rotate spine (twist each way)

Lumbar spine (think degenerative disease, ankylosing spondylitis & sciatica)

Movement (2 planes)	1. flex (touch toes) & extend back 2. bend to each side (lateral flexion) - schober test: measure 10cm above & 5cm below dimples of venus & mark, when patient attempts to touch their toes measure distance between marks, normal flexion would have >5cm change
Function	- watch gait
Neuro/special tests	- sciatic stretch test: lay patient flat, tell them to keep their leg straight whilst you lift it off the bed & at the same time dorsi flex their foot (push foot upwards towards head) ⇒pain which can go down the whole leg past the knee to the foot, suggests sciatic nerve irritation/compression (sciatica) - femoral stretch test: patient lies on their front, bending the knee causes thigh slight pain, lifting their same leg off the bed exacerbates the pain = indicates femoral nerve compression (L2-L4)

Hips

N.B. a way to remember this examination is 'I've Got To Prepare Student Teaching Monthly': Inspection, Gait, Trendelenburg's, Palpation, Shortening, Thomas' test, Movements

Inspection	- scars, swellings, erythema, deformities - N.B. a neck of femur fracture usually presents as a painful hip + a shortened externally rotated leg
Palpation	- palpate around trochanter (joint is too deep to easily palpate) + surrounding muscles for tenderness & assess temp
Shortening	- assess leg shortening by seeing if bottom of feet are at same level - N.B. maybe due to pelvic tilting so check pelvis is also level
Thomas' test	- looks for a fixed flexion deformity: put hand under patient's back, flex the opposite hip to the one you are examining until their lumbar spine is flat on your hand, the test is +'ve if the leg you are examining has lifted off the bed
Movement (3 planes)	1. flexion = "keeping your leg straight lift it off the bed" (normal range = 0-135°), someone with neck of femur fracture cannot usually straight leg raise 2. abduct leg away to the side then adduct past the other leg (normal abduction 0-45°, normal adduction 0-30°) 3. internal/external rotation: can either roll the hip with the leg flat on the bed or flex + support knee & move ankle left then right (normal = 0-40° each way)
Trendelenburg test	- stand on the good leg, lift the other off the floor, put your hands on the patient's pelvis to stabilise, test = +'ve if pelvis dips on the good side (suggesting weakness of abductors on the opposite side) - N.B. remember 'good side goes'
Gait	- painful hip (⇒patient limbs to avoid weight bearing), short leg, 'swinging' gait (due to weakness in hip muscles, *see trendelenburg test*)

Knee

Inspection	- look for valgus deformity (ankles deviate away from midline), varus deformity (towards midline), fixed flexion deformity, scars, swelling, erythema, gait
Palpation	- palpate knee, behind knee (for bakers cyst) & around joint line (when knee bent) + assess joint temp - bulge sign for effusion: milk fluid up & round patellar - patellar tap: milk fluid downwards & tap patellar, this detects a larger effusion
Movement & special tests	- flex & extend with hand on knee to assess for crepitus (normal range = 0-130°) - ask patient to straight leg raise = a good test for quadriceps power & function - cruciate ligaments: with knee flexed & foot flat on bed (sit next to patient's foot to fix it's position, so you have both hands free) pull tibia towards & then push away = anterior & posterior drawer tests - collateral ligaments: hold/support knee at ~20° flexion, move ankle left then right whilst supporting just above thee knee (can also perform this by placing their foot/ankle under your arm pit & pushing the knee left then right) - meniscal tests: mcmurray's test is the most common = with one hand on foot flex knee to 90°, place other hand on the lateral side of the knee & push knee medially (=valgus force), then extend & externally rotate the knee at the same time, pain +/- clicking indicates medial meniscal tear, for lateral tears push the knee laterally (=varus force) extend & internally rotate, N.B. you are unlikely to have to perform meniscal tests in your exam as they can cause pain

Foot and Ankle

Inspection	- close inspection for any abnormalities, arches (flat foot =pes planus, high arch =pes cavus), muscle wasting, scars, check calf muscles, big toe bunion (hallux valgus), toe deformities (claw =toes curl under, hammer =middle of toe points upwards ⇒inverse 'V' shape, & mallet =tip points downwards), calluses on soles show abnormal weight bearing - remember foot has 3 parts: hindfoot (back), midfoot & forefoot (front e.g. toes)
Palpate	- ankle joint line, hindfoot (including achilles tendon insertion), mid foot, & compress forefoot (if elicit tenderness usually due to RA, OA, or morton's neuroma = thickening of nerve) - assess temp
Movement	- dorsiflex (upwards) & plantarflex the ankle - support the heel, abduct & adduct then invert & evert to assess midfoot movements
Neuro/special tests	- simmon's test: detects an achilles tendon rupture, get patient to kneel on a chair (or lay on front with foot hanging off bed), squeeze the calf muscle, if the foot moves down (plantarflexes) the achilles is intact - N.B. the nerve supply to the foot & ankle is complex, it is unlikely you get asked them in the exam

Gait

Observe walking	- spasticity = stiff & jerky on a narrow base - parkinson's disease = shuffling gait - cerebellar ataxia = broad base + unstable - sensory ataxia = broad base & high stepping - foot drop = high stepping gait - hemiplegia = plantar flexed foot with leg swung in arc

Osteoarthritis (OA)	- due to: trauma, gradual wear & tear, avascular necrosis, haemochromatosis/haemophillia ($\Rightarrow$bleeding into joint $\Rightarrow$inflammatory process $\Rightarrow$cartilage destruction) & hyperparathyroidism ($\Rightarrow\uparrow$osteoclast activity $\Rightarrow\downarrow$bone density & $\uparrow$Ca in blood) - hand joints affected: DIP ($\Rightarrow$heberden's nodes), PIP ($\Rightarrow$bouchard's nodes), 1st carpometacarpal (sublux/squaring of thumb base) - large joints affected: hips, knees & lumbar/cervical spine - X-ray findings (4 to remember): 1. joint space narrowing =$\downarrow$cartilage $\Rightarrow\downarrow$chondroctyes $\Rightarrow$cartilage fissures $\Rightarrow$microfractures in bone $\Rightarrow$ 2. boney cysts, followed by bone repair $\Rightarrow$ 3. subchondral sclerosis & 4. osteophytes - symptoms: joint pain (during activity, relieved by rest, worst at end of day), stiffness/gelling following inactivity, asymmetric joint involvement, locking due to loose bodies, crepitus, $\downarrow$range of movement - tests: bloods (show normal inflammatory markers = WCC, CRP & ESR) & synovial fluid are usually normal, check for haemochromatosis ($\uparrow$Fe) & hyperparathyroid ($\uparrow$PTH) - treatment: analgesia, $\downarrow$weight, exercise/physio, surgery (e.g. joint replacement) & occupational health support - N.B. when assessing joint pain remember these causes: monoarthritis (=septic arthritis, gout, pseudogout, OA) & polyarthritis (=reactive arthritis, RA)
Septic arthritis	- identify route of infection: remote site spread, local spread (osteomyelitis, skin, soft tissue), introgenic spread (from needle therapies or diagnostics performed recently) or trauma - this condition is a surgical emergency - diagnosis: bloods (infection screen, inc. blood cultures if patient has a temp >38°), aspirate joint (send sample to microbiology), X-ray, further imaging (MRI or ultra sound) - treatment: antibiotics, immobilize +/- surgical washout - N.B. before starting antibiotics it is best to get the microbiology samples first
Osteoporosis	- $\downarrow$ bone matrix components $\Rightarrow$ fractures with little/no trauma - common fractures: distal radius (colles), neck of femur & wedge fracture of spinal vertebrae (in thoracic region $\Rightarrow\downarrow$height & kyphosis/dowager's hump) - primary causes = postmenopausal oestrogen deficiency, $\downarrow$intake of Ca/vitamin D, $\uparrow$alcohol & $\downarrow$exercise - can be secondary to: thyrotoxicosis, cushing's disease, hyperparathyroid & steroid therapy - X-ray findings: narrow "pencilling" of bones outer layer - bone densitometry is used to calculate bone density - treatment: stop smoking, $\downarrow$alcohol/caffeine, Ca & vitamin D supplements, bisphosphonates (inhibit bone reabsorption $\Rightarrow\downarrow$ bone turnover), exercise, hormone replacement therapy (in post menopausal women) & prevent fractures
Osteomyelitis	- bone infection - can be due to local spread (e.g. open fracture) or from a remote site of infection - presents with bone pain + fever - diagnose with: bloods + blood cultures, imaging (X-ray +/- CT), bone biopsy, & radioisotope scan (will show $\uparrow$bone activity in region of infection) - treatment: long term antibiotics +/- surgical removal of infected bone

Fracture complications	- immediate: bleeding, damage to organs, nerves & vessels - early: wound breakdown, infection, compartment syndrome *(see below)* - late: delayed/mal/non-union of the fracture, stiffness & contracture, complex regional syndrome, avascular necrosis (necrosis due to lack of blood supply, commonly seen in hip fractures), usually suffer with OA in later life if the fracture effects a joint
Charcot's joint	- patient cannot feel pain or repeated trauma due to nerve damage and loss of joint sensation - associated with diabetes, MS and other neurological diseases
Perthe's disease (in children)	- interruption of blood supply to hip/femoral head ⟹avascular necrosis (parts of bone start to die) - symptoms: pain & limping, unable to weight bear, can ⟹fracture - can affect both legs - needs X-ray +/- MRI scan - surgery maybe necessary
Colles fracture	- a type of distal radius fracture in osteoporotic bone within 1 inch of the wrist joint, common in post menopausal women - usually due to Fall On Out Stretched Hand (FOOSH) - check neurovascular status (median nerve can be damaged) - if displaced reduction is needed with plaster cast immobilisation + internal/external fixation in more severe fractures

Neck of femur fracture
 	
1
 	
2
 	
3
 	
4
	- intracapsular = just below the femoral head but within the capsule, blood supply can be damaged
	- extracapsular (intertraochanteric) = at level of or below trochanters, blood supply to hip usually intact
	- patients present with hip pain + leg is usually shortened & external rotated
	garden's classification for intracapsular hip fractures:
	  1. incomplete fracture of the neck
	  2. complete without displacement
	  3. complete with partial displacement, fragments are still connected by posterior retinacular attachment
	  4. complete femoral neck fracture with full displacement, the proximal fragment is free & lies correctly in the acetabulum so that the trabeculae (bone lines) appear normally aligned
	- this classification mentions displacement which is relevant because the blood supply to the femoral head runs around the base of neck & goes from distal to proximal (femoral circumflex artery) ⟹avascular necrosis in 30% of displaced & 10% of undisplaced fractures
	- treatment: resus, analgesia, X-rays, blood (inc. clotting + group & save, i.e. prepare for surgery), keep nil by mouth (NBM), surgery (dynamic hip screw fixation if extracapsular or for more severe/intracapsular fractures a hemi/total hip replacement maybe needed)

Ankle fracture
 	
A
 	
B
 	
C
	- common injuries, usually caused by the ankle rolling inward/outward or a crush type injury (e.g. car accident or hard landing)
	weber classification (based on involvement of fibula):
	  A. fibula fractured below the tibio-fibula syndesmosis (as a result of an abduction or adduction injury), the syndesmosis (tibio-fibula) ligaments are intact, these fractures are usually stable after reduction
	  B. oblique fibular fracture starting at level of the syndesmosis/joint line, the syndesmosis ligaments can be damaged, but are usually intact
	  C. fibular fracture above the syndesmosis, usually due to abduction injury, these are unstable fractures ⇒rupture of syndesmosis ligaments
	- N.B. you also need to assess for talar shift = joint widening between the tibia & the talus on the medial side of the ankle = deltoid ligament maybe damaged ⇒unstable fracture
	- treatment: analgesia, reduction (in A&E if any neurovascular damage), bloods (if surgery required), NBM, surgery (unstable fractures will require open reduction & internal fixation)

Compartment syndrome	- swelling/bleeding within a compartment of the arm/leg ⇒ischaemia & necrosis of surrounding tissue - causes: fractures, soft tissue trauma, compression, bleeding, burns - symptoms: a tense compartment (e.g. calf) + the 6 Ps: Pain (in this case out of proportion to injury), Paraesthesia (↓sensation), then in later stages Pulseless, Pallor, Perishing cold & Paralysis - treatment: resus + emergency surgery (fasciotomy = opening of compartments to release the pressure, this is left open for 5 days so pressure does not rebuild)

Salter harris classification
(in children)
	- used in fractures affecting the growth plates in children
	types:
	  1. transverse fracture through growth plate
	  2. fracture through growth plate & metaphysis (section before bone forms into the shaft)
	  3. fracture through growth plate & epiphysis (bone head)
	  4. fracture through all 3 areas
	  5. compression deformity
	- there is a neumonic to remember this, SALTeR = Slipped, Above, Lower, Through & Reduced
	- N.B. the dark line in the diagram = the growth plate
	
	    1 2 3 4 5

Carpal tunnel syndrome	- compression of median nerve as it passes through the carpel tunnel ⇒pain (worse at night), paraesthesia & wasting of thenar eminence muscle - causes: idiopathic, pregnancy, rheumatoid arthritis (RA), tumours, endocrine diseases (common in diabetes & acromegaly) - associated with a +'ve phalen's & tinel's sign (see 'Musculoskeletal Examination' section) - treat with: NSAIDs , splinting +/- surgical decompression

Dupuytren's contracture	- hypertrophy & contraction of palmar aponeurosis/fascia, usually effects the ring finger ⇒fixed flexion deformity - causes: alcoholic liver disease (cirrhosis), diabetes or idiopathic (=unknown) - treatment: surgery + treat underlying disease
Back Pain	- causes: mechanical, inflammatory, infective (e.g. TB or osteomylitis), neurological, referred, or sinister (e.g. boney metastases) - take full history + do musculoskeletal & neuro limb exam - most pain resolves using the following treatments by 6 months: physio, analgesia +/- NSAIDs, lifestyle advice (inc. chair position & correct lifting techniques) - if pain not settling or any sinister symptoms then investigate: bloods (inc. ESR & ↑calcium), PSA (if prostatic cancer suspected), spinal X-ray (looking for boney mets or fractures) +/- spinal MRI - cord compression: progressive neurological deficit = lower motor neurone signs at level of lesion + upper motor neurone signs below - cauda equina syndrome (surgical emergency) = compression of cauda equina, causes (disc prolapse, tumour, fracture or abscess), symptoms (pain, muscle weakness, ↓sensation especially in the saddle, urinary/bowel disturbance & ↓anal tone when PR performed), needs urgent MRI +/- surgical decompression - N.B. be suspicious of an aortic aneurysm *(see 'Cardiovascular Revision' section)* in central back pain
Metastatic Bone Cancer	- most common primary bone cancer is multiple myeloma - secondary metastases are common from the following primaries (a weird way to remember them is that they almost all start with B): Breast, Brostate (prostate), Bronchus, Byroid (thyroid), Bidney (kidney) & Bowel - investigations: bloods (may have ↑calcium due to ↑bone turnover), X-rays (bones have circular dark/↓density looking lesions), CT all areas to find primary - N.B. 66% of secondary bone cancers are due to breast or prostate primarys

Rheumatoid Arthritis (RA)	- autoimmune disorder $\Rightarrow$chronic, symmetric & erosive arthritis of synovial joints
	- joints effected in order of most common first: MCPJs (metacarpal phalangeal joints of fingers = knuckles), carpus (wrist), MTPJs (metatarsal phalangeal joints of toes), PIPJs (proximal interphalangeal joints of fingers), elbows, knees, shoulders, ankles, hips & cervical spine
	symptoms:
	  1. joint swelling/pain/stiffness/$\uparrow$temp worse in morning, improves throughout day
	  2. ulnar deviation = sublux/dislocation of MCPJ
	  3. swan neck deformity = hyperextension of PIPJ + flexion of MCPJ
	  4. boutonniere deformity = flexion of PIPJ + extension of DIPJ & MCPJ
	  5. Z thumb
	  6. trigger finger is usually due to tenosynovitis = thickening of flexor sheath $\Rightarrow$tendon cannot run smoothly through sheath $\Rightarrow$locking, treated with steroid injections or surgical release
	  7. muscle wasting (especially the thenar muscle at base of thumb on palm of hand)
	  8. others manifestations: palmar erythema, elbow nodules, carpal tunnel syndrome (median nerve compression), vasculitis ($\Rightarrow$ischaemic ulcers), splenomegaly, distal neuropathies, dry eyes, renal disease (due to treatment medication) & general symptoms of illness (fatigue, $\downarrow$appetite, lethargy, etc.)
	- blood shows: signs of inflammation ($\uparrow$ESR/CRP) + anaemia of chronic disease ($\downarrow$Hb + normal MCV, *see 'Haematology' section*), look for rheumatoid factor (RF, identified using rose waaler test, found in 85% of cases, is not diagnostic) & anti-nuclear antibodies (ANA, found in 30% of cases)
	- X-ray findings: $\downarrow$joint space, bony erosions, subluxation/dislocation & soft tissue swelling
	- multi-disciplinary treatment: physio, occupational health, NSAIDs (if long term use always give with a COX2 inhibitor e.g. omeprazole $\Rightarrow\downarrow$GI side effects), steroids during flare ups, in later stages give disease modifying drugs (methotrexate, sulfasalazine, gold salts, cyclosporine, all are very toxic) +/- surgery
	- N.B. rheumatoid hands are common in OSCEs so remember & be able to spot the deformities mentioned above

Gout	- $\uparrow$ uric acid (due to diet, alcohol, diuretics, aspirin) $\Rightarrow$monosodium urate crystals (have $-$'ve birefringence when viewed via a microscope) in the synovial joint capsule - symptoms: acute onset, red/swollen/warm/painful joint - usually effect one joint at a time (monoarticular), the 1st metatarsophalangeal MTPJ (big toe) being the most common - uric acid crystals deposited in the kidneys can $\Rightarrow$nephropathy & renal stones - in chronic conditions X-rays show structural changes $\equiv$ OA + punched out lesions, if acute X-rays may just show soft tissue swelling - diagnosis: blood (can show $\uparrow$urate concentration + $\uparrow$inflammatory markers) + joint aspirate microscopy (monosodium urate crystals) - treat with: NSAIDs, steroids (can be injected directly into joint), prophylactic allopurinol ($\downarrow$uric acid formation in blood) & diet control (e.g. $\downarrow$alcohol intake) - N.B. a septic/infected joint needs to be ruled out, bloods would show signs of infection + joint aspirate would grow organisms

Pseudogout	- calcium pyrophosphate dihydrate crystals (+'ve birifringence) in the synovial joint capsule - symptoms similar to gout but not as severe & usually affects larger joints e.g. wrist, knee or shoulder - can be due to: dehydration, diabetes, wilson's disease ($\uparrow$copper), hypothyroid, haemochromatosis ($\uparrow$iron) & hyperparathyroidism - diagnose as above, but aspirate shows dihydrate crystals - treat with: NSAIDs & intra-articular steroids
Osteomalacia	- 'soft bones' = $\downarrow$mineralization of osteoid matrix - $\downarrow$calcium due to vitamin D dietary deficiency &/or vitamin D metabolic abnormality (liver/renal failure) also $\downarrow$sunlight has some effect - can $\Rightarrow$ hyperparathyroidism ($\downarrow$Ca in the blood $\Rightarrow\uparrow$parathyroid hormone release $\Rightarrow\uparrow$osteoclast activity = Ca removed from bones & put into blood) - results in skeletal deformities in children (rickets), bone pain, fractures & proximal muscle weakness in adults +/- parathyroid gland swelling - tests: X-rays show looser's zones/pseudofractures (horizontal areas of radiolucency), bloods (check for $\downarrow$phosphate, $\downarrow$calcium & $\uparrow$parathyroid hormone $\Rightarrow\uparrow$alkaline phosphatase due to bone breakdown) - treat by giving vitamin D supplements + fracture prevention education
Paget's disease	- chronic $\uparrow$osteoclastic bone reabsorption/breakdown ($\Rightarrow$lytic lesions) followed by $\uparrow$disordered osteoblastic bone formation $\Rightarrow$ weak bones prone to fracture + overgrowth deformities - skull involvement can $\Rightarrow$ tam o'shanter appearance (protruding large forehead/skull) & deafness due to compression of auditory nerve by $\uparrow$bone size, if the disease effects the spine can $\Rightarrow$paralysis - diagnosis: blood shows $\uparrow\uparrow$ alkaline phosphatase (due to $\uparrow$osteoblastic activity), X-rays, isotope bone scan & bone biopsy - treat with bisphosphonates (inhibit bone reabsorption $\Rightarrow\downarrow$ bone turnover), calcitonin (inhibits osteoclasts) & surgery for fractures & to relieve compressions due to bone overgrowth
Ankylosing spondylitis	- disease of lumbo-sacral spine, usually effects young men $\Rightarrow$lower back/buttock pain/stiffness/inflammation, "?" posture & restricted spinal bend (identified using schober's test, *see 'Musculoskeletal Examination' section*) - associated with: reiter's syndrome (=urethritis, conjunctivitis & sero negative arthritis = RF –'ve, e.g. ankylosing spondylitis, reactive arthritis, etc.), aortic regurge, achilles tendonitis & plantar fascitis - investigations: this is a rheumatoid factor/sero –'ve spondyloarthropathy (therefore RF is –'ve) & has HLA-B27 antigen present in >90% of cases, bloods (=$\uparrow$inflammatory markers), spinal MRI + isotope bone scan - treat with: physio, NSAIDs, steroids & disease modifying drugs (e.g. methotrexate)
Reactive arthritis	- autoimmune disease of joint due to previous/ongoing infection - usually results in non-infective inflammation of a single joint - tests: rheumatoid factor/sero –'ve, HLA-B27 antigen is present in 70% of cases, bloods (=$\uparrow$inflammatory markers), culture everything (inc. joint aspiration if possible) & image joint - treat with: physio, NSAIDs, steroids +/- disease modifying drugs, antibiotics (if other part of body still infected)

Vasculitis	- inflammation of blood vessel walls ⇒ischaemic damage to organs + systemic signs of inflammation (fever, weight loss, lethargy & anorexia)
	classification:
	  1. giant cell arteritis effects large vessels
	  2. polyarteritis nodosa effects medium sized vessel (e.g. those supplying organs, skin, the gut, joints & kidneys)
	  3. wegener's gramulomatosis effects small vessels (e.g. respiratory tract & gomerulus of kidneys)
	- can be primary or secondary to RA, SLE, cancer or infection
	- tests: tissue biopsy + look for specific autoantibodies (e.g. RF or ANA) + bloods (=↑inflammatory markers)
	- treatment: because this is an autoimmune inflammatory process give NSAIDs +/- steroids

Temporal arteritis	- due to giant cell arteritis/vasculitis - severe headache, scalp/temple tenderness ("pain when putting on glasses") +/- visual disturbance & systemic symptoms - bloods (=↑inflammatory markers) + blood vessel biopsy shows 'giant cells' - give instant high dose steroids due to risk of blindness
Systemic lupus erythematosus (SLE)	- multi system autoimmune connective tissue disorder, relapsing & remitting in nature, 10 times more common in women, usual age of onset 20-40 years - symptoms: joint pain, lymphadenopathy, butterfly rash on face, photosensitivity, ↑risk of infections, vasculitis (⇒vital organ damage) - auto-immune antibodies are present in 90% of cases (anti-double stranded DNA antibodies are specific to SLE), rheumatoid factor +'ve in 40% of cases, ↑inflammatory markers (CRP & ESR) & normochromic normocytic anaemia (anaemia of chronic disease) - treat with: anti-inflammatories (NSAIDs), during flare ups (steroids +/- disease modifying drugs) & UV/sunlight protection - N.B. SLE is associated with CREST (systemic sclerosis) = <u>C</u>alcinosis (calcium deposits throughout body in soft tissue), <u>R</u>aynaud's (vascular condition effecting blood flow to extremities), o<u>E</u>sophageal dysmotility (damage to smooth muscle of oesophagus ⇒scar tissue ⇒↓transport efficiency), <u>S</u>clerodactyly (thickening & tightness of skin usually in hands & feet), <u>T</u>elangiectasia (dilation of small vessels in skin), also ⇒pulmonary fibrosis

Raynaud's	- colour, sensation & temp changes when hands & feet exposed to cold
	- long term disease ⇒ muscle wasting, can ⇒ gangrene at tips
	  1. primary (raynaud's disease) = digital artery vasospasm
	  2. secondary (raynaud's syndrome) = digital artery obstruction, vibration injury or secondary to systemic sclerosis (CREST) therefore investigate for autoimmune problem (e.g. bloods for ANA, ESR, etc.)
	- if unilateral & patient >40 yrs old check for peripheral arterial disease
	- treat by keeping hands warm & nifedipine medication (vasodilator)

Polymyalgia rheumatica	- autoimmune inflammation of proximal muscles ⇒stiff painful shoulders/thighs, usually effects patients >60yrs - unknown cause but disease is associated with giant cell arteritis - symptoms: morning stiffness, general lethargy & weight loss - bloods =↑inflammatory markers (CRP & ESR) - treatment: anti-inflammatories (NSAIDs), steroids + medication to protect bones (e.g. Ca/vitamin D supplements &/or bisphosphonates)

Ear, Nose & Throat

The Ear

Anatomy	can be split into 3 parts: 1. external ear: outer ear, ear canal & ear drum 2. middle ear: this contains air & is connected to the nose via the Eustachian tube (acts as a drain + air equalizer), it's job is to transfer sound energy from air to the fluid medium of the inner ear, this is done via 3 small bones/ossicles (malleus, incus & stapes) 3. inner ear: contains the semicircular canals (3 loops each in a different plane = bodies balance organ) & the cochlea (the organ of hearing in which hair cells convert transmitted vibrations to into nerve impulses), both are connected to the 8th cranial nerve
Tests	- auriscope: pinch the ear softly & elevate it upwards & backwards, then slide the scope into ear canal - audiometry: this uses headphones (air conduction) and a vibrator placed on the mastoid process (bone conduction), noises are then played via both at different frequencies ⇒graph with hearing level on y-axis & frequency on x-axis, from this you can see at what frequencies hearing is worst/lost & whether bone (sensorineural) or air (conductive) is effected, different diseases will give different results tuning fork tests (performing both these tests lets you distinguish between a conductive &/or sensorineural loss, use 512Hz fork): 1. rinne's test: compares air conduction with bone conduction, "which is louder", fork next to ear canal or base of fork touching the mastoid process, in a normal ear air conduction is best which = a +'ve result, a conductive loss would = −'ve result 2. weber's test: base of fork is placed on centre of forehead, a conductive deafness in the left ear means the sound will be heard louder on the left, a sensorineural deafness in the left ear would cause the sound to be heard loudest in the right
Hearing loss	conductive: - wax build up, use sodium bicarbonate or olive oil ear drops to loosen then syringe or suck wax out - drum perforations: usually from infection (otitis media) or trauma, heals naturally or can be repaired via graft surgery (tympanoplasty) - otosclerosis: excessive bone growth in ossicles (e.g. paget's disease, *see 'Rheumatology Revision' section*) ⇒inability to conduct sound sensorineural: - presbyacusis: gradual loss of hair in the cochlea with age, high frequencies lost first - noise exposure: prolonged or acute (e.g. bang), starts with tinnitus ⇒high frequency loss first - acoustic neuroma: this should be investigated via MRI scan for with anyone who presents with increasing unilateral sensorineural loss

Otitis externa	- infection of external ear: starts with a red tender ear canal ⇒discharge ⇒hearing loss when canal inflames & discharge accumulates - treat usually with topical drops, get swabs first (for culture), clean out pus (aural toilet) + can insert a otowick (=foam that expands in the canal when drops put on it = holds canal open) - malignant (is not cancer just a severe form of otitis externa) = spread of infection to temporal bone (=osteomyelitis), usually effects immunocompromised, treat as above & give oral/IV antibiotics +/- surgical washout
Otitis media	- infection of the middle ear: usually follows an upper respiratory tract infection which spreads via the eustachian tube - pus in middle ear ⇒pressure build up ⇒severe pain & bulging of ear drum, can ⇒ear drum rupture (=blood & pus discharged from ear), also anything effecting the middle ear can cause problems with the semicircular canals (⇒problems with balance, can be tested for as it causes nystagmus & +'ve romberg's test, *see 'Cranial Nerve Exam' section*) - treat with oral/IV antibiotics - children who suffer a number of these attacks can be treated with grommet insertion (= a small tube inserted into the drum ⇒balances out pressure by allowing pus/inflammation to escape) - can ⇒mastoiditis (infection of mastoid bone), facial paralysis, cerebral meningitis/abscesses - N.B. all infections usually have systemic features e.g. fever, ↑HR, N&V, etc.
Herpes zoster = shingles (ramsay hunt syndrome)	- viral infection that can affect the facial nerve ganglion - ⇒painful vesicles in ear canal +/- facial palsy (= bell's palsy) - treat with antivirals (e.g. acyclovir) +/- steroids - N.B. this type of facial palsy = a lower motor neuron lesion therefore the forehead muscles are not spared as they would be if due to a stroke (=upper motor neuron lesion)
Meniere's disease	- disease of body's balance system - usually effects young to middle aged & happens in attacks - symptoms: vertigo (feels like room is spinning), hearing loss & tinnitus (ringing in ears) - difficult to treat cause, but can try anti-emetics to help with symptoms

The Nose

Allergic rhinitis	- can be due to a number of precipitants/allergens (e.g. pollen, pets, dust, etc.) which ⇒a type 1 hypersensitivity reaction by binding to immunoglobulin E (IgE = antibody) which in turn binds to/activates mast cells ⇒local inflammatory response (in nose/upper airway) by releasing histamine - treat with systemic antihistamines or local steroids (e.g. beclometasone spray) - can result in flare ups of asthma & nasal polyps (areas of oedematous mucosa)
Epistaxis (nose bleed)	- mainly due to bleeding from kiesselbach's plexus in the nose (area dense in blood vessels and supplied by internal & external carotid) - causes: local trauma/infection/inflammation, high BP, clotting disorders - check for signs of excessive blood loss/shock (↑HR, ↓BP) - treatment: ice, local compression (by squeezing or insertion a nasal pack or inflatable balloon), cauterization, if severe check bloods (FBC, clotting, group & save, etc.), may need fluids or blood transfusion

Sinusitis	- infection/inflammation of the facial sinuses (maxillary, frontal & sphenoidal, these drain into the nose via the ethmoid sinus) - treat with local/systemic anti-inflammatories or antibiotics depending on the cause
Adenoids	- this is a collection of lymph tissue at the back of the nose, due to their position adenoidal hypertrophy can ⇒nasal obstruction & blockage of eustachian tube (can ⇒recurrent otitis media) - treat by surgical removal (adenoidectomy)
Various nasal surgeries	- septoplasty: performed if a deviated septum is causing nasal obstruction - rhinoplasty: plastic surgery of the nose - otoplasty: plastic surgery of the ears

The Throat

Anatomy	sections: 1. oral cavity: the mouth (inc. anterior 2/3 of tongue) 2. pharynx: comprises of the nasopharynx (posterior section of the nose + soft palate), oropharynx (base of tongue + tonsils) & hypopharynx (junction between trachea & oesophagus), because food & air passes through the pharynx there are 2 mechanisms to stop food going the wrong way = soft palate blocks of the nasopharynx & the epiglottis closes over the trachea (part of the larynx) 3. larynx: blocks food entering the trachea (via the epiglottis) & contains the vocal cords salivary glands: 1. parotids: anterior & inferior to ears, these are the largest of the salivary glands, produces mainly serous fluid, duct opens into the mouth at the 2nd upper molar tooth 2. sublingual: found at the floor of the mouth, produce mainly mucus & enter via a number of ducts into the floor of the mouth 3. submandibular: located between the other 2 glands, produce both serous & mucus (makes up 70% of saliva in the oral cavity), ducts also enter via the floor of the mouth - *see 'Cranial Nerve Exam' for the nerve supply to this region* - direct examination of the nose & throat is performed using a flexible rhinolaryngoscope - N.B. an emergency airway can be created via the cricothyroid membrane (gap between cartilages surrounding the larynx), this can be changed for a tracheostomy if needed long term
Dysphonia (voice changes/loss)	causes: - inflammation/infection = laryngitis, acid reflux - laryngeal or lung/breast cancer (the laryngeal nerve comes off the vagus nerve which passes near the lung/breast), if any systemic signs of cancer get a chest X-ray +/- chest CT - myasthenia gravis: *see 'Neurology Revision' section* - systemic problems: mainly hypothyroid & rheumatoid arthritis

Stridor	- noisy breathing due to a narrowing of the upper airway, depending where the narrowing is will produce either inspiratory, expiratory or biphasic stridor
	level of narrowing:
	  1. supraglottis (above vocal cords) = inspiratory, in children the most severe is epiglottitis (caused by haemophilus influenza B) this is an emergency, give nebulised adrenaline + get an anaesthetist involved straight away (may need intubation or emergency airway)
	  2. glottis (level of cords) = biphasic
	  3. bronchial narrowing = expiratory
	- N.B. in children the most common cause of stridor is foreign bodies

Tonsillitis	- most sore throats are viral in nature, the presence of pus on tonsils + them being red & swollen = bacterial (usually β haemolytic strep) - other symptoms: systemically unwell ($\uparrow$temp, etc.), dysphagia, halitosis, swollen cervical lymph - tests: bloods ($\uparrow$WCC) & throat swabs - treat with analgesia (paracetamol also reduces temp) + antibiotics (penicillin V) - N.B. if suffered with recurrent infections can have tonsillectomy
Mumps	- RNA paramyxovirus (droplet spread) - symptoms: painful salivary gland swelling (usually the parotid), malaise, fever +/- rash, can also result in a painful testicular swelling (orchitis) - common in children, usually resolves without treatment after 5-10 days - patient can be immunized against using the MMR vaccine (*see 'Paediatric' section*) - N.B. in adults can $\Rightarrow\downarrow$fertility
Mononucleosis (glandular fever)	- usually effects teenagers with fever, sore throat & swollen tonsils +/- hepatosplenomegaly - caused by epstein-barr virus (EBV) - diagnosis = +'ve monospot test - treat with advice + analgesia & $\uparrow$fluids - N.B. if mistaken for tonsillitis & ampicillin (amoxicillin) is given can $\Rightarrow$maculopapular skin rash
Peritonsillar abscess (quinsy)	- pus collection between tonsils & surrounding muscles - symptoms: severe unilateral sore throat, dysphagia, systemic features - treatment: incision & drainage of abscess + IV antibiotics + analgesia

Eye Examination

This examination is virtually the same as that found in the 'Cranial Nerve Examination' section, but with a little more detail

Introduction	- wash your hands - approach the patient and introduce yourself - check patients name & that they are appropriately positioned (=sitting upright) - explain to patient what you are going to do & gain verbal consent
Inspection	- comment on patient's general appearance - comment on presence/absence of obvious ptosis, cranial nerve palsies, a squint, signs of pathology & whether the patient is wearing glasses
Vision A D F H Z P T X U D Z A D N H P N T U H X	- ask the patient if they normally wear glasses, if so assess without (=vision) then with (=visual acuity) - assess distant vision (using snellen chart) & near vision (e.g. read a book), perform these examinations using one eye (monocularly) then both (binocularly) - calculating snellen fraction: top number =distance from chart in meters, (normally 6m, can bring closer if patient unable to see chart or if small exam room), second number =distance at which a 'normal' eye can see the letter (e.g. 6/6 = good), so if the patient is standing 6m away from chart & the lowest they can read = 3rd line from top ≡ what a normal eye can read at 18m, vision = 6/18) - N.B. 20/20 = the american equivalent (measured in feet) of 6/6
Colour vision	- standard test = ishihara plates (series of coloured dots resembling numbers with other coloured dots surrounding), N.B. the first plate can be seen by everyone - perform test on one eye at a time = will elicit colour vision defects - congenital defects will be binocular - a quick alternative if suspicious of a uniocular nerve lesion is to compare 'colour de-saturation', i.e. ask if a red pen top looks equally red in both eyes, or if less red in one eye
Visual fields & inattention	- assess using the confrontation method = compare your vision with the patient, positioning & explanation are important, sit so you can test vision half way between you & the patient - visual inattention: both eyes open, "is my finger moving on one or both sides simultaneously", inattention = cannot see both sides move simultaneously, test in upper & lower quadrants, can be impaired by stroke etc. - visual field defects: cover eye not being tested, you cover your apposing eye, bring finger in diagonally from upper then lower quadrants & L then R sides, "tell me when you can see my finger" (*for specific symptoms see 'Visual Field Defects' section of appendix*) - assess blind spot: start at 10° temporal to central point of vision, with slow movements find boundaries within the x & y axes, this will be enlarged with papilloedema & chronic glaucoma, *this is difficult to perform therefore it is usually not assessed in your OSCE exams*
Ocular movements	- eye movements, test both eyes at same time - "keep your head still & follow my finger with your eyes", trace out H shape then I shape down centre, *see diagram* - look for nystagmus (e.g. ask patient to look to their extreme L and hold ⇒slow drift to R then fast correction to L = L horizontal nystagmus), NB. the nystagmus is the fast correction - look for an obvious squint, if there is one perform the cover test (ask patient to

	focus on object then cover the good eye should ⇒the squinting eye should then straighten & fixate on the object) - ask about double vision - oculomotor (3rd nerve) controls all eye muscles apart from superior oblique (supplied by 4th nerve, moves eye inwards + down) & lateral rectus (6th nerve, moves eye outwards), a strange way to remember this is via the mnemonic = O_3 SO_4 LR_6, trust me it works! - the oculomotor nerve also supplies the muscles that open the eye lid & constrict the pupil - N.B. ↑ICP can ⇒6th nerve palsy
Pupillary reflexes R L ➡ ◉ 1 ◉ ◯ 2 ◯ ⬅ ➡ ◉ 3 ◉	- there is both a direct (in eye light is being shone into) & consensual (in other eye) pupillary light reflex - afferent component = via optic nerve to brain, efferent component = oculomotor nerve, think of it like this if there is an afferent defect the signal that light creates when it hits the eye cannot travel to the brain so nothing will happen in either eye, if there is an efferent defect the signal reaches the brain but will only cause a response in the eye in which the efferent branch is intact - ask patient to look into the distance & 'swing' torch in from the lateral side, first look for a direct reflex then perform again looking for a consensual reflex - the diagram shows a relative afferent pupillary defect (RAPD or marcus gunn pupil), this is most commonly associated with optic neuritis (related to MS), 1 = light shone into right eye (healthy optic nerve, both pupils constrict), 2 = swing light to left eye (damaged optic nerve, both pupils stay fixed or slightly dilate), 3 = swing light back to right (both pupils constrict again)
Accommodation	- accommodation (both eyes at same time) - focus on distant point then on examiners finger, eyes converge + pupils constrict
Ophthalmoscopy	- explain that you will be using a bright light to examine the eyes - examine for red reflex (from a distance): absence in elderly is most likely due to a cataract, in children be mindful of rare retinoblastoma (cancer of the retina, quick onset & can be fatal) - being comfort with an ophthalmoscope is essential, practice placing it in your eye socket & rotating the magnifying lens as to move closer into the eye, ensure you can see through aperture (can adjust magnification depending on your visual acuity), when examining a patient's right eye look through it with your right eye & vice versa, N.B. a good technique is to place your hand across there forehead and rest you forehead on the back of the same hand - approach the patient from slightly superior & temporal, start from about 10cm away looking at the external appearance of the eye, then move closer, ensuring that the light continues to shine through the pupil, if you stay in this line you should hit the optic disc - to find the optic disc follow the vessels within the eye as they generally converge at this point, there are 4 main vessels leaving the optic disc, as you get better try and follow each vessel in turn towards the periphery, then return to the disc before following the next - to examine the macular (=directly temporal/lateral to the disc) ask the patient to look directly into the light, this can be uncomfortable for the patient so perform it at the end of the examination & only for a short period of time, in older patients the macular maybe darkened & pigmented (= macular degeneration) - N.B. at the end of the examination thank the patient & present your findings to your examiner

Conjunctivitis	- inflammation/infection of the conjunctiva (a thin transparent layer overlying the sclera), visual acuity (VA) should be unchanged causes: - viral = most common, self resolving - bacterial = purulent discharge (pus), treat with antibiotic eye drops/ointment (e.g. chloramphenicol) - N.B. reiter's syndrome: triad of symptoms = inflammatory arthritis, inflammation of the eyes (conjunctivitis or uveitis) & urethritis
Glaucoma	- group of diseases causing ↑intraocular pressure (IOP) ⇒damage to retinal ganglion cells at the optic disc ⇒deterioration in visual fields ⇒'tunnel vision' & eventually can ⇒blindness - characteristic changes to the disc = the cup (central light coloured section of the disc) becomes wider & deeper + the surrounding rim becomes paler types: 1. chronic 2. open angle: triad of symptoms = ↑IOP, visual field defect & changes to optic disc appearance (see above), treat with topical eye drops to ↓IOP, e.g. betablockers & latanoprost (⇒↑outflow of aqueous fluid from the eyes) +/- surgery 3. acute closed angle: is an ophthalmological emergency, presents with acute onset red eye, severe pain, N&V, cloudy cornea (= oedema) & a fixed dilated pupil, treatment = acetazolamide (⇒↓fluid production in eye ⇒↓IOP) +/- laser iridotomy (surgically cut a hole in the iris to release the pressure)
Cataracts	- most common cause of blindness worldwide - is age related, but also caused by steroid use, trauma, congenital & diabetes - treat via surgery = phacoemulsification (ultrasonic destruction) of lens & replace with artificial lens, is minimally invasive & can be done under a local anaesthetic
Diabetic retinopathy	- ↑sugar in the blood gets deposited in the small vessels of the eyes - is the most common cause of blindness in the working age population levels of retinopathy severity: 1. background: microaneurysms (tiny red dots), haemorrhages (blots) & hard exudates (lipid deposition in retina due to vessel leakage), no specific eye treatment required (apart from diabetic control of blood sugar) + annual review 2. preproliferative: cotton wool spots (fluffy edged white areas of ischaemia), needs regular review + aim for maximal control of diabetes 3. proliferative: new vessel formation (neovascularisation) ⇒↑immature vasculature (these can be easily damaged) ⇒bleeding, can ⇒retinal detachment, significant haemorrhage & glaucoma, treatment = laser photocoagulation (destruction of new immature blood vessels) 4. macular oedema: fluid & protein deposits on the macula of the eye ⇒thickening & swelling, is most common cause of visual impairment in diabetics
Hypertensive retinopathy	- high BP damages delicate retinal vessels & can ⇒blindness signs: 1. arterial nipping (arteries cutting across veins) 2. silver wiring (↑arterial musculature) 3. flame haemorrhages (blood explodes out of capillaries due to ↑BP) 4. cotton wool spots (areas of ischaemia) 5. papilloedema (swelling around optic disc ⇒optic disc ischaemia) - treat by controlling patient's BP (*see 'Cardiovascular Revision' section*)

Macular degeneration	- most common cause of blindness of all ages in the UK, is age related
	- starts with gradually loss of central vision (at the macula) & distorted vision (metamorphopsia), mainly due to retinal atrophy - ⇒general decrease in visual acuity (VA) - tests: can use amsler grid (see diagram) to pick up early signs (focusing on dot in centre ⇒lines look distorted if macular degeneration present) two types (both typically start monocular but become binocular): 1. dry: common (90% of cases), gradual deterioration in central vision, presence of drusen (yellow deposits that are difficult to distinguish from hard exudates except for their distribution = focused over the macular) 2. wet: rarer (10%), rapid onset, quick decline in VA, due to neovascularisation (see diabetic retinopathy above)
Optic neuritis	- inflammation of the optic nerve - signs: subacute ↓VA, associated with ocular pain on movement (due to stretching of the inflamed optic nerve) + can get a relative afferent pupillary defect (RAPD = light shone in the affected eye will produce less pupillary constriction than light shone in the unaffected eye) & impaired colour vision, N.B. the optic disc may appear normal - may need an MRI to exclude multiple sclerosis - most patient's recover without treatment but steroids can be used
Anterior uveitis (iritis)	- inflammation of the iris (can affect the whole uveal tract = iris, ciliary body & choroid) - symptoms: unilateral, red, painful eye, photophobia & slight visual deterioration - associated with inflammatory diseases e.g. RA, inflammatory bowel disease, etc. - typically responds to topic steroids
Trauma	- blow out fracture: blunt trauma to anterior orbit ⇒increased pressure in orbit ⇒fracture in weakest wall (typically the orbital floor), may require surgery to avoid diplopia due to muscle entrapment in floor - penetrating injury: "something went in my eye" ⇒symptoms, use fluorescein drops & a UV light look for aqueous leakage (seidel test) this indicates penetration, can also perform an X-ray or orbital CT - a foreign body underneath the eyelid shows vertical striae (when fluorescein drops & a UV light are used) where blinking has eroded the corneal epithelium
Vessel Occlusion	- both arterial & vein occlusion can affect the central (⇒entire visual field defect) or branch (⇒segmental field defect) vessels 1. retinal artery occlusion: sudden, profound loss of vision with little chance of improvement, retina can appear pale, most commonly caused by a local atherosclerotic emboli or carotids stenosis (can ⇒emboli) 2. retinal vein occlusion: sudden profound loss of vision, reasonable prognosis (50% have reasonable vision after 6 months) - amaurosis fugax: do not forget that a transient loss of vision is TIA until proven otherwise, see 'Neurology Revision' section for management
Loss of vision	- acute differential: central retinal vein/artery occlusion, acute closed angle glaucoma, retinal detachment, giant cell arteritis, wet macular degeneration or macular haemorrhage - gradual differential: chronic glaucoma, cataracts, dry macular degeneration or optic atrophy
Red Eye	- differential: conjunctivitis, anterior uveitis, acute closed angle glaucoma, foreign body, corneal ulceration

Dermatology Revision

Describing a Rash	- dermatology is all about recognising a rash from it's appearance, so look at as many examples as you can, if you have not seen the condition before the best thing you can do is describe it's characteristics - symptoms: ask about general health (temp, N&V, recent contacts, etc.) + distribution (exactly where it is found on the body & the history of the spread), painful, itchy, raised/flat, colour, discharging (pus or clear), blanching (=application of pressure e.g. via a glass makes rash become clearer, if it stays the same = non-blanching) characteristics: - macule = flat coloured lesion, e.g. rubella - papule = raised solid lesion, e.g. insect bite - maculopapular = mixture of 2 above, e.g. measles & rubella - vesicle = raised fluid-filled lesion, e.g. chicken pox - wheal = firm, elevated swelling of the skin, pale red in colour, e.g. urticaria/hives usually due to an allergy - haemorrhagic = areas of bleeding under skin (called purpura, or if tiny called petchiae), purplish colour, are non-blanching, e.g. meningococcal septicaemia & henoch-schonlein purpura
Measles	- RNA paramyxovirus (droplet spread, very infectious) - symptoms: starts with fever, conjunctivitis, blue/white koplic spots in mouth & a cough, then 3-5 days later a maculopapular rash appears usually on face first then spreading down the body - remember the 3 Cs = cough, conjunctivitis, & coryza (=symptoms of head cold e.g. nasal congestion) - child is infectious for several days before & after the rash - diagnosis: if needed can look for IgM antibodies in saliva - treatment: analgesia, ↑fluids, advice on infection spread (isolate + vaccinate unvaccinated contacts), has to be reported to CDC - N.B. MMR vaccination given to children for <u>M</u>easles, <u>M</u>umps *(see 'ENT')* & <u>R</u>ubella
Rubella (german measles)	- RNA virus (droplet spread) - 2-3 week incubation period, child is infectious for 1 week before rash - symptoms: fever, pink macular rash starting on the face & scalp spreading downwards, upper respiratory tract symptoms & ↑lymph - diagnosis: if needed can look for IgM antibodies in saliva - treatment: analgesia, ↑fluids & advice (stay away from pregnant women) - NB. rubella is teratogenic during the 1st trimester of pregnancy ⇒congenital rubella syndrome
Herpes simplex virus (HSV ⇒ cold sores)	- fluid filled vesicles ⇒ crust over & heal < 2 weeks - HSV type 1 effects oral/lip region, HSV type 2 effects genital area - tests: viral culture + serology - treat with topical acyclovir (an antiviral)

Herpes zoster (chickenpox + can ⇒shingles)	- varicella zoster virus - 2 week incubation period before rash - chickenpox symptoms: usually an itchy vesicular rash starting on face, trunk, & back + general signs of infection, can ⇒secondary skin infections & scarring if scratched - treatment: advice (highly infectious after first few days) + oral acyclovir in immunocompromised - once acute infection is over the virus hibernates in dorsal root ganglia, when body run down/immunocompromised can reactivate ⇒shingles =effects the nerves usually on one side of body (can be contained in one dermatome) resulting in neuralgic pain & a vesicular rash, can ⇒complications if the ophthalmic division of the trigeminal nerve is involved (e.g. blindness), treat with acyclovir + educate on contact precautions
Scarlet fever	- due to group A strep toxin produced during a strep throat (tonsillitis) ⇒erythrogenic toxin ⇒cutaneous vasodilatation ⇒rash - symptoms: apart from the swollen pus filled tonsils & fever, there is a diffuse red blanching maculopapular rash & a strawberry red tongue - treatment: antibiotics (penicillin) + analgesia & ↑fluids
Slapped cheek (fifth disease)	- caused by parvovirus B19 (erythrovirus) - symptoms: fever, sore throat & bright red macular rash on face which can spread to body - treat with advice + analgesia & ↑fluids
Scalded skin syndrome	- reaction to toxin produced by staph infection - symptoms: generalized erythema, shredding of skin & large fluid filled blisters (skin looks like it has been scalded) + generally unwell - diagnosis is via typical skin appearance, bloods (=signs of infection) + can perform biopsy to rule out other causes - treat with analgesia & fluids (skin looses fluids much in the same way burnt skin would, keep eye on electrolyte balance) + IV antibiotics - N.B. known as ritter's disease in newborn
Henoch-schonlein purpura (HSP)	- an autoimmune systemic vasculitis ⇒deposition of immune complexes containing IgA antibodies in the skin, joints & kidneys - occurs mainly in young children & usually follows a viral illness - symptoms: purpuric haemorraghic rash over buttocks & thighs + arthritis, abdominal pain & can ⇒glomerulonephritis - diagnosis: typical rash pattern + bloods (=↑inflammatory markers CRP/ESR & deranged U&Es due to kidney damage, normal platelet count), skin biopsy can be performed to rule out other causes - treat symptoms, usually self limiting - N.B. has similar characteristics to idiopathic thrombocytopaenic purpura, but in HSP the platelet count = normal
Idiopathic thrombocytopaenic purpura	- usually due to an autoimmune reaction following a viral illness ⇒antibodies against platelets - symptoms: purpuric haemorraghic rash, skin may also show bruising + prolonged bleeding time - tests: bloods (↓platelet count) - N.B. a low platelet count can ⇒intercranial bleed, therefore platelet transfusions maybe needed

Atopic dermatitis (eczema)	- atopy is an inherited tendency to develop type 1 hypersensitivity reactions $\Rightarrow\uparrow$IgE $\Rightarrow\uparrow$histamine release from mast cells $\Rightarrow$inflammation in skin (eczema), lung (asthma), or nose (hay fever) depending on the irritant - eczema = erythematous scaly patches on face & flexor sites - scratching $\Rightarrow$skin thickening (lichenification) & can $\Rightarrow$infection - usually a family history of atopy - treatment: education, avoid irritants, emollients (keep skin moist), anti-histamines, topical steroids (during flare ups), phototherapy - N.B. anaphylaxis (e.g. to peanuts, bee stings, etc.) is also an IgE reaction but is usually systemic instead of local, treat like above i.e. with antihistamines, steroids, & if severe IM adrenaline
Seborrhoeic eczema	- due to an abnormal reaction to pityrosporum yeasts - symptoms: eczema rash on scalp, face, chest, back & groin - treat with steroids + antifungal cream - NB. long term steroid use can $\Rightarrow$ local skin necrosis & systemic cushing's features
Contact dermatitis	split into: 1. irritant eczema: usually only found at sites of contact with an irritant substance, has a rapid onset 2. allergic eczema: can spread away from contact site, more gradual onset (over a day or so) - investigate by doing patch testing - treat with topical steroids +/- antibiotics if secondary infection & education
Urticaria (hives)	- skin swelling due to leaky capillaries $\Rightarrow$ itchy red (erythematous) wheals - caused by mast cell degranulation due to a type I immunological reaction $\Rightarrow$ release of histamine etc. - when severe can $\Rightarrow$ oedema in face, tongue & larynx - investigate for infection - treat with antihistamines + steroids if severe
Psoriasis	- chronic autoimmune inflammatory condition effecting skin & joints - symptoms: red plaques with silvery scales mainly on extensor surfaces, nail changes (onycholysis) + can effect joints - biopsy shows clubbed rete pegs and inflammatory signs - treat similar to eczema
Acne vulgaris	- chronic disorder of sebaceous ducts $\Rightarrow\uparrow$sebum production, duct hyperkeratinisation, inflammation & abnormal symbiotic relationship with commensal bacteria - can $\Rightarrow$ scarring - sebaceous glands are driven by androgens (sex hormones), therefore investigate for PCOS, cushing's etc. - treat depending on severity: antibiotics, anti-androgenic hormones, oral vitamin A derivatives (influence follicle lining cells lifecycle helping prevent hyperkeratinisation $\Rightarrow\downarrow$blockage, e.g. retinoic acid, side effects =eczema, conjunctivitis, mood disturbance & is teratogenic)
Rosacea	- instability of facial vasculature $\Rightarrow$ red flushed face - can be brought on by coffee, spicy foods, alcohol etc. - treat with: topical medications to reduce inflammation

Vitiligo	- autoimmune condition $\Rightarrow$ depigmentation ($\downarrow$melanocyte) - areas can be seen with woods UV lamp - associated with other autoimmune conditions e.g. diabetes, addisons, pernicious anaemia, thyroid disease - treat with fake sun tan, UV therapy, steroids (may $\Rightarrow\uparrow$pigmentation but have side effects e.g. skin thinning & sensitivity to light)
Impetigo	- superficial skin infection caused mainly by strep but also by staph organisms - vesicles form that discharge $\Rightarrow$golden dry crusts - treat with antibiotics + education as very infectious
Cellulitis	- an infection of connective tissue with severe inflammation of the dermal & subcutaneous layers of the skin - usually infects area of skin trauma or chronic inflammation - tests: bloods (raised infective & inflammatory markers), swab areas of discharge - treatment: antibiotics (if infective organism unknown usually start with oral flucloxacillin but in more severe cases IV maybe needed) + fluid resus if septic - necrotizing fasciitis (flesh-eating disease): severe form of cellulitis $\Rightarrow$quick progression to tissue death/necrosis (dusky purple appearance), is a surgical emergency needs IV antibiotics, fluid resus & surgical removal of infected areas
Human papillomavirus (HPV $\Rightarrow$ warts)	- causes proliferation of keratinocytes sealing the virus from elimination $\Rightarrow$a wart - treat with keratolytics (salicylic/retinoic acid) or cryptotherapy (freezing) - N.B. genital warts $\Rightarrow\uparrow$risk of cervical cancer
Fungal infections	- candida: common cause of thrush, can affect mouth in immunocompromised - dermatophytosis (ring worm): affects groin, feet, axillae & nails (onychomyosis), have characteristic lesions which are circular with a clear centre, some show up under woods lamp - athlete's foot (tinea pedis): causes scaling, flaking, & itching, can spread to other areas e.g. the groin - treat with topical/oral antifungals
Parasites	- scabies: symmetrical rash & intense itching, mites usually burrow between fingers (can be seen on examination), skin scraping show female mite (sarcoptes scabiei) or her eggs - head lice (pediculus humanus): these suck blood from the scalp & lays eggs on hair shaft (these eggs are visible on examination, use a fine toothed comb to collect them) $\Rightarrow$itchy rash - these spread quickly so all the family needs educating & treatment with topical insecticides
Nails	- iron deficiency (koilonychia), chronic disease (clubbing), infective endocarditis (splinter haemorrhages & clubbing), psoriasis (pitting & onycholysis), chemotherapy (beau's lines), chronic liver (leukonychia & clubbing)
Hair	- $\uparrow$ (hirsutism) = polycystic ovarian syndrome, drugs, adrenal carcinoma, menopause - $\downarrow$ (alopecia) = autoimmune (related to addison's, pernicious anaemia, etc.)
Keratoacanthoma	- benign variant of squamous cell carcinoma - rapid growth on light exposed skin - smooth/regular margins & dome-shaped with centre crater of keratinaceous material

Premalignant disease	- bowen's disease: intraepidermal carcinoma in situ, looks like eczema, but no itching & does not respond to topical steroids - congenital melanocytic naevi: large pigmented lesions from birth, can $\Rightarrow$ malignant melanoma
Basal cell carcinoma	- never metastasizes - usually on face, head & neck due to sun exposure - late presentation may $\Rightarrow$ deep invasion
Squamous cell carcinoma	- sun exposed area in elderly or multiple tumours in young patients with xeroderma pigmentosor (due to DNA repair defect) - slow growing, 'fleshy' lesion with central ulcer - common on ear, lower lip & back of hand - can metastases to local lymph - treat with surgery +/- radiotherapy
Malignant melanoma	- risks: UV exposure, family history, freckles/moles 3 types: 1. superficial: first growth in horizontal plane $\Rightarrow$ new or changing mole, then invades locally & metastasizes to lymph nodes early on 2. nodular 3. acral: found on palms, soles & under nails - be concerned during history/exam if: rapid increase in size, itching, bleeding, irregular margins/colour, lymph enlargement, more lesions over body - treat with surgery (leave large border on excision) +/- radio/chemotherapy

Gynaecological History

Introduction	- approach politely and introduce yourself - patients name, DOB & occupation

Menstrual cycle	- age at first period (menarche), age periods ended (menopause) - first day of last period - normal period compared with what it is now: length, cycle regularity, heaviness (passing clots or flooding), sanitary use (type & number) - bleeding between periods - bleeding after intercourse
Urinary incontinence	- how often - brought on by cough, straining, laughing, etc. (stress incontinence) - urgency (urge incontinence/detrusor instability) - do you wear a pad - number of times pass water per day & amount passed - nocturia - difficulty emptying bladder (normal flow, dribble afterwards) - burning sensation on passing water - abdominal tenderness
Sexual History	- do you or your partner use any birth control - difficulties with intercourse (pain, bleeding) - frequency of intercourse
Vaginal discharge	- length of complaint - colour - smell - amount - itching - does partner have any symptoms - is the timing related to periods - abdominal tenderness
Infertility	- should interview both husband & wife - how long have you been trying to conceive - how often do you have sex - partner's problems (erection or ejaculating)

PMH	- list PMH (inc. appendicitis & ectopic pregnancies) + DEAR J SMITH
Medications, allergies, smoking & alcohol	- if ex smoker ask smoking history
FH	- are parents/brothers/sisters alive, if so do they suffer from any diseases, if they have passed away, sympathise and then ask age & cause of death
Social/occupational history	- who is at home & how does this condition effect their life - expand on occupation

Gynaecological Examination

Introduction	- always have a chaperone & document the identity of that person in the notes - wash hands - approach politely and introduce yourself - patient's name & DOB - explain to patient what you are going to do & obtain verbal consent - expose patient after asking
General examination	- general appearance, height, weight, BMI, BP, pulse, urine dip (inc. pregnancy test), facial & body hair, pallor, examine heart & lungs - N.B. you should also perform a breast exam in the over 35s
Abdominal exam	- *see 'Gastroenterology Examination' section*
Pelvic examination	- get all your equipment ready before you start (speculum, swabs, brushes) & label all pots/slides etc. so that you look professional & do not fumble about - examine the vulva for redness, swelling, ulceration, warts, discharge - examine the urethral meatus & ask patient to cough (look for signs of incontinence) - speculum examination (done first to avoid contamination with lubricant), involves passing a cusco's speculum into vagina (twist speculum onto its side to insert, once in slowly twist back to horizontal position), then open the blades of the speculum to visualise the cervix, note the cervix's appearance (any tears, polyps, bleeding, discharge, etc.), then take any swabs/smears that are necessary, the vaginal wall can be visualised by withdrawing the speculum slowly with the blades held slightly apart, N.B. a sims' speculum is used when a prolapse is suspected (with patient lying on her side) - examine the vagina digitally by passing your lubricated index & middle finger into the vagina up to the level of the cervix, a bimanual examination involves using the other hand to press on the abdomen above the symphysis pubis (compressing the pelvic organs onto the examining fingers) use this technique to feel around & build up a mental picture of what lies inside the pelvis, be sure to feel laterally into both fornices feeling for ovarian enlargement - a rectal examination is not always performed but may be desirable in some situations *(see 'Gastroenterology Examination' section)*
When finished	- cover the patient up, advise them the examination is over & allow them to get dressed before explaining any findings
Breast lumps	examination: 1. inspection: with arms raised, then hands on hips + press inwards (puts tension on pectoralis muscle), then finally whilst patient is leaning forward 2. palpation: in concentric circles starting at edge and moving inwards 3. examine nipple do not attempt to produce nipple discharge just ask about it - breast cysts (fibrocystic disease): symptoms are cyclic (linked to menstrual cycle), lumps are smooth edged & mobile = cobblestone texture in the breasts +/- bilateral breast pain, treatment with the oral contraceptive pill helps with symptoms in most women - fibroadenomas: an encapsulated benign tumour = a single, rubbery, smooth, solid, mobile mass, usually found in young women, if worrying can be removed by surgery - because breast cancer is the most common malignancy in women, if unsure about a breast lump perform triple diagnosis, *see 'breast cancer' below*

Gynaecological Revision

Puberty	- as hypothalamic region develops it begins releasing gonadotropin releasing hormone (GnRH) which stimulates the pituitary to release luteinizing hormone (LH) & follicle stimulating hormone (FSH), these then work on the ovaries $\Rightarrow$release of oestrogen & progesterone and the menstrual cycle begins - these sex hormones effect the whole body: thelarche = breast development (8-10yrs), adrenarche = pubic & axillary hair (11-12yrs), menarche = 1st menstruation (12-13yrs)

Precocious puberty	- puberty <8yrs
	types:
	  1. primary: due to premature development of hypothalamic/pituitary region, e.g. idiopathic or pituitary tumours $\Rightarrow\uparrow$FSH/LH $\Rightarrow\uparrow$oestrogen
	  2. secondary: is independent of the sex hormones produced by brain, e.g. ovarian tumours $\Rightarrow\uparrow$oestrogen
	- can $\Rightarrow$short stature (early grow $\Rightarrow$bones fuse earlier)
	- tests: bloods (TFTs, LH/FSH, oestrogen & progesterone levels), image ovaries with pelvic USS & brain with CT/MRI
	- treat: GnRH agonists, surgery, radio/chemo therapy

The menstrual cycle	- begins at the menarche & ends at the menopause - at birth a female contains approximately 2 million follicles which reduces to 300,000 by time of menarche, each contains a oocyte/egg surrounded by thecal cells (stimulated by LH) & granulosa cells (stimulated by FSH), only one develops each menstrual cycle - 1st day of menstruation = 1st day of menstrual cycle proliferative phase: - as the follicle develops it produces oestrogen, when oestrogen reaches a certain level $\Rightarrow$surge mainly of LH but also FSH, both are released from pituitary due to stimulation by gonadotropin releasing hormone (GnRH) from hypothalamus luteal phase: - LH surge $\Rightarrow$ovulation = follicle split into egg (releases oestrogen) & corpus luteum (releases progesterone which prepares endometrium for implantation) - if no implantation (i.e. egg not fertilized) $\Rightarrow$corpus luteum degeneration $\Rightarrow\downarrow$hormones $\Rightarrow$menstruation (shedding of endometrial lining) & the cycle begins again - if implantation occurs the embryo will start producing human chorionic gonadotropin (βhCG) which prevents menstruation & the corpus luteum will form into the placenta - N.B. pregnancy tests measure levels of βhCG, also it is important to realise that negative & positive feedback mechanisms control the levels of these hormones

Amenorrhoea	- the absence or stopping of menstruation
	primary (menstruation not started by 16yrs) causes:
	  1. gonadal failure: ovaries fail to develop $\Rightarrow$nil or decreased ovarian sex hormone (oestrogen) produced $\Rightarrow$breasts do not develop, is usually due to chromosomal abnormalities (e.g. turners syndrome = XO sex chromosomes), some diseases can be treated with oral contraceptives (COCP)
	  2. hypothalamic dysfunction: $\downarrow$GnRH $\Rightarrow\downarrow$LH/FSH $\Rightarrow\downarrow$oestrogen, can be due to a brain lesion, perform a CT/MRI scan, treat with oral contraceptives +/- surgery & radio/chemotherapy

	3. vaginal underdevelopment, abnormalities or obstruction: menstruation takes place but the products cannot be expelled due to a blockage, patients usually suffer with dysmenorrhoea, image region (e.g. pelvic USS) 4. testicular feminisation: due to androgen insensitivity (mutation of androgen receptor gene) $\Rightarrow$XY genotype but female phenotype, patient usually has undescended testes (must be removed after puberty as $\uparrow$risk of testicular Ca) secondary (absence of periods for >6 months in woman who usually has a regular cycle) causes: 1. pregnancy 2. polycystic ovarian syndrome 3. pituitary disease: prolactin-secreting tumours or sheehan syndrome (pituitary necrosis due to blood loss & hypovolemic shock during/after childbirth), can treat with hormone replacement therapy (HRT) &/or surgery depending on the cause 4. hypothalamic dysfunction: can be due to stress, excessive weight loss & some drugs, treat with COCP & lifestyle advice 5. ovarian failure: early menopause (<40yrs), number of causes, treat with HRT
Abnormal vaginal bleeding	- menorrhagia (long heavy periods), polymenorrhea ($\downarrow$interval between bleeding), oligomenorrhea ($\uparrow$interval between bleeding) causes: 1. within the gynaecological organs: pregnancy, cancer, contraceptive use, endometriosis or fibroids 2. systemic: thyroid disease, bleeding disorders + liver disease ($\Rightarrow\downarrow$clotting factors) - tests: pregnancy test, bloods (inc. FBC, LFTs, clotting & TFTs) & pelvic USS - treatment: if systemic treat cause, COCP helps most women, mefenamic acid (an anti-inflammatory $\Rightarrow\downarrow$bleeding), surgery (dilatation & curettage, removal of lesions, hysterectomy)
Pelvic inflammatory disease (PID)	- chronic or acute infection that can involve any gynaecological region - symptoms: pain, discharge, irregular bleeding & systemic symptoms of infection (fever, N&V, etc.) - treatment depends on cause: antibiotics or surgical draining (e.g. abscesses) - can $\Rightarrow$scaring & adhesions which can $\downarrow$fertility
Endometriosis	- due to endometrial glands/cells finding their way outside the uterus, these cells are controlled by progesterone & therefore proliferate as the progesterone levels increase each month (the same as the endometrial lining) - $\Rightarrow$cyclic symptoms which vary in severity throughout the menstrual cycle depending on where the endometrial cells end up: abdominal/pelvic pain, dysmenorrhoea (uterine pain during menstruation), dyspareunia (pain during sex), bladder & rectal problems (if cells effect those regions), also can $\Rightarrow$infertility - diagnosis: inspection + biopsy, lesions have typical 'powder burn' appearance - treatment: because the cells are controlled by sex hormones if these hormones can be reduced $\Rightarrow\downarrow$symptoms, start will simple contraceptives that stop ovulation, can also use GnRH agonists, finally can surgically remove specific lesions or perform hysterectomy - N.B. known as adenomyosis if the endometrial cells are found in the myometrium (uterus muscle wall layer)

Polycystic ovarian syndrome (PCOS)	- is not known whether the primary pathology is in the ovaries or the hypothalamus but results in ↑oestrogen & ↑GnRH - this in turn effects the FSH & LH levels in the body therefore interfering with the normal menstrual cycle - ↑oestrogen ⇒↑LH (+'ve feedback) & ↓FSH (-'ve feedback) ⇒chronic elevated LH & suppressed FSH ⇒chronic anovulation - also results in ↑testosterone ⇒hirsutism (male like hair growth) - this mechanism is amplified in obese people because oestrogen is also produced in adipose/fat tissue - symptoms: enlarged cystic ovaries, menstrual irregularities (can ⇒anovulation/amenorrhoea), hirsutism, infertility & ⇒↑risk of endometrial Ca + diabetes - treatment: weight loss, COCP, metformin (↑sensitivity to insulin ⇒↑oestrogen uptake into cells ⇒↓circulating oestrogen), surgery (ovarian drilling destroys sections of ovary ⇒↓oestrogen)
Fibroids	- also called myomas or leiomyomas, these are the commonest pelvic benign tumours - they are oestrogen sensitive benign fibromuscular swellings arising from the muscle wall of the uterus & tend to grow during pregnancy & regress after menopause - 20% of women over 30yrs have fibroids, can be single or multiple, ranging from microscopic growths to football sized tumours - symptoms: can be asymptomatic (found incidentally on examination), pressure can cause urinary frequency & poor stream, constipation (if they form posteriorly), pain, menstrual disturbances (such as menorrhagia, irregular bleeding, etc.), submucosal fibroids distorting the endometrial cavity can cause infertility & abortion (due to interference with the process of implantation) - management: for small asymptomatic fibroids no treatment is required except annual examination, manage pain with analgesia, women wishing to become pregnant can be given GnRH agonist for 6 months (the withdrawal of oestrogen will shrink the fibroid, effects are not long lasting and fibroids will grow back, also long term usage ⇒↓bone density), uterine artery embolization (passing a cannula into the uterine artery via the femoral artery then injecting small silicone particles cause the fibroids to degenerate), if the above fail or heavier/longer periods are present surgical removal is considered (myomectomy), N.B. in women over the age of 40 not wishing to have further children hysterectomy is preferred
Urinary incontinence	- involuntary loss of urine, associated with bladder/urethral dysfunction, or fistula formation types: 1. true incontinence: continuous loss of urine through the vagina, commonly associated with fistula formation but can be a manifestation of urinary retention with overflow 2. stress incontinence: due to bladder sphincter weakness, brought on when ↑bladder pressure (cough, laugh, sneeze, etc.), is characterised by a short spurt of urine which can then be controlled, caused by old age, spinal cord trauma/compression, MS, pelvic floor damage after childbirth, vaginal degeneration (post menopause due to ↓oestrogen) 3. urge incontinence: due to detrusor instability (i.e. an overactive bladder

	muscle) $\Rightarrow$ sudden urge to urinate which usually happens before patient can get to the toilet, treat with behavioural/bladder training or antimuscarinic drugs ($\Rightarrow\downarrow$ bladder muscle innervation)
	4. overflow incontinence: loss of urine when the bladder is overfilled, usually associated with an obstruction to the bladder neck (past surgery scaring/strictures) or denervation of detrusor muscle (due to extensive pelvic surgery, neurological defects or diabetes)
	- tests: urodynamic assessment of incontinence is via an input/output diary or via cystometry to measure bladder pressures
	- general management can be conservative via pelvic floor exercises, weight loss & reduction of physical exertion, if these fail surgery can be considered
Vaginal prolapse	- pelvic organs descend into vaginal canal, can $\Rightarrow$ a portion of the vaginal canal protruding from the opening of the vagina
	- causes: vaginal trauma (pregnancy $\Rightarrow$ damage to pelvic support structures), $\downarrow$ oestrogen $\Rightarrow$ deterioration of pelvic collagen fibres (e.g. post menopause), connective tissue disease or chronic steroid use
	- treat using ring pessaries or if more severe surgery
	types (each $\Rightarrow$ different symptoms depending on organs involved):
	- uterine: uterus herniates into the vagina
	- cystocele: bladder herniates into the vagina
	- rectocele: rectum herniates into the vagina
	- enterocele: small bowel herniates into the vagina
Contraception	- barrier contraceptive: condom, diaphragm, etc.
	- combined oral contraceptive pill (COCP): synthetic oestrogen & progesterone $\Rightarrow$ inhibits LH surge preventing ovulation, start taking on 1st day of period, take for 21 days then stop for 7 days $\Rightarrow$ withdrawal bleed, barrier contraceptives need to be used for 1st month, contraindications (history of thromboembolic disease, liver disease, pregnancy & oestrogen dependant cancer e.g. breast Ca), should take care prescribing to women who smoke, suffer with chronic migraines, heart disease or diabetes
	- depo: long acting progesterone intra-muscular injection, lasts for 12 weeks, prevents LH surge, side effects vary between women (vaginal bleeding, weight gain, $\downarrow$ libido & sometimes depression)
	- implanon: slow release progesterone capsules inserted under the skin, lasts 3 years, side effect similar to depo
	- intrauterine devices (IUD): copper IUD works by creating a local inflammatory reaction in uterus so sperm/egg cannot survive, mirena IUD works in similar way to copper but also contains progesterone
	- emergency contraceptive: is basically the same as the COCP but contains a much larger dose (can use up to 3 days after sex), can also have an IUD fitted (up to 5 days after sex)
Sterilization	- female: there are a number of methods which $\Rightarrow$ either fallopian tube ligation/cutting or tube occlusion (via clipping or banding)
	- male (vasectomy): much safer than female sterilization, patient's are not sterile until 3 months after the procedure, semen analysis should be performed before having unprotected sex
Infertility	- defined as failure to conceive after one year of unprotected sex at frequent intervals, ranges from around 12% in europe to 50% in some african communities
	- male causes: impotence, premature ejaculation, poor sperm motility,

	azoospermia/oligospermia ($\downarrow$concentration of sperm in ejaculation), investigation of the male partner includes semen analysis (=volume, sperm concentration, total sperm count, sperm motility & morphology) - female causes: ovarian dysfunction, narrowing or occlusion of tubes due to infection, PCOS, peri-menopause, vaginal or uterine malformations, investigation of the female includes detection of ovulation (0.5°C rise in body temp during luteal phase, increased production of low viscosity mucous during follicular phase & peak in urine/blood FSH/LH approximately 20 hours before ovulation), USS of ovaries to identify follicular growth, direct visualisation of ovary via laparoscopy, it also involves investigating tubal patency by using radiopaque dyes, or coloured dyes at laparoscopy
Assisted reproduction	- there are three main assisted reproductive techniques, all involve sperm preparation & superovulation (drug-induced production of multiple eggs) 1. in-vitro fertilization (IVF): ovaries are stimulated with intramuscular gonadotrophins to produce a large number of follicles, oocytes are then harvested transvaginally, the eggs & sperm are brought together in a culture medium & incubated at body temp for 24-48 hours, the 3 best zygotes are selected & re-introduced into the uterine cavity, success rate for fertilization can be as high as 90% although this corresponds to a live birth rate of ~15%, N.B. sperm can also be injected into the oocyte in a process called intracytoplasmic sperm injection (ICSI) 2. gamete intrafallopian tube transfer (GIFT): ovaries are stimulated in the same way as IVF, oocytes retrieved via laparoscopy under GA & the best 3 oocytes examined microscopically are mixed with sperm & re-introduced into the fallopian tubes, the success rate is slightly lower than IVF 3. in-utero insemination (IUI): here washed semen are injected high into the uterine cavity to meet an oocyte by travelling up the fallopian tube as happens naturally - other alternatives are donor semen, donor oocytes & surrogate mothers
Menopause	- defined as the cessation of menstruation for more than one year, the average age of onset is between 49-50 yrs (spontaneous cessation of periods before the age of 40 years is defined as premature menopause) - there is a marked reduction in ovarian production of oestrogen this $\Rightarrow$excessive release of FSH & LH which can be detected in the blood - signs & symptoms: hot flushes (in around 80% of women, that can persist for up to 5 years after menopause), osteoporosis, vaginal dryness/atrophy, loss of libido, atrophy of breast structure, the decrease in oestrogen also takes away the protection it gives against heart disease
Hormone replacement therapy (HRT)	- artificial oestrogen &/or progesterone - aims to reduce the symptoms of oestrogen (& to a lesser extent progesterone) deficiency & reduce the risk of both osteoporotic fractures & cardiovascular disease - but it also $\Rightarrow\uparrow$risk of developing breast cancer, endometrial cancer & CVAs, therefore it is not recommended to prescribe HRT to women who do not have significant symptoms - HRT can be administered orally, transdermally (gels and patches), via implants or vaginally - immediate side effects can include breast tenderness & abdominal bloating

General cancer staging	- histology (biopsy) = grade & subtype - spread: T (size), N (lymph involved), M (metastases)
Ovarian cancer	- types: mainly cystomas, epithelial (related to CA125 marker), sex cord & germ cell (teratoma) - risks: BRCA 1 & 2 gene mutations (i.e. family history of ovarian or breast cancer), null parity (had no children), infertility & early menarche - symptoms: all gynaecological cancers can ⇒irregular bleeding, abdominal pain, general lethargy & weight loss - spread: via lymph →pelvis, via blood →lung, brain, liver, bone & vagina staging: - 0 carcinoma in situ - I limited to ovaries - II local invasion, present in pelvis - III presence outside pelvis - IV distant mets - treat all cancer with surgery +/- radio/chemo therapy or palliative treatment, in this case due to high risk if BRCA gene mutation detected prophylactic ovarian removal is sometimes offered
Cervical intraepithelial neoplasia (CIN)	- this is a pre malignant condition (dyskariosis) that usually occurs at the cervical transformation zone = columnar-squamous junction (uterus = columnar cells, cervix = squamous cells), these junctions have ↑risk of malignancy (e.g. similar to the transformation zone at base of oesophagus) - screening performed using a PAP smear which removes a thin layer of cells from the cervix which is then analysed, in UK women have 1st at 25 or when sexually active then every 3-5 years till 65 - risks: ↑sexual partners, early intercourse, human papillomavirus (HPV) & smoking staging: - CIN 1 = 1/3 of epithelium shows abnormalities (cell features =↑nuclear:cytoplasmic ratio, loss of polarity, ↑mitotic figures, hyperchromatic nuclei) - CIN 2 = 2/3 - CIN 3 > 2/3 - if result comes back as positive a colposcopy is performed (microscopic visualisation of cervix) +/- biopsy of lesion - treatment: remove/destroy lesion - N.B. there is now a vaccine available that immunizes against several strains of the human papillomavirus (HPV), this can be offered to teenage girls who are not yet sexually active
Cervical cancer	- main cause = human papillomavirus (HPV) therefore is usually a disease of young sexually active women, also linked to prolonged pill use, smoking, etc. - types: squamous cell (80-90%), adenocarcinoma (15%) - staging ≡ ovarian
Endometrial/uterine cancer	- due to excess oestrogen with no progesterone e.g. obesity, PCOS, post menopause, tamoxifen medication (↓oestrogen effects on breast tissue but ↑oestrogen effect on uterus), also has a genetic component - is mainly an adenocarcinoma - 80% found in post menopausal women - staging ≡ ovarian

Vaginal cancer	-	usually squamous cell
Vulval intra-epithelial neoplasia	-	pre malignant condition of squamous cells
	-	HPV is the major cause
Breast cancer	-	because the breast is a gland which consists of columnar cells this is usually an adenocarcinoma
	-	risks: age, oestrogen exposure (early menarche, late menopause, HRT, etc.) , family history (2 close relatives), genetic = breast cancer (BRCA) 1 & 2 genes
	-	screening: UK women are offered a mammogram every 3yrs from 50yrs of age
	-	triple diagnosis (performed urgently if breast cancer is a differential diagnosis): clinical examination, biopsy (fine needle or excisional) & imaging (mammogram or CT)
	-	staging: see 'general cancer staging' above
	-	treatment: tamoxifen ($\downarrow$oestrogen effects on breast tissue but $\uparrow$oestrogen effect on uterus = $\uparrow$risk of uterine Ca) + surgery (ranges from lumpectomy to radical mastectomy = breast + surrounding lymph removed) +/- radio/chemotherapy
	-	N.B. carriers of the BRCA gene have approximately 70% chance of developing breast cancer, in some cases prophylactic mastectomies are offered
Candidiasis albicans (thrush)	-	fungal infection
	-	symptoms: very itchy, sore, 'cottage cheese' discharge
	-	vaginal pH < 4.5
	-	can be detected under microscope & cultured using sabouraud's medium
	-	treat with: antifungal pessary + antifungal cream (e.g. canesten) or oral fluconazole if more severe
	-	if > 4 episodes in a year investigate for diabetes, immunodeficiency, and regular antibiotic/steroid use
Chlamydia trachomatis	-	symptoms: can be asymptomatic to start $\Rightarrow$purulent discharge, lower abdominal pain & postcoital/intermenstrual bleeding
	-	vaginal pH > 4.5
	-	can $\Rightarrow$pelvic inflammatory disease $\Rightarrow$infertility
	-	can be detected using: DNA probe test (nucleic acid amplification) or enzyme immunoassy (ELISA)
	-	treatment: antibiotics (e.g. doxycyline)
	-	N.B. as with most vagina infections also consider contact tracing & screening for other STIs + education (lifestyle advice)
Bacterial vaginosis	-	overgrowth of anaerobic bacteria
	-	symptoms: thin white fishy discharge +/- pain & itching
	-	vaginal pH > 4.5
	-	clue cells seen on culture = +'ve whiff test
	-	treat with antibiotics (e.g. metronidazole)
	-	N.B. can $\Rightarrow$$\uparrow$risk of preterm labour & intra amniotic infections
Trichamonas vaginalis	-	due to a motile flagellate/protozoan (parasite that looks like sperm)
	-	symptoms: frothy green fishy discharge + haemorrhages (can $\Rightarrow$postcoital/intermenstrual bleeding)
	-	diagnosis: infection can be seen via a microscope on wet film & vaginal pH>4.5
	-	treat with antibiotics (e.g. metronidazole)

Neisseria gonorrhea	- due to gram −'ve diplococcus - symptoms: purulent urethral discharge or asymptomatic - can ⇒systemic features of infection (e.g. fever + N&V), cervicitis, urethritis & bartholin's gland inflammation - can be detected under microscope & cultured using thayer-martin agar - treat with antibiotics (e.g. ciprofloxacin)
Bartholin's cyst/abscess	- blockage of one of the pair of bartholin's glands that releases lubricating mucus - this can be treated with antibiotics, if this fails incision & drainage of pus may be necessary
Herpes simplex virus (HSV ⇒ cold sores)	- fluid filled vesicles which crust over & heal over a few weeks - HSV type 1 effects oral/lip - HSV type 2 effects genital area - tests: viral culture + serology - treat with acyclovir (antiviral)
Genital warts	- due to human papillomavirus (HPV) - symptoms are usually asymptomatic - diagnosis: inspection, colposcopy +/- biopsy - treatment = local destruction e.g. freezing or laser - N.B. HPV has strong links with cervical cancer
Swabs	- high vaginal (collects squamous cells): candida, bacterial vaginosis & trichamonas vaginalis - endocervix (collects columnar cells): chlamydia & gonorrhoea
Gynaecological surgery	- dilatation & curettage (D&C): the cervical os is dilated by passing stainless steel rods of increasing diameter then a curette is passed into the uterus which is used to scrape away the outer layers of endometrium, is used to evacuate the uterus of the products of conception or in the investigation of menorrhagia or post menopausal bleeding - hysterectomy: the removal of the uterus, this can be performed through the abdomen via a laparotomy (TAH), vaginally, or laparoscopically (smaller abdominal incision, uterus removed through vagina), the ovaries can also be removed (oophorectomy) - ablation of the endometrial lining of the uterus: most commonly done to manage dysfunctional uterine bleeding, it can be achieved by thermal ablation (a balloon passed into the uterus & heated with 80°C water), microwave ablation (microwave probe passed into the uterus) or hydroablation (free flowing water at a temp of 98°C passed into uterus, it can also be achieved using electrocoagulating loops & with a laser

Obstetric History

When it comes to your OSCE exams you will probably not be asked to perform an obstetric or gynaecology examination, it just would not be fair on the patient. Therefore, I have not gone over either of these examinations in as much detail as the rest in this book, but this should be all you need during your studies. What you could get is communication stations covering various obs & gynae topics: general pregnancy advice, counselling a patient who wants an abortion or who wants to be sterilized, talking to someone who wants to be put on the oral contraceptive pill but has a history high BP, or talking about the risks/benefits/results of an investigation e.g. amniocentesis. Just spend some time thinking logically about what clinical conditions can be replicated enough times that every medical student in the year can be examined on them.

Introduction	- approach politely and introduce yourself - patients name, DOB & occupation

Current pregnancy	- first day of last menstrual period (LMP) - length of menstrual cycle = days between first day of each period (28 days for most women but 21-42 days is normal) - age at onset of periods (menarche) - can calculate estimated delivery date (EDD) from LMP (use a gestational wheel or subtract 3 months from date of LMP then add 10 days) tell her this is an 'estimate' only, 40% of women will deliver within 5 days each way of their EDD - explain & reassure patient that symptoms such as N&V, urinary frequency, tiredness & breast tenderness are normal in early pregnancy, also it is normal not to feel fetal movements until 20 weeks - women may also find that they have a strong desire for certain foods
Past obstetric history	- gravida = pregnancy (primigravida = 1st pregnancy, multigravida = has been pregnant many times) - parity = patient has given birth to a baby (alive or dead) older than 24 weeks or weighing >500g, nulliparous = never given birth to viable baby - example: a pregnant woman who has had 2 viable babies & 1 miscarriage would be described as gravida 4, para 2 (this can be recorded shorthand as G4 P2^{+1}, the superscript +1 represents the miscarriage) - enquire about problems during previous pregnancies - did she have vaginal deliveries or a caesarean section - were the babies healthy (inc. weights) & at how many weeks were they born

PMH	- list PMH (inc. appendicitis & ectopic pregnancies) + DEAR J SMITH
Medications, allergies, smoking & alcohol	- if ex smoker ask smoking history - some medications can be teratogenic to a growing fetus
FH	- are parents/brothers/sisters alive, if so do they suffer from any diseases, if they have passed away, sympathise and then ask age & cause of death - in this case you also have to ask about the father's health + family history
Social/occupational history	- who is at home & how does this condition effect their life - expand on occupation

Obstetric Examination

Introduction	- always have a chaperone & document the identity of that person in the notes - wash hands, approach politely and introduce yourself - patient's name & DOB - explain to patient what you are going to do & obtain verbal consent - expose patient after asking
General examination	- general appearance: height, weight, BMI, pulse, BP, pallor (e.g. anaemia) - examine any areas that have obvious problems - N.B. to be complete you should: check the breasts for any lumps (if nipples are inverted can hamper breast feeding) & examine the heart for murmurs (flow murmurs are common in pregnancy & usually have no significance)
Abdominal examination	- inspection: stretch marks (striae gravidarum, white = old, red/purple = new), N.B. the linea alba is a white line running vertically down the middle of the abdomen if this becomes pigmented it is then called the linea nigra - palpate for organomegaly (the uterus cannot be felt until 12 weeks as it lies behind the pelvis until this point) - palpate for the fetus (fetal anatomy is not usually palpable before 24 weeks): head (hard & round), bottom (soft & round), spine (firm & uniform) & limbs (non uniform projections), try to determine the fetal lie - fetal lie (=relationship of long axis of fetus to long axis of uterus): longitudinal lie (fetus parallel to uterus), oblique (fetus at 45° to uterus), transverse (fetus lying at right angles to uterus), head down (cephalic presentation), bottom down (breech presentation) - near end of pregnancy the fetus will engage (descend into the pelvis), at this point if in cephalic presentation the head cannot be fully palpated or balloted - auscultate for fetal heart sounds: for a cephalic presentation listen at ~8cm above the pubic symphysis, for breech listen at the level of the umbilicus, the fetal heart will be much faster than the mothers (feel mother's pulse simultaneously if unsure), N.B. the fetal heart rate is often determined with a sonicaid (handheld ultrasound device) but in exams you may be asked to use a pinnard stethoscope (looks like a champagne flute/glass) ways to estimating gestational age: 1. palpate for the fundus (≡top) of the uterus, the fundus should first become palpable at 12 weeks, at 20 weeks it should be at the level of the umbilicus & at 36 weeks it is palpable at the level of the xiphisternum 2. find the fundus & measure vertically down to the top of the symphysis pubis, number of centimetres ≡ weeks of gestation
Pelvic examination	- lay patient on their back (supine), heels together + feet drawn up towards their bottom & knees allowed to relax to the sides - examine external genitalia for lesions & scars from previous pregnancies (tear or episiotomy = incision made to enlarge the vagina & assist childbirth) - lubricate a speculum & pass (described in 'Gynaecology Examination' section) - examine the cervix for pathology & note the shape of the cervical os (nulliparous women usually have a round os, parous women will have a slit shaped os maybe with a tear) - perform a digital examination & bimanually examine the uterus, remember to feel the shape & size of the bony pelvis (critical for delivery of the fetus)
When finished	- cover the patient up, advise them the examination is over and allow them to get dressed before explaining any findings

Pre-pregnancy care	- this involves the mental & physical preparation of both partners before conception, it consists of education & tests that should ⇒a healthier baby, a safer delivery & a happier couple - recommend folic acid supplements (400mcg daily) at the time of conception & up to 12 weeks gestation =helps to prevent neural tube defects - mother's baseline weight, BP, past pregnancy/medical history, etc. advice on the avoidance of: 　1. teratogens (alcohol, ACE inhibitors, methotrexate, tetracycline) 　2. certain foods: soft cheese (can ⇒listeria), liver (may have too much vitamin A), shellfish, only drink pasteurised milk & make sure any meat or eggs are cooked properly 　3. excessive heat, cat litter (can contain toxoplasmosis), feverish children & ionising radiation (X-rays/CT scans) - introduce the couple into antenatal care & parentcraft classes - *for more information on infertility & assisted reproduction see 'Gynaecology Revision' section*
Fertilization	- fertilization usually occurs in a fallopian tube within a few hours of ovulation resulting in a zygote with 46 chromosomes (XX female or XY male), implantation then takes place in the uterus - after 10 weeks the conceptus is no longer called the embryo, it is now the fetus
The fetus	- placenta: transfers nutrients & O_2 from mother to fetus & clears fetal waste, it does this using placental villi (⇒large surface area), it also synthesizes hormones & proteins - circulation: before birth all O_2 is supplied via the umbilical cord, a hole between the atria of the fetal heart (the foramen ovale) bypasses the lungs, after birth this closes & the vessels connecting the umbilical cord to the child's blood supply constrict/atrophy - respiratory: the lungs are bypassed until birth, a special substance called surfactant found in fetal lungs lowers the alveoli surface tension preventing them from collapsing & making them easier to expand during those first breaths, N.B. in premature babies there maybe ↓surfactant which can ⇒respiratory distress syndrome - fetal blood contains fetal haemoglobin (HbF) which has a higher affinity for O_2 than adult Hb therefore 'pulling' O_2 from mother's blood, after birth HbF gradually switches to the adult form
Intrauterine growth retardation (IUGR)	- this is fetal growth significantly less than normal implying pathology, is determined from the measurements taken via USS, causes include placental dysfunction, chromosomal abnormality, infection, congenital abnormality, vascular diseases (e.g. SLE) & pre-eclampsia - can narrow down cause due to IUGR pattern: a problem early on in pregnancy (e.g. infection) ⇒symmetrical growth retardation (small head & body), if later on in pregnancy (e.g. problems with placenta) ⇒asymmetrical growth (normal sized head + small body) - other causes include smoking, genetic syndromes, etc. - N.B. macrosomia (big baby syndrome) is due to poorly controlled/gestational diabetes

Amniotic fluid/liquor	- is a nourishing & protecting liquid, later in pregnancy liquor is made up mainly of fetal urine
	disorders in liquor volume
	1. increased (polyhydramnios): maternal DM ($\Rightarrow$fetal hyperglycemia $\Rightarrow\uparrow$fetal urine) or fetal anomalies that impair swallowing (the fetus normally swallows the amniotic fluid)
	2. decreased (oligohydramnios): usually due to fetal urinary tract abnormalities, e.g. renal disease, fetal polycystic kidneys or urinary outflow obstruction
	3. absent (anhydramnios): ruptured membranes, placental dysfunction or impaired fetal renal function
Other fetal disorders	- *for chromosomal, cardiovascular & central nervous system abnormalities see 'Syndromes' section of appendix & 'Paediatrics Revision' section*
Antenatal screening	- general health check up & healthy living advice
	- dating scan (12 weeks): fetal measurements (length + head/abdomen circumference) $\Rightarrow$calculate number of weeks gestation, see if carrying twins, some spinal & head abnormalities are visible, position of placenta, can also measure nuchal skin thickness for down's screening
	- anomaly scan (18-20 weeks): looks for abnormalities & rechecks fetal measurements, can also perform umbilical cord blood flow doppler studies & can look for fetal heart congenital abnormalities
	- quadruple test: blood sample from mother looking at certain markers: alpha-fetoprotein (AFP), βhCG, inhibin-A & oestiol, N.B. this will only calculate risk, for a definitive diagnosis amniocentesis &/or chorionic villus sampling are used

	AFP	βhCG	oestiol	inhibin-A
open neuro-tube defects (e.g. spina bifida)	$\uparrow\uparrow$	normal	normal	normal
down's syndrome	$\downarrow$	$\uparrow$	$\downarrow$	$\uparrow$
edward's syndrome	$\downarrow$	$\downarrow$	$\downarrow$	$\downarrow$

	- amniocentesis: ultrasound guided removal of amniotic fluid, done between 16-18 weeks, small chance of miscarriage (0.5-1%), sample sent for genetic analysis
	- chorionic villus sampling: ultrasound guided sampling of placental tissue at 9-12 weeks, risk of miscarriage 1-2%
	- umbilical blood sampling: ultrasound guided, miscarriage risk 1-5%
	- mothers should be thoroughly counselled before consenting to the above tests, they must have thought through what they would do (e.g. abortion) if the tests come back +'ve, if they would keep the baby then the risk of miscarriage outweighs the benefit of the test
	- N.B. screening is also performed for sickle cell disease, thallasemia, & cystic fibrosis
Pregnancy termination	medical:
	- if <7 weeks = mifepristone (progesterone receptor antagonist $\Rightarrow$detachment of embryo from uterine wall)
	- 16-24 weeks = intra-amniotic infusion of saline +/- prostaglandin, both followed by misoprostol (promotes uterine contractions)
	surgical:
	- up to 16 weeks = dilation & curettage (D&C, dilate cervix & suck/scrape products out)

Miscarriage	- spontaneous expulsion of conception products <24 weeks gestation, N.B. don't use the term 'abortion' as it can be upsetting to some women - 15-20% of confirmed pregnancies will miscarry in the first 12 weeks - if USS shows a fetal heartbeat after 7 weeks there is an 85% survival rate - early miscarriage <12 weeks, late miscarriage 12-24 weeks - causes: maternal pathology (diabetes, trauma, drugs, severe hypertension, septicaemia), congenital fetal abnormalities, faulty implantation - if in 1st trimester usually due to fetal chromosomal abnormalities or endocrine disorders with mother (e.g. diabetes), in 2nd trimester main causes = structural abnormalities (e.g. fibroids or cervix incompetence) - tests: bloods (inc. FBC & βhCG) + group & save (G&S), imaging (e.g. pelvic USS) types of miscarriage: 1. threatened: usually present with bleeding & no pain, cervix is closed, patient should be advised rest 2. inevitable: heavier bleeding & crampy lower abdominal pains, cervical os is open, miscarriage is usually inevitable, treatment is analgesia & in some cases removal of the products if they do no pass naturally 3. incomplete: some products of conception remain in the uterus $\Rightarrow$continued bleeding, crampy pains & passing of clots, can be treated conservatively by giving prostaglandins ($\Rightarrow$uterus contracts) or surgically 4. complete: all products of conception have passed & the uterus is left empty, bleeding should subside & the cervix will close 5. missed: the embryo dies during early development, it is then reabsorbed leaving an empty gestational sac, these women will initially have a +'ve pregnancy test but βhCG levels will then drop, cervical os will be closed, can be managed conservatively (watch & wait) or surgically 6. recurrent: 3 consecutive miscarriages, needs to be investigated
Ectopic pregnancy	- implantation of egg anywhere but endometrial lining - $\uparrow$risk if egg does not have clear smooth path to uterus, usually due to scarring & adhesions from infection/inflammation (e.g. pelvic inflammatory disease) or surgery - tubal ectopic pregnancies account for around 0.5% of UK pregnancies - symptoms: abdominal pain, irregular/absent vaginal bleeding, shoulder pain (due to irritation of diaphragm), can $\Rightarrow$rupture (surgical emergency) $\Rightarrow$haemorrhage $\Rightarrow$shock ($\uparrow$HR & $\downarrow$BP) - tests: pregnancy test (βhCG is released by implanted egg, a –'ve test excludes ectopic), ultrasound & laparoscopy (key-hole surgery to diagnoses & treat) - treatment: methotrexate (inhibits the metabolism of folic acid, can also be used to induce abortion), if haemodynamically unstable treat with resus ABCs + surgery (for a fallopian tube ectopic a salpingectomy is usually performed = complete or partial removal of damaged section of tube)
Pre eclampsia	- is a triad of symptoms during pregnancy: $\uparrow$BP, proteinurea +/- oedema ($\downarrow$protein $\Rightarrow$blood less concentrated $\Rightarrow$fluid/water diffuses from circulation to surrounding tissues) - usually occurs after 20 weeks gestation - diagnosed by $\uparrow$BP (systolic BP >140mmHg or diastolic >90mmHg on 2 separate occasions) + $\uparrow$protein in urine - cause is poorly understood, but usually occurs in primigravida (first pregnancy) - other symptoms: visual disturbances, headaches, N&V, $\downarrow$urine output, &

	papilloedema, can $\Rightarrow$eclampsia - the only cure is to deliver the baby - can be controlled by giving anti-hypertensives *(see 'Cardiovascular Medication' section)*, also magnesium sulphate is given to help prevent fitting (i.e. to prevent disease progressing to eclampsia)
Eclampsia & HELLP syndrome	- epileptic fits associated with $\uparrow$BP in pregnancy - prevalence in UK = 1:3000 pregnancies - treat with ABCs + turn patient onto their side, maintain the airway & if not settling give magnesium sulphate &/or diazepam - the only cure is to deliver the baby - HELLP syndrome (<u>H</u>aemolysis, <u>E</u>levated <u>L</u>iver function and <u>L</u>ow <u>P</u>latelets) can $\Rightarrow$disseminated intravascular coagulation (DIC, *see 'Haematology Revision' section*) & bleeding, blood transfusions & fresh frozen plasma (contains clotting factor) may be needed
Gestational diabetes	- those women in whom diabetes is discovered for the first time during pregnancy, N.B. women who are already diabetic remain diabetic during pregnancy - pregnancy $\Rightarrow$state of relative insulin resistance due to hormonal changes ($\uparrow$oestrogen, progesterone, etc.) + changes in insulin receptors in the mother's body - can $\Rightarrow$miscarriage, polyhydramnios ($\uparrow$amniotic fluid), big baby syndrome, premature delivery, congenital abnormalities, $\uparrow$BP + $\uparrow$risk of developing DM post pregnancy - *see 'Endocrine Revision' section* for tests & treatment (must be tightly controlled)
Rhesus (Rh) incompatibility	- mother mounts an immune response against antigens on fetal RBCs that enter her circulation, in this case the mother is Rh $-$'ve so when fetal Rh $+$'ve blood enters her bloodstream $\Rightarrow$immune response creating anti-D antibodies, N.B. fetal blood can enter the mothers circulation during delivery, miscarriage, placental abruption & trauma - the anti-D antibodies are created during the first pregnancy but do not usually effect that pregnancy, but in future pregnancies (if another Rh $+$'ve fetus) $\Rightarrow$the anti-D antibodies cross the placenta & bind to fetal RBCs causing haemolysis $\Rightarrow$haemolytic anaemia & can $\Rightarrow$death of the fetus (known as haemolytic disease of newborn) - treatment: anti-D immunoglobulin is given to all Rh $-$'ve women at 26 and 40 weeks gestation, this reacts with the fetal Rh $+$'ve RBCs before they stimulate mom to produce anti-D antibodies, babies born with haemolytic disease of newborn may need an exchange blood transfusion (to replace diseased blood)
Anaemia	- during pregnancy the blood volume increases by 40%, but RBC mass does not increase by as much $\Rightarrow\downarrow$Hb concentration, therefore more folic acid & iron is required, the body's iron stores & dietary intake are usually sufficient - iron deficiency anaemia affects around 10% of pregnant women - treat with oral iron supplements, only a small amount need blood transfusions
Infections during pregnancy	- rubella, cytomegalovirus, toxoplasmosis, syphilis & herpes zoster are all teratogenic (can $\Rightarrow$abnormal development & miscarriage of the fetus) - screening for these infections is important so that mother can be treated before pregnancy or measures can be taken to $\downarrow$transmission

Normal labour	- expulsion of the fetus & placenta from the uterus, divided into three stages: 1. dilatation: from the onset of labour until the cervix has reached full dilatation, further divided into the latent phase (can last up to 7 hours =cervix dilates to around 4cm) & active phase (more rapid, cervical dilation of around 1-2cm per hour) 2. expulsive: from full dilation of the cervix until expulsion of the fetus, at this stage the mother has the desire to push, once the fetus is delivered an injection of oxytocin ($\Rightarrow$uterine contraction) & ergometrine (causes smooth muscle tissue in the blood vessel walls of uterus to narrow $\Rightarrow\downarrow$bleeding) is usually given to aid in the delivery of the placenta & reduces risks of haemorrhage 3. placental: begins with the delivery of the child ending with expulsion of the placenta, gentle traction may be applied to the cord to aid expulsion of the placenta, rubbing of the uterus can initiate contraction & minimise bleeding - pain relief in labour: breathing entonox (50% nitrous oxide, 50% O_2), opioids (can be used but may $\Rightarrow$neonatal respiratory problems) or epidural anaesthesia - N.B. 3 mechanical factors determine the progress of labour, the degree of force expelling the fetus (Power), the dimensions of the pelvis (Passage)& the dimensions of the fetal head (Passenger), remember 3 Ps
Abnormal labour	- premature labour: onset of labour before 36 weeks gestation, dexamethosone (a steroid) is given in order to accelerate surfactant production in the fetal lungs (makes it easier for the baby to take its first breaths), N.B. 50% of babies born in the UK at 26 weeks survive, mainly due to high level care in neonatal ICU - prolonged labour: is more common in primigravida, induction of labour can be performed using prostaglandin gels or pessaries ($\Rightarrow\uparrow$cervical os opening + uterine contraction), amniotomy (surgical rupture of waters), oxytocin ($\Rightarrow$uterine contractions) or cervical sweeping with a finger
Breech presentation	- when the buttocks present in the lower part of the pelvis instead of the head - accounts for ~3% of pregnancies, there is an $\uparrow$risk of breech in preterm pregnancies (mainly because the fetus is smaller) - can $\Rightarrow$intracranial damage (due to rapid delivery of the head), hypoxic injuries (due to prolapsed cord or slow delivery of the head) & $\uparrow$mortality (2-3 times higher than for cephalic presentations, some due to fetus being pre-term) - external cephalic version (ECV): after 37 weeks can attempt to disengage the breech from the pelvis & rotate it in a summersault fashion
Operative & instrumental delivery	types 1. caesarean section: delivery of the fetus through the abdominal wall, accounts for 25% of deliveries in the UK, usually performed under a spinal anaesthetic, the common approach is via a transverse incision through the lower segment (is safer because is extraperitoneal, compared with old fashioned vertical incision) 2. ventouse (vacuum extractor) delivery: using a cup shaped device with a handle to which a vacuum is attached, this sucks onto the fetal head allowing traction to be applied 3. forceps delivery: involves placing the two curved blades of the forceps around the fetal head to apply traction

Cardiotocography (CTG)	- CTG records fetal heart rate simultaneously with uterine activity & fetal movements the mnemonic DR C BRAVADO is used to interpret it: - Define Risk: high or low - Contractions: frequency & length - Baseline RAte: fetal baseline HR should be between 110-160bpm, bradycardia suggests congenital heart disease, tachycardia suggests fetal distress - Variability: should be 5-15bpm from the baseline - Accelerations = rise in fetal HR of 15bpm above baseline lasting for at least 15 seconds (1-2 accelerations in 20mins are normal, no accelerations = no labour) - Decelerations: in the absence of a uterine contraction a deceleration in fetal HR is of serious significance, baby will need to be delivered quickly - Overall impression: is it reassuring, suspicious or pathological, then act on it!
Post partum haemorrhage	- blood loss > half a litre within 24 hours of delivery - causes: atonic uterus, retained placenta & trauma to the lower genital tract during delivery - management: resus ABCs + fluid/blood, give IV ergometrine (causes smooth muscle tissue in the blood vessel walls of uterus to narrow $\Rightarrow\downarrow$blood flow) & vigorously massage the uterus to cause contractions, may need emergency surgery
Multiple pregnancies	- twins = 1 in 100 pregnancies, triplets = 1 in 10,000 - identical twins (monozygotic) result from mitotic division of a single zygote into identical babies (1 sperm + 1 egg = 2 identical babies), N.B. late & incomplete division $\Rightarrow$conjoined twins - non identical twins (dizygotic) result from fertilisation of two different oocytes by different sperm (2 sperm + 2 eggs = 2 non identical babies) - fetal mortality & long term risk of disability is greatly increased in multiple pregnancies, also congenital abnormalities are 2-4 times more common - pre-eclampsia, anaemia, gestational diabetes & post partum haemorrhage are all more common in multiple pregnancies
The puerperium	- the 6 week period following delivery - in this period the woman's body returns back to the pre-pregnant state - lactation will begin & mothers should be encouraged to breastfeed as there are many benefits to mother & baby *(see 'Paediatric Revision' section)* complications may arise in this period: - secondary post partum haemorrhage (occurs after 24 hours) is due to endometriosis +/- retained placental tissue - thromboembolic disease (PE or DVT) is the leading cause of maternal death - postpartum pyrexia = $\uparrow$temp (over 38°C) in the first 14 days post partum, is usually due to infection - urinary retention, urinary tract infection & incontinence can all occur - pain occurs in 40% of women after birth & can continue for more than 8 weeks in some women - postnatal depression affects 10% of women

Paediatric History

Paediatrics sometimes can fell like a whole field of medicine on its own, but most of the time everything you have learnt from this book will also apply to patients under the age of 16. Try to approach paediatric medicine in the same way you do with adults, obtain a detailed history (in this case that maybe from the parents), after which you need to examine the child (you will need to learn new techniques for this which will come with practise), from your findings come up with differential diagnosis then order investigations to prove/disprove these, and finally discuss the management options with the patient/parents. To perform these tasks it is always worthwhile interacting with the child from the start to build a rapport and familiarity.

In keeping with the idea behind this book, in this chapter I will only be covering what is specific to paediatrics, everything else you need to know can be found in the other chapters, for example asthma can be found in the Respiratory section, tonsillitis in ENT, chickenpox in Dermatology etc.

When it comes to your OSCE exams be logical, the odds are that you will not end up having a young child to examine, what young kid do you know that will sit quiet & still whilst countless students examine them, but what you may get are 'communication stations' with a child's parent, as much of paediatrics is educating & counselling parents.

General advice	- approach politely and introduce yourself to parents & child (if old enough to understand) - obtain patient's name & DOB - if child old enough to ask them questions try to be at their eye level when you do so, in paediatrics it is essential to build a good rapport with both child & carer - as with all histories start with open ended questions and progress onto closed - always be observing the child & their behaviour
Areas to cover	- basically the same structure as with adults (*see other history sections*) but if dealing with younger children you need to ask a few extra questions 1. presenting complaint (PC) 2. history of presenting complaint (HPC) 3. past medical history (PMH) 4. antenatal & birth history: abnormal scans or tests during pregnancy, gestation (term or preterm), birth problems, admission to special care baby unit, etc. 5. developmental history: did the child reach the developmental milestones at the correct age (*see below*) 6. medications + immunization history & allergies 7. family history (FH): including genetic diseases running in family 8. social history: who lives at home & do they smoke, any pets - N.B. in an OCSE type situation end each history or examination with a brief summary of your findings

Paediatric Examination

Introduction + general advice	- wash hands - take into account child's age when approaching - approach politely and introduce yourself to parents & child (if old enough to understand, get down to their level to gain rapport) - obtain patient's name & DOB - explain what you are going to do and gain verbal consent - expose patient after asking, for older children consider using a chaperone - it is best to examine infants whilst still in their parents arms or babies lying on a bed with their parent nearby, always ask the parent for help when dealing with infants/babies - examining a child can be very difficult so the more you practise the better, sometimes you need to take opportunities while you can & try to leave distressing exams till the end (e.g. children hate the ENT examination)
the specific examinations for a child are virtually the same as for an adult, except you leave out some of the stages depending on the age of a child, I have therefore not included every section of the paediatric exam, please find individual examinations in there corresponding chapters	
Neurological exam in an infant	- of course infants cannot walk or talk so you have to observe them whilst handling them - any obvious general observations - palpate fontanel (soft spots in the skull which allow flexion during birth, they ossify after ~2 years): good for assessing dehydration (severe ⇒fontanel depression) & assessing ↑ICP (⇒bulging) assess tone & posture: - hypotonic: baby is floppy, sometimes will see them in the 'frog leg' position - hypertonic: baby resists passive limb moment, sometime will see them cross/scissor their legs - moro reflex: when babies head is allowed to drop backwards ⇒abduction then adduction of arms, last <4 months, absence (or presence after 5 months) indicates a disorder of the motor system - palmar grasp: rubbing baby's palm ⇒hand grasp, last <4 months - plantar reflex: stroking bottom of foot ⇒toes curl downwards, an upwards movement (babinski sign) suggest an upper motor neuron disorder - rooting reflex (to aid breast feeding): stroking cheek ⇒newborn infant will turn their head towards stimulus - suck reflex

Paediatric Revision

At birth	- full term = 37-42 weeks, premature <37 weeks - weight: average = 3kg, put on small baby pathway if <2kg - vernix = white substance found all over newborn - meconium = baby's faeces, if delivery is causing distress baby may pass more which it can then aspirate (breath in) ⇒respiratory problems - clamping the umbilical cord stops the baby receiving oxygen from the mother ⇒stimulates breathing - surfactant within the lungs ⇒↓surface tension ⇒lungs expand easier (N.B. preterm babies may have ↓surfactant ⇒respiratory distress) - vitamin K is usually given a birth = prevents haemorrhagic disease of the newborn (vitamin K deficiency ⇒↓production of clotting factors)
Apgar score	- score ≡ general health of baby at time of birth - normal = 7-10, anything less may need monitoring +/- resuscitation

	score	0	1	2
<u>A</u>ppearance	skin colour	white	blue extremities	pink
<u>P</u>ulse	heart rate	absent	<100	>100
<u>G</u>rimace	reflex to irritation	none	grimace	cough/sneeze/pulls away
<u>A</u>ctivity	muscle tone	limp	some flexion	active movement
<u>R</u>espiration	breathing	absent	irregular or weak	strong

Premature babies	small/preterm babies have ↑risk of: - hypothermia: due to ↓fat, ↑surface area to volume ratio & immature skin which does not hold in heat or fluid well - hypoglycaemia: due to ↓glycogen stores - cerebral palsy: due to immature cerebral blood vessels - ↓nutrient absorption: due to immature GI system - respiratory distress syndrome (RDS): due to ↓surfactant & ↑risk of infection, N.B. in RDS a CXR will show a ground glass picture due to alveolar collapse, also steroids are given to mother if baby is at risk of being preterm to ↑amount of surfactant in its lungs - retinopathy: due to immature vasculature of the retina - baby may need time in incubator (a warm, humidified, clean environment)
Breast feeding	- ↑milk production by breast alveoli is due to ↑prolactin levels at birth + stimulated by infant sucking - nipple stimulation ⇒oxytocin released from pituitary ⇒breast releases milk - is still considered the best form of nutrition for children for a number of reasons, e.g. good balance of fat/protein, mother transfers some of her immunity to child, good for mother-child bond, etc. - a child should be weaned from breast/bottled milk onto pureed foods at 6 months
Record keeping	types: - child health record (red book) is given to parents and is for them to keep up to date with health checks, immunizations, developmental observations, hospital visits etc. - special register = social services record of any child with chronic illness or

	- special needs - child protection register = record of any abused/neglected children, N.B. if you believe a child is at risk of, or has been abused, ask for senior help straight away and they will inform social services
Growth charts	- are used to assess growth development & to compare a child with the rest of the population, there are 3 measurements that need to be taken then plotted (y-axis = specific measurement, x-axis = age) - after plotting the measurements with a dot you can then see how the child compares with the rest of the population due to each area being split into centile lines, if the measurement lies on the 50th centile = median/average for population, if below = less than average 1. height/length (cm): is measured lying down until ~2 yrs old 2. weight (kg) 3. head circumference (cm): take average of 3 measurements - if weight or height is below the 2nd centile or falls down 2 centiles this needs to be investigated - failure to thrive = failure to grow or develop (intellectually & emotionally), this can be due to acute/chronic illness, genetic, social, or psychological problems - N.B. if the baby is born premature then you plot their gestational age, e.g. if born at 32 weeks gestation (8 weeks premature) and is now 18 weeks old their corrected age on the chart = 10 weeks, use this corrected age until the child reaches 2 years of age
Developmental milestones	- 6 weeks: smiles - 6-7 months: sits up + crawling - 9-10 months: can use pincer grip - 12 months: walks + can say a few words - 18 months: can build tower of several cubes - 24 months: can speak in small sentences - N.B. remember that these are only rough guides
Immunization schedule	types: - DTaP/IPV/Hib = IM injection containing diphtheria (D), tetanus (T), pertussis (aP), polio (IPV), H Influenza B (Hib) - pneumococcal (PCV) = IM injection against organisms that can cause pneumonia & meningitis - MenC = IM injection against organism that can cause meningitis - MMR = a live attenuated vaccine against measles, mumps & rubella, do not give to immunocompromised + be careful in children with egg allergy (vaccine is grown using chick embryos) - BCG = protects against tuberculosis, patient is usually left with a scar schedule (in UK): - 2 months DTaP/IPV/Hib + PCV - 3 months DTaP/IPV/Hib + MenC - 4 months DTaP/IPV/Hib + PCV + MenC - 12 months Hib + MenC - 13 months MMR + PCV - 3-5 years DTaP/IPV + MMR - 13-18 years DT/IPV + BCG

Congenital heart disease	- there are a number of problems that can arise during the heart's development, all will result in a pump that does not function properly ⇒↓oxygen carrying capability ⇒ a number of symptoms *(please review the cardiovascular chapters)* including failure to thrive in children
	- tests (virtually same as adults): ECG, CXR, echo, etc.
	- N.B. all will need prophylactic antibiotics for certain surgical procedures
	types:
	  1. ventricular septal defect (VSD): hole in septum between the ventricles ⇒shunting of blood from L (more powerful side) to R ⇒heart failure, in large defects cardiomegaly + enlarged pulmonary vessels (can be seen on CXR), & a harsh pansystolic murmur, may need surgery
	  2. atrial septal defect (ASD): hole between atria ⇒similar symptoms as in VSD but less severe
	  3. patent ductus arteriosus (PDA): before birth this duct shunts blood from the pulmonary artery to the aorta to bypass the lungs (O_2 comes from mother until birth), if it does not close at birth due to the change in pressure (aorta >pulmonary) blood starts shunting the other way from aorta to pulmonary system ⇒heart failure & pulmonary oedema + a continuous 'machinery' murmur & collapsing pulse, usually treated medically but may need surgery
	  4. coarctation/narrowing of aorta ⇒↓blood supply/oxygen to lower limbs & vital organs ⇒acidosis & impalpable/weak femoral pulses
	  5. tetralogy of fallot (comprises of 4 disorders): 1. VSD, 2. an overriding aorta (sits on top of the ventricular septum), 3. R ventricular outflow obstruction (≡pulmonary stenosis ⇒ejection systolic murmur) ⇒4. R ventricular hypertrophy (seen on ECG), CXR =boot shaped heart, needs surgery to correct
	  6. transposition of great arteries: aorta & pulmonary artery switched (aorta connected to R ventricle & pulmonary to L), only way oxygenated blood can get into the circulation is via PDA (or VSD/ASD if there is one), needs urgent surgery (initially the atrial septum can be cut open creating an artificial ASD, later the vessel need to be switched back)

Spina bifida	- in latin means 'split spine' - a neural tube defect = during growth in the uterus the neural tube does not develop correctly ⇒sections of spinal cord/brain do not close over ⇒varying degrees of disability (& death) depending on area effected - spina bifida occulta: mildest form, some of the vertebrae do not completely close, can be closed via surgery (this will not cure any neurological symptoms) - anencephaly: severe form of disease, cranial section of neural tube left open ⇒brain does not develop ⇒death - using folic acid (needed in DNA replication) supplements before & during pregnancy have reduced incidence of spina bifida
Cerebral palsy	- disorder of movement due to a non-progressive brain lesion - causes can be during pregnancy (infection, malformation), during delivery (hypoxic event, prematurity), postnatal (any illness/trauma that can ⇒brain damage) - symptoms & severity depend on the region effected, can result in learning & speech difficulties, epilepsy, visual problems, etc. - perform MRI &/or CT brain to image the lesion - multidisciplinary management + education

Haemolytic disease of newborn	- an immune response by mom against components in fetal blood that have crossed the placenta ⇒IgG antibodies created by mom which can pass back across the placenta reacting with fetal antigens ⇒haemolysis (RBC destruction) in fetus, can ⇒anaemia, jaundice & death types: 1. rhesus incompatibility: mom = Rh −'ve, baby = Rh +'ve, mom will have created an immunity due to a previous pregnancy where child was Rh +'ve (the first pregnancy is not effected but subsequent ones will be), N.B. Rh −'ve moms are now given anti-D which is an antibody that reacts with the fetal Rh +'ve RBCs before they stimulate mom have an immune response 2. ABO incompatibility = similar to rhesus but milder - tests: both of these will give a +'ve coombs test (looks for the IgG antibodies or the antigens attached to the fetal RBCs) - treat anaemia & jaundice, in severe case give exchange blood transfusion (can now be done before birth via the umbilical cord)
Jaundice *(also see 'Gastroenterology' section)*	- needs investigating if within 24hrs of birth or lasting >2weeks - as with adults the causes of jaundice can be split into pre-liver, within the liver & post-liver, the type of bilirubin found in the blood helps identify this (e.g. unconjugated =pre liver) - if severe can also ⇒infection & sepsis - treat cause + phototherapy (works by converting the insoluble unconjugated bilirubin to biliverdin which is water soluble & therefore can be excreted by kidneys), in more severe cases give blood transfusion, if due to ↑conjugated bilirubin refer to liver specialist - N.B. keep eye on clotting as long-term jaundice can ⇒↓vitamin K (⇒↓clotting factors) pre-liver (unconjugated bilirubin) - immune mediated haemolysis (↑breakdown of RBCs): mainly due to rhesus & ABO incompatibility, N.B. both of these will give a +'ve coombs test - non-immune mediated haemolysis: will give a −'ve coombs test, e.g. disorders of G6PD enzyme (X linked + Heinz bodies seen on blood film) & pyruvate kinase enzyme (autosomal recessive + prickle cells seen on blood film) - infection can ⇒haemolysis liver (unconjugated bilirubin) - physiological: immature liver enzymes ⇒↓ability to conjugate bilirubin, usually settles in a week - in some cases breast milk can inhibit liver enzymes, starts ~1 week after first feeding & can last for months liver (conjugated bilirubin) - hepatitis *(see 'GI Revision)*, will have abnormal LFTs post-liver (conjugated bilirubin) - usually due to a blockage/narrowing/immaturity of bile ducts (in some cases e.g. biliary atresia the bile ducts do not form), stools = white coloured
Pyloric stenosis	- due to hypertrophy of pyloric muscle (sphincter muscle separating stomach from duodenum) ⇒↓flow from stomach to intestine ⇒projectile vomiting during/after a feed - the vomit does not contain bile (bile enters the intestines at duodenum level), also due to loss of stomach acid the child can suffer with metabolic alkalosis - ↓food absorption ⇒↓weight & dehydration

	- during/after feeding a hard mass can sometimes be palpated in the epigastric region (=a full stomach), diagnosis is via USS - investigate as you would any N&V + abdomen pain: bloods, ABGs, abdomen imaging (X-ray, USS, etc.) - treat with fluids + surgery (split overgrown pyloric muscle)
Intussusception	- when one section of bowel folds into another - symptoms may include: N&V, abdominal pain, redcurrant jelly stools (=blood mixed in) - this usually happens at the point where the small bowel becomes large bowel (the caecum), therefore a child may have a palpable mass in the RIF - ultrasound scan shows: bowel within bowel (the doughnut sign) - treat by reducing either by giving a barium enema, by forcing air into the bowel via the rectum, or by surgery
Gastroenteritis *(see 'Gastroenterology Revision' section)*	- usually viral in children (rotavirus is the most common & very contagious), but can be bacterial also (e.g. e-coli) - excessive diarrhoea can ⇒loss of bicarbonate/alkali ⇒metabolic acidosis, excessive vomiting can ⇒loss of stomach acid ⇒metabolic alkalosis - main symptom is dehydration, therefore you must push oral fluids (in severe cases may need IV fluids) - N.B. in children a lot of illnesses ⇒D&V
Bronchiolitis	- usually due to respiratory syncitial virus (RSV), epidemics in winter - symptoms of general infection (fever, etc.), widespread wheeze + crackles on chests auscultation - treatment of symptoms with paracetamol/ibuprofen, small amount of cases need hospital admission for respiratory support - N.B. airways are narrower in children ⇒wheeze more common
Whooping cough	- due to bordetella pertussis (can be identified by nasal swab) - symptoms: general illness + busts of coughing in quick succession with fast inspiration in between, can ⇒capillary rupture especially in eyes (= petechiae) due to the ↑pressure when coughing - treatment depends on severity: paracetamol/ibuprofen & ↑fluids, O$_2$ if needed + antibiotics & can give steroids in severe cases
Croup	- due to para influenza virus ⇒ upper respiratory tract infection - general illness/fever + wheeze, stridor & a 'barking' cough - treatment depends on severity: usually just analgesia & ↑fluids + can give steroids &/or salbutamol, some need ventilation support

Cystic fibrosis	- genetic disorder of water & salt transport
	- caused by autosomal recessive gene (chromosome 7 genetic deletion), carrier rate 1:25, disease rate 1:2500
	- general symptoms: failure to thrive, malabsorption & recurrent chest infections (can ⇒bronchiectasis)
	- diagnosis: guthrie test (↑immune reactive trypsin), sweat test (↑Na & Cl) & genetic analysis
	specific symptoms + treatment:
	  1. lungs: thick secretions ⇒↓cillary clearance ⇒recurrent infection + restrictive disorder, treat with daily physio, bronchodilators & prophylactic antibiotics
	  2. pancreas: diabetes (due to ↓insulin production) + ↓enzyme production (lipase, amylase, protease) ⇒malabsorption & steatorrheoa (fatty stools), treat with oral pancreatic enzyme supplements & a diet high in calories & protein
	  3. gut: ↑risk of meconium ileus (meconium is the earliest stools of an infant, in this

	case they become thickened & congested ⇒obstruction in ileus), constipation, & intussusception 4. reproduction: men (infertile due to thick secretions from vas deferens), women (↓fertility) - general treatment: multidisciplinary approach & regular reviews
Genetic syndromes	- *see 'Syndromes' section in appendix*
Urinary tract infections *(see 'Renal Revision' section)*	- usually due to e coli - recurrent UTIs can ⇒renal scaring ⇒problems in later life (e.g. ↑BP & renal failure) - tests: culture & dip MSU + bloods (can be ↑WCC & CRP = infective & inflammatory markers) - after first UTI most children will have a kidneys USS, if recurrent UTIs need more detailed investigations (see below) + whilst awaiting these tests should get prophylactic antibiotics, the investigations look for problems within the kidneys or in the ureters, bladder & urethra - micturating cystourethrogram (MCUG): contrast (a radiopaque liquid =can be detected by X-rays) is injected into the bladder via a catheter, images then taken show any reflux into kidneys or bladder outflow obstruction - DMSA isotope scan: specific contrast is injected into the blood & taken up by the kidneys ⇒picture of kidney where areas of low intensity =scarring/damage
Febrile convulsions	- usually effect children <5yrs - viral or bacterial infection ⇒fever which can then ⇒convulsion - treat by educating parents as may happen again (recovery position + maintain airway) + identify cause of fever & cool child (both paracetamol & ibuprofen will reduced a temperature) - N.B. a small % may ⇒status epileptics (*see 'Neurology Revision' section*)
Developmental dysplasia of the hip	- the hip socket (acetabulum) does not cover enough of the head of the femur ⇒↑risk of dislocation (or subluxation =partially dislocated) 2 clinical exams can be performed: 1. ortolani test: if dislocated there will be difficulty abducting the hip & when doing so a click maybe felt = hip relocated 2. barlow test: with child lying on a bed, pushing the hip backwards into the bed will ⇒dislocation if disorder is present
Breath holding	- I remember this well, my brother used to do it when upset, usually whilst crying he would hold his breath until his lips turned blue, which seemed to last forever, but he always would resume breathing normally afterwards
Dermatology	- *children can be infected by a number of diseases that show signs in the skin, see the 'Dermatology Revision' section for more information*
Nappy rash	- due to ↑moisture & waste in region + irritation from modern nappies & chemicals types: - contact dermatitis = erythematous lesions with spared skin folds, can get secondary infections, treat with steroid cream + education (keep area clean & dry) - candida = red rash + surrounding satellite lesions (small macular red areas), skin folds are effected, treat with antifungal cream (e.g. nystatin) + education

Mental State Exam

Introduction	- approach politely and introduce yourself - obtain patient's name & DOB - explain interview & get verbal consent

Immediate recall	- give patient a name & address and ask them to repeat it back to you (maximum of 3 attempts, if cannot try objects) - explain that you will ask for this address again at the end of exam (assesses short term memory)
Orientation in time, person & place	- what is the: day, month, year - who am I - where are you now (building, city & country)
Concentration & attention	- serial 7s (100 – 7 – 7….), "please can you recite to me 100 – 7 & keep going, e.g. 100, 93, 86" - if cannot perform above try days of the week in reverse or spell WORLD backwards
Recent long term memory	- something in the news, something that happened recently, or prime minister of England
Remote long term memory	- distant memory (e.g. dates of start & end of world war 1 or 2), of course if patient is not old to remember these you enough need to ask something relevant
Short term memory	- recall address or objects from beginning of interview

Suicide Risk Assessment

This must be performed whenever a patient has attempted suicide to assess whether they will be at risk if allowed to leave the hospital. Also remember that whenever you are performing a mental health history, even if the patient has not attempted suicide yet, you should always ask if they have any thoughts of self harm (perform shortened version of assessment, i.e. focusing on past history, current intent & future plans)

Suicide risk assessment	- ask about time line of events (past, present & future): 1. past self harm 2. mental illness 3. drug/alcohol use 4. seriousness of attempt (advanced planning, severity of attempt, suicide note left, etc.) 5. regrets about the attempt 6. current intent 7. why patient will not do it again 8. support network (family & friends) 9. what has changed since attempt 10. future plans (holidays, something to look forward to, etc.) - a question the patient always asks at the end of the consultation in OSCE exams is "can I go home?", the answer is NO if you believe they are at risk + say "I need a second opinion from a senior colleague"
Overdose	- it is important to get a good history (find out exactly what was taken & the quantity as your treatment will depend on this) - look up the symptoms, investigations, treatment & monitoring of the specific overdose in the hospital policies &/or via online systems like 'toxbase' - monitoring: bloods (look for organ damage + some substances can be measured e.g. paracetamol), ABGs (look for acidosis & hypoxia), ECG (for arrhythmias) - general treatment: ABCs, fluids + if substance was taken recently use activated charcoal (mops up toxic substances within the stomach stopping them entering the blood stream) or gastric lavage (large tube into stomach to washout any tablets) can be performed to reduce further damage to body - paracetamol overdose: $\uparrow$intake $\Rightarrow \uparrow$paracetamol metabolites which deplete the substance within the liver (glutathione) that normally breaks down paracetamol, these free metabolites then start damaging liver cells, treat with N-acetylcysteine (replenishes glutathione helping body break down the paracetamol, should be used within 8 hours of ingestion), in severe cases can $\Rightarrow$liver failure then patient may need a liver transplant - aspirin overdose: broken down into salicylate in the blood (the level of this can be measured), nil specific treatment, patients need to be monitored & symptoms treated accordingly - if intentional attempt patient should be referred to the psychiatric team + you should assess patient's future suicide risk (*see above*)

Mental Health Revision

Mental health acts	section 5 (2) = holding order (lasts 72hrs): - must be performed by SHO or above - patient = inpatient under doctors care (i.e. not in A&E) - patient has a mental illness - patient held so can have assessment by psychiatric team, as you are concerned they maybe a risk to themselves or others section 2 = assessment order (lasts 28 days): - performed by psychiatrist or section 12 approved doctor + another approved health worker who knows the patient - can be done anywhere - patient has a mental illness - is a risk to themselves or others - has no insight - N.B. to administer treatment must progress to a section 3 order section 3 = treatment order (order lasts 6 months): - same as section 2, but also aloud to treat patient + section can be renewed common law: - can be performed by any doctor on patient anywhere (does not need to be an inpatient) - does not need to have a mental illness - is a risk to themselves or others N.B. no matter what the patient's condition cannot treat with hormones or do brain surgery without consent
Dementia	- this is a progressive decline in cognitive function beyond that of normal aging, all can be investigated via brain imaging (CT/MRI) - alzheimer's: most common cause of dementia, disorientation in time & place, short term memory loss (as disease progresses long term memory can be effected), usually a family history of the disease, common in down's syndrome, thought to be associated with amyloid plaques & tangles in the brain, can image brain to rule out more sinister causes, no cure available - lewy body: lesions/structures found throughout the brain $\Rightarrow$ parkinsonism symptoms (tremor, rigidity, bradykinesis, *see 'Neurology Revision' section*), drop attacks (spontaneous falls with quick complete recovery) & visual hallucinations - vascular (multi-infarct): neurological signs, stepwise deterioration (i.e. worsened by each infarct) & nocturnal confusion - huntington's: autosomal dominant inheritance, disease mechanism =degeneration of basal ganglia $\Rightarrow$ $\downarrow$GABA & ACh but normal dopamine levels, onset usually = 30-40yrs of age, symptoms = ataxia (lack of coordination), involuntary movements & $\downarrow$mental abilities - pick's: frontal lobe atrophy results in $\downarrow$intelligence & judgement, personality change, disinhibition, patient keeps repeating words & also cannot remember words (e.g. when shown a pen would not remember what it is called) - normal pressure hydrocephalus: slow acting chronic condition so body adapts slightly which means gradual $\uparrow$ICP but symptoms are not acute, i.e. ataxia, incontinence, nystagmus, headaches, & mental decline

Psychosis	symptoms: - delusion (unshakeable false belief not normal for patient's culture) - hallucinations (sensory perception with no external stimuli) - thought alienation = composed of insertion (thoughts being inserted into patient's mind), withdrawal (thoughts being removed), broadcast (ability to insert thoughts into other people's minds) & echo (patient hears his thoughts being repeated out loud) - passivity/made act (believes actions are controlled by an external force)
Schizophrenia	- abnormal perception of reality types: - paranoid: paranoid delusions, auditory hallucinations, rapid onset - hebephrenic: slow onset, personality change (childlike, laughing inappropriately), formal thought disorder (disorganized behaviour & speech) - acute/transient: stress induced, nor adrenaline receptors malfunction, clears up quickly with medication & cognitive behavioural therapy (CBT) - N.B. severe depression/mania can $\Rightarrow$ psychosis
Antipsychotic medication & side effects	- antipsychotic drugs are dopamine antagonists, they are used to treat psychosis which is linked to $\uparrow$dopamine production - there are 2 types of medication: the first created are known as 'typical' (e.g. haloperidol & chlorpromazine), more modern day antipsychotics are known as 'atypical' (e.g. olanzapine & clozapine), both $\Rightarrow$ numerous side effects but the atypicals have less side effects of all antipsychotics (mneumonic = LATPAN): 1. Lithium toxicity (of course only if lithium is being used): acts like a poison ($\Rightarrow$vomit/diarrhoea, $\uparrow$urination $\Rightarrow$kidney damage $\Rightarrow$$\downarrow$urination + neurological signs) 2. Akathesia: restless (can $\Rightarrow$$\uparrow$suicide risk) 3. Tardive dyskinesia: repetitive involuntary movements (e.g. chewing motion) $\Rightarrow$difficultly moving properly 4. Parkinsonian: rigidity & tremor (this side effect is not found with the new 'atypical' medication), N.B. parkinson's disease is due to $\downarrow$dopamine therefore antipsychotics can mimic its symptoms 5. Acute dystonic reaction: $\uparrow$muscle tone & muscle spasm can $\Rightarrow$jaw lock 6. Neuroleptic malignant syndrome: hyperthermia ($\uparrow\uparrow$sweating)
Alcohol	signs of alcoholism (seriousness increases as you go down the list) 1. stereotyped behaviour 2. narrowed repertoire (drinks certain type of alcohol) 3. primacy (puts drinking first) 4. tolerance 5. withdrawal 6. relief drinking 7. craving 8. abstinence 9. reinstatement - withdrawal symptoms (within 8-12hrs of abstaining) $\Rightarrow$delirium tremors (~48hrs post abstaining) $\Rightarrow$wernicke's encephalopathy ($\downarrow$thiamine due to malnutrition $\Rightarrow$brain damage, staggering gait, nystagmus, ataxia & disorientation) - if not treated can $\Rightarrow$korsakov's (permanent short term memory loss)

	- acute treatment: sedation (librium) & thiamine + vitamin B_{12} supplements - if encephalopathic (signs of brain damage, in this case due to metabolic irregularities) stop sedation + give lots of lactulose $\Rightarrow$expel toxins - N.B. short form of above history = CAGE questionnaire: have you thought about <u>C</u>utting down, do you get <u>A</u>nnoyed by people criticizing you, do you feel <u>G</u>uilty & do you need an <u>E</u>ye opener in the morning - medications: anti drinking drugs (e.g. antibuse & disufiram $\Rightarrow$side effects if alcohol is consumed), dependence drugs (e.g. acamprosate, help $\downarrow$addiction) & thiamine + vitamin B_{12} (due to malnourishment)
Depression	psychological: - $\downarrow$ concentration/self esteem/self confidence - feeling guilt & unworthiness - pessimistic future view - cognitive distortions - N.B. is important to assess self harm risk is all patients with depression biological: - low mood - $\downarrow$ energy/libido/appetite/weight/pleasure in normally pleasurable activities - early morning wakening - diurnal mood variation (change in mood depending on time of day) - self harm ideas - treatment for depression = counselling, medication, cognitive behavioural therapy (CBT) & ECT - usually patients get a mixture of depression types (psychological + biological) - N.B. reactive depression (e.g. following bereavement or relationship breakdown) is an acute form of depression that usually settles naturally as the patient comes to terms with their loss, in some cases this can $\Rightarrow$long term depression
Antidepressants	types: 1. selective serotonin reuptake inhibitors (SSRIs): $\uparrow$levels of the neurotransmitter serotonin by inhibiting its reuptake, usually the 1st line medication for depression (e.g. citalopram & fluoxetine) 2. tricyclic: blocks serotonin & norepinephrine transporters $\Rightarrow\uparrow$concentrations of these, used 1st line in patients who also complain of chronic pain (e.g. amitriptyline) 3. monoamine oxidase inhibitors (MAOIs): used as last line of defence due to them having a number of dietary & drug interactions (e.g. phenelzine) - a normal course of antidepressant medication lasts at least 6 months - remember that antidepressants only help with the physiological symptoms of depression, where possible patients should also be encouraged to undergo a course of cognitive behavioural therapy (CBT) which will help them deal with the negative emotions involved in depression

Mania	- this is usually seen in manic depression where patients flick between being severely depressed to having moments of mania
	symptoms:
	- elevated mood
	- grandiosity
	- impaired judgement
	- disinhibited behaviour
	- flight of ideas (when patient speaks they jump from one topic to the next)
	- ↓sleep
	- easily distractibility (poor concentration, check by doing serial 7s in mini mental exam)
	- pressure of speech
	- euphoria
	- ↑libido
	- irritability
	- medication: mood stabilizers (e.g. lithium) are good for bipolar disorders & mania
Anxiety	- tension headaches
	- ↓ concentration
	- sweating
	- ↑urination & diarrhoea
	- palpitations & panic attacks
	- tremor
	- insomnia
	- medication: benzodiazepines (e.g. diazepam) should only be give for a short period due to dependence

Appendix

Contents	Page

ABG Interpretation

Everyone finds ABGs difficult to understand but knowing certain principles makes them much easier

pH (norm = 7.35 – 7.45) ↓pH = acidic ↑pH = alkali	- this is the first thing to assess, if acidic or alkali you then need to identify whether it is due to a respiratory or metabolic cause - the pH can be normal if the body is compensating, e.g. in chronic COPD a respiratory acidosis (↑pCO_2) is compensated for by a metabolic alkalosis (↑bicarbonate) $\Rightarrow$ normal pH - because pH is calculated using a Log scale of H^+ concentration a small change in its valve = a massive change in the amount of H^+ in the blood, e.g. a 0.3 drop in pH $\equiv$ double the normal H^+ concentration in the body - remember in the blood $CO_2 \equiv$ +'ve ion = acidic, bicarbonate $\equiv$ –'ve ion = alkali
pO₂	- if this is low the patient is in respiratory failure
pCO₂	- if this is normal or low (& ↓pO_2) the patient is in type 1 respiratory failure - if this is high (& ↓pO_2) the patient is in type 2 respiratory failure - if this is low the patient is hyperventilating, this maybe a compensatory mechanism, e.g. diabetic ketoacidosis (DKA) $\Rightarrow$metabolic acidosis, the body compensates by ↑RR $\Rightarrow$blowing off body's CO_2 stores creating a respiratory alkalosis, neutralising the metabolic acidosis to some extent
Bicarb & base excess	- these are both –'ve ions - ↓ = metabolic acidosis (think of it as acidosis = ↑+'ve ions combine with the –'ve ions in the bloods $\Rightarrow$↓–'ve ions) - ↑ = metabolic alkalosis - these changes can be primary or due to a secondary compensation mechanism

ABGs are not just used for respiratory diseases, most severe disease processes (e.g. sepsis & DKA) will $\Rightarrow$ a metabolic acidosis, ABGs are used to monitor the progression of these diseases

	pCO₂	Bicarbonate
Metabolic acidosis (e.g. sepsis & DKA)	↓ (compensation)	↓
Metabolic alkalosis (e.g. vomiting)	↑ (compensation)	↑
Acute respiratory acidosis (e.g. pneumonia)	↑	small ↑ (compensation mechanism only has a short period to produce excess bicarbonate)
Chronic respiratory acidosis (e.g. COPD)	↑	larger ↑ (long time for compensation mechanism to adjust)
Acute respiratory alkalosis (e.g. hyperventilation)	↓	small ↓ (compensation)
Chronic respiratory alkalosis	↓	larger ↓ (compensation)

For respiratory causes see the 'Respiratory Revision' section & for metabolic cause see the 'Renal Revision' section

It is difficult to tell just from the ABG result which system (respiratory or metabolic) is the primary & which is compensation, therefore these results must always be combined with a clinical examination, history & any other tests performed

Advanced Trauma Life Support (ATLS)

ATLS is the universally accepted way of managing trauma and is used in almost all A&Es in the UK, this is a brief overview of ATLS theory and management

Initial assessment
1. preparation: pre-hospital and in-hospital phase
2. triage: sorting patients based on treatment priority & resources
3. primary Survey: ABCDEs
4. resuscitation: managing life & then limb threatening injuries
5. adjuncts to primary survey & resuscitation: pulse oximetry (SATS), bloods (inc. ABGs), ECG, catheter, NG tube, X-rays (chest, pelvis, c-spine, etc.), diagnostic studies (e.g. peritoneal lavage & portable USS of abdomen)
6. secondary survey: head-to-toe evaluation & history (if possible)
7. adjuncts to the secondary survey: other X-rays/scans/invasive tests & monitoring tools
8. continued monitoring & re-evaluation
9. definitive care

Primary survey
Airway management & cervical spine control
Breathing & ventilation
Circulation & haemorrhage control
Disability & neurologic status
Exposure
FG = don't forget glucose

N.B. although ABCDE is the order of priority in which to assess the patient, in a hospital setting, the trauma team is usually present so these can often be done simultaneously

	Assessment & management
A	airway: - foreign body in mouth/obstruction, abnormal breath sounds/hoarseness, obvious facial fractures - airway maintenance: either chin-lift/head tilt or jaw thrust (do if C-spine injury suspected as C-spine must be immobilised) - high flow oxygen should be given at all times (15L = mask with reservoir bag, don't forget to put your finger over the air inlet to fill the reservoir bag first) - use suction if vomit or aspirate present - is a definitive airway needed (number of adjuncts can be used including intubation = tube into trachea), if unable to intubate a surgical airway is needed (tracheostomy), a GCS < 8 always needs a definitive airway - N.B. ventilation should take place in-between intubation efforts with a bag & mask, also avoid using a nasotracheal airway if a base of skull fracture is suspected cervical spine: - initially stabilise with collar & blocks until cleared both clinically (may not be possible if unconscious/confused) & radiologically (X-rays/CT scan) - N.B. C-spine X-rays = AP & lateral views + make sure that C1-7 can be seen, inc. T1 junction

B	look, listen & feel the chest: 1. look: for bruising, cyanosis (fingers =peripheral, lips/tongue =central), respiratory rate (RR) 2. listen: to chest (↓breath sounds = lung collapse, pneumothorax or haemothorax) 3. palpate: for chest expansion (if not symmetrical = possible pneumothorax/collapsed lung), rib tenderness (fractures), surgical emphysema (air in the subcutaneous tissue suggesting a punctured lung communicating with it, feels like 'bubble wrap' under the skin) - get chest X-ray & perform ABGs some conditions: - tension pneumothorax: a 'one-way valve' between pleural space & lung or chest wall ⇒mediastinum displaced to opposite side, decreasing venous return & compression of opposite lung ⇒pain, respiratory distress, tachycardia, hypotension, tracheal deviation (away from pneumothorax), absent breath sounds & hyperresonant percussion on side of pneumothorax, requires immediate treatment = insertion of a large venflon/needle (into the 2nd intercostal space mid-clavicular line), when immediate treatment complete convert to a chest drain (into the 5th intercostal space mid-axillary line) - open pneumothorax: a 'sucking chest wound' defect (=one way valve) in the chest wall causing air to go in but not escape out, an occlusive dressing is needed over the defect (=dressing taped on only 3 sides to act as a one-way valve letting air out but not in) - flail chest: when a segment of the chest wall moves independently to the rest of the chest, usually due to multiple rib fractures, the independent segment usually moves in the opposite direction to the rest of the chest wall due to the pressures involved during inspiration & expiration, give analgesia, O_2 & ventilate if necessary
C	- heart rate & rhythm, blood pressure, capillary refill time (CRT <2secs =normal), skin colour (pallor = ↓perfusion to skin) - heart sounds (muffled suggests blood/excess air in the way, e.g. pericardial tamponade or pneumothorax) - assess level of shock *(see below)* - identify obvious external sources of bleeding, external haemorrhage should be managed by applying direct pressure (only use a tourniquet in cases of mangled limbs with exsanguinations) - catheterise = urine output - aim to get 2 large bored (grey or green coloured) IV cannulas (usually into anterior cubital fossa = at level of elbows) and start 2 litres of fluid running - take bloods (can be taken via cannula before it has been used): FBC, U&Es, clotting & cross match 2-4unit of blood (depending on scenario) - N.B. young people show signs of shock late due to their ability to compensate, but elderly patients have a reduced ability to increase their HR in response to blood loss (⇒↓BP) some conditions - massive haemothorax: rapid accumulation of blood into the chest, a chest drain is needed for decompression +/- blood transfusion - cardiac tamponade: penetrating or blunt injury causes pericardium to fill with blood affecting electrical activity & cardiac filling, diagnosed using beck's triad = 1. pulsus parodoxus (BP decrease >10mm Hg with inspiration), 2. muffled heart sounds & 3. ↑JVP, a portable USS or pericardiocentesis (needle aspiration of blood from the pericardium) aids diagnosis, cardiothoracic specialist input is needed for definitive management
D	- if GCS is deteriorating or <8 needs definitive airway - blood glucose (finger prick measurement), manage glucose levels as appropriate, e.g. sliding scale (=blood sugar level measured regularly & insulin/dextrose infusion altered depending on the result)

E	-	abdomen: look for bruising & lacerations, palpate to assess for guarding & rebound tenderness (suggests peritoneal irritation e.g. bowel perforation), percussion (tympanic/hyperresonant if obstructed =excess gas), auscultate (↓sounds = paralytic ileus, ↑=obstruction), N.B. common injuries with blunt trauma are spleen & liver lacerations
	-	pelvis: assess pelvic stability (if unstable will need a pelvic binder/sheet tied around the greater trochanters of hips, may need temporary external fixation inserted later on), common injuries are 'open book' (unstable pelvic ring) & 'vertical shear' (hemi-pelvis sheared vertically ⇒unstable in the vertical plane), N.B. the pelvis should only be stressed once as repeated manoeuvres can cause a large pelvic clot which is preventing more internal bleeding to be dislodge (⇒tamponade effect lost)
	-	limbs: always remove dressings to assess injury & neurovascular status, is there an open/compound fracture, splint the region (e.g. with plaster or traction) to provide pain relief & reduce blood loss, N.B. before any dressing/plaster is put over an open fracture take a picture of it so that the surgeons do not need to keep removing it
	-	investigations: X-ray all suspected fractures (AP & lateral + joint above & below), portable abdominal ultrasound scan or diagnostic peritoneal lavage (to look for intra-peritoneal haemorrhage)

Shock classification	Class 1	Class 2	Class 3	Class 4
blood loss (ml)	<750	750-1500	1500-2000	>2000
blood loss (%)	<15	15-30	30-40	>40
pulse rate	<100	>100	>120	>140
blood pressure	normal	normal	decreased	decreased
pulse pressure	normal/increased	decreased	decreased	decreased
respiratory rate	14-20	20-30	30-40	>35
urine output (ml/hr)	>30	20-30	5-15	negligible
mental state	anxious (slightly)	anxious (mildly)	anxious/confused	confused, lethargic, or LOC
fluid replacement	fluid	fluid	fluid & blood	fluid & blood

You do not need to remember the different shock classifications, I have included this table so you can see generally how the body reacts to blood loss

Glasgow coma scale (out of 15, worst score possible = 3)	eye opening: 1. none 2. to pain 3. to voice 4. spontaneous	motor response 1. none 2. extension to pain 3. flexion to pain 4. localising pain 5. moves to command 6. spontaneous	verbal response 1. none 2. unrecognisable sound 3. inappropriate words 4. confused conversation 5. normal speech

N.B. special circumstances such as trauma in pregnancy, paediatric trauma, injuries due to heat/cold & trauma in the elderly all have separate requirements when assessing & managing these patients

Antibiotics

These are the recommended antibiotics for some common infections at the time this book was published (if infection is severe give IV antibiotics to get control then can switch to oral)

Tonsillitis	- penicillin V (erythromycin if allergic) - do not give amoxicillin because if this is glandular fever instead of tonsillitis will ⇒a rash - N.B. think penicillin for most strep infections
Ear infections	- otitis externa can be treated with chloramphenicol drops if not overly severe - otitis media = oral amoxicillin (erythromycin if allergic)
Eye infections	- conjunctivitis = chloramphenicol eye drops/ointment/cream
Chest infections	- upper respiratory tract: amoxicillin (erythromycin if allergic) - lower respiratory tract (inc. community acquired pneumonia, COPD exacerbation & bronchitis): 1st line = amoxicillin (erythromycin if allergic), 2nd line = co-amoxiclav - to assess the severity of community acquired pneumonia & therefore the antibiotic needed (& whether it is given oral or IV) use CURB 65 score: Confusion, Urea >7mmols/L, Respiratory rate >30, BP <90 systolic, age >65 - hospital acquired pneumonia: depends on hospitals policy as maybe resistant to certain treatments, broad spectrum antibiotics are used & usually given IV
Skin infections	- usually due to staph infection, therefore use flucloxacillin - N.B. if skin/soft tissue trauma may consider augmentin (= combination of 2 antibiotics also known as co-amoxiclav)
GI infections	- h. pylori eradication = proton pump inhibitor (PPI) + 2 antibiotics (e.g. omeprazole + clarithromycin + metronidazole) - abdominal sepsis (give multiple antibiotics to cover different types of bacteria) = amoxicillin, ciprofloxacin & metronidazole - clostridium difficile = metronidazole - travellers diarrhoea = ciprofloxacin
Meningitis	- IV benzylpenicillin
Infective endocarditis	- IV benzylpenicillin + gentamycin
UTI	- usually due to e. coli, 1st line = nitrofurantoin, 2nd line = trimethroprim, if severe also give IV gentamycin
Fungal infections	- can usually treat with a topical fungicidal cream - if systemic & severe = IV fluconazole

N.B. these guidelines are always changing & maybe different between trusts, it is a good idea to check your hospital's antibiotic guidelines

Just remember to culture where possible before giving initial antibiotics then alter treatment according to result & if in doubt in your exams say you would contact the hospitals microbiologist for advice

Investigations	- bloods (inc. infection & inflammatory markers) - culture (MSU, blood, faeces, sputum, wound, etc.) - immunology (viral studies) - ABGs (assess for acidosis, can show the severity of the disease) - imaging (X ray, USS, CT, MRI etc. depending on severity)

Assessing an Ill Patient

These are the steps you must follow when assessing an ill patient, only the investigations relevant to the complaint need to be performed

A (airway)	- patency + ability to maintain
B (breathing)	- respiratory rate - SATS (% of O_2 in blood) - O_2 requirements - listen to chest investigations: - ABGs - imaging: CXR, etc.
C (cardiovascular)	- HR & rhythm - BP - capillary refill - heart sounds/murmurs - fluid input & urine output = fluid balance - if requires fluids/IV drugs get IV access, N.B. you can take blood via a venflon before it is used investigations: - ECG - Bloods
D (drugs & disability)	- AVPU = <u>A</u>lert, responds to <u>V</u>oice, responds to <u>P</u>ain, <u>U</u>nconscious (or GCS *see 'Neurology Revision' section*) - medication (is patient on any drugs that can $\Rightarrow\downarrow$consciousness) - pupils (size & reaction)
E (everything else)	- temp (if >38° do blood cultures) - head to toe examination/review (inc. drains, stomas, wound sites, etc.) investigations: - cultures (blood, sputum, urine, faeces, etc.) - imaging: abdo X-ray, etc.
FG	- don't <u>F</u>orget <u>G</u>LUCOSE

Basic Life Support (BLS) & Advanced Life Support (ALS)

I've included this & the ATLS chapter in the appendix to give you a feel for what happens in an acute situation. For your exams you will only be expected to perform BLS, but in the real world (on your first day of the job) you should know ALS, which is the next step up from BLS because you assess the patient and then actually do something about it. Below is the ALS arrest algorithm, you will probably do the course in your first year as a doctor, during which you will also be taught how to manage a patient with tachycardia (give amiodarone &/or adenosine) & bradycardia (give adrenaline &/or atropine), *see 'Cardiovascular Medications' section for more information on arrest medication.*

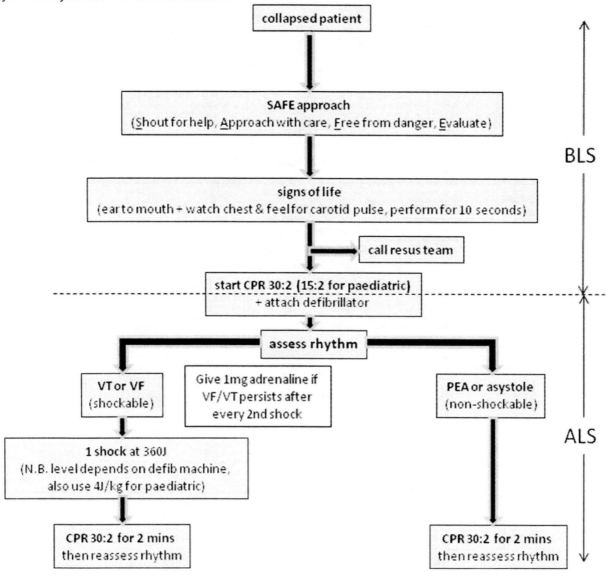

Whilst the arrest is running you should also be thinking about correcting 'reversible causes' (4Hs & 4Ts):
1. Hypoxia: give O_2
2. Hypovolaemia: get IV access & give fluids
3. Hypo/hyperkalaemia (metabolic): send of bloods + performing an ABG gives you a quick potassium measurement, a recent ECG may show peaked T waves = ↑K
4. Hypothermia: check temperature, if low cover patient with blankets + can give warmed IV fluids
1. Tension pneumothorax: listen to chest, check chest expansion, insertion of a large venflon/needle into the 2nd intercostal space mid-clavicular line
2. Tamponade cardiac: diagnosed using beck's triad = 1. pulsus parodoxus (BP decrease >10mm Hg with inspiration), 2. muffled heart sounds & 3. ↑JVP
3. Toxins: is there a witness who states patient has taken an overdose
4. Thrombosis: recent history that may point to ↑risk of coronary or respiratory blood clot & check patient's calves for DVT

Blood Test Interpretation & Urinalysis

Blood results can seem very complicated, to make things easier the trick I use is instead of trying to remember how each specific disease effects the blood think of the organs involved. Look at the blood results and work out which organ is malfunctioning then match this to the history and examination you have performed.

As I keep saying to you, keep things simple! In an exam situation when you are stressed, panicking and your mind goes blank, it is these basic principles from which you can build an answer that will pull you through.

Below are the main blood abnormalities arranged by the organ each result focuses on:

Kidneys (U&Es)

Sodium (Na) – there are a number of causes if this is abnormal, think fluid balance & endocrine disease

Potassium (K) – very important for optimal muscle function, especially in the heart, if abnormal can $\Rightarrow$ arrhythmias *(see 'ECG Interpretation' section)*

↑ Creatinine – a muscle metabolism waste product, increases due to ↓excretion in kidney failure/damage

↑Urea – a liver metabolism waste product, increases due to ↓excretion in kidney failure/damage

Liver (LFTs) – *see 'Gastroenterology Revision' section for more information*

↑AST & ALT – leak from damaged liver cells (hepatocytes)

↓albumin ($\Rightarrow$oedema) & ↑prothombin time ($\Rightarrow$↑bleeding) - ↓synthetic production by liver (e.g. chronic liver disease)

↑γGT – liver damage especially alcoholic

Pancreas

↑amylase – pancreatic cell damage

↑glucose – due to ↓insulin (e.g. diabetes or chronic pancreatic disease)

Gall Bladder

↑alkaline phosphatase – damage to the cells lining the gall bladder

↑bilirubin $\Rightarrow$jaundice (unconjugated =pre-liver disease e.g. haemolysis, conjugated =drainage obstruction e.g. gall stones)

Full blood count (FBC)

↓Haemoglobin (Hb) – anaemia (using MCV can pinpoint cause)

↓MCV – microcytic anaemia = iron deficiency (associated with ↓ferritin & ↑transferrin/TIBC)

↑MCV – macrocytic anaemia = folate/vitamin B_{12} deficiency $\Rightarrow$ impaired DNA synthesis

↔MCV – normocytic anaemia = chronic disease (if associated with ↑bilirubin = haemolysis)

↑WBC – infection, if ↑↑ = leukaemia or severe systemic infection (sepsis)

Thyroid (TFTs)

↑T_3 & T_4 – hyperthyroid (usually associated with ↓TSH)

↓T_3 & T_4 – hypothyroid (↑TSH = primary cause i.e. within thyroid gland, ↓TSH = secondary e.g. pituitary disease)

Cardiovascualr

↑Tropinin T – MI (test performed 12 hours post chest pain = when tropinin T would be at its highest)

Inflammation

↑CRP or ESR

Clotting

↑Platelets (PLT) – inflammatory response, smoking, cancer

↓ Platelets (PLT) – thrombocytopaenia, infection, bone marrow failure

↑INR – due to ↓clotting factors (e.g. haemophilia & liver disease) or warfarin medication (treatment range usually 2-3, prosthetic valve/recurrent blood clots 3-3.5)

↓factor 8 – haemophilia A

↓factor 9 – haemophilia B

Specific diseases

↑Copper (Cu) – wilson's disease

↑Iron (Fe) – haemochromatosis

↓Hb/WBC/PLT (pancytopenia) – bone marrow failure

↓cortisol – adrenal failure

↑cholesterol – atherosclerosis (LDL = bad, HDL = good)

↑calcium – hyperparathyroid or bone tumour/metastasis

↑Hb – polycythaemia = COPD or erythropoietin secreting tumour

Urinalysis	
	- appearance (cloudy suggests bacteria, brown suggests blood or ↑bilirubin =jaundice), unpleasant odour (infection), urine volume (indicator of core perfusion & increased in diabetes)
	- specific gravity ≡ concentration (tests renal function)
	- proteinuria (>2g/day) = glomerular disease
	- microalbuminuria = 30-300mg of albumin/day (early stage kidney disease, e.g. diabetes)
	- bence-jones proteins = myeloma
	- haematuria = infection, trauma, renal stones, tumours, etc.
	- nitrite & leucocytes suggest infection (gram –'ve bacteria convert nitrate→nitrite)
	- urine microscopy looks for RBC, WBC, epithelial cells (from renal tubule due to UTI &/or inflammation), bacteria
	- urinary casts (dead material): hyaline casts (essential hypertension, renal disease), granular casts (glomerulonephritis, ↑BP, diabetic nephropathy), red cell casts (prove that the haematuria is due to glomerular disease), white cell casts (infection/inflammation & occurs in pyelonephritis)
	- crystals: urate (gout), oxalate (renal stones), cystine (cystinuria)

Burns

As a student you are probably not required to know how to manage burns patients but I decided to include it because it covers some basic principles

Burn thickness	types:
	1. partial thickness ($\equiv$second degree): this type of burn effects the epidermis & dermis depending on its severity, it does not affect anything below this level, therefore the nerve supply to the skin is left intact $\Rightarrow$ a painful, red, blistered area
	2. full thickness ($\equiv$third degree): the burn penetrates the epidermal & dermal layers $\Rightarrow$nerve & vessel damage $\Rightarrow$ a painless, white/grey region
Rule of 9s	- to formulate a management plan it is important to assess what percentage of the body has been burnt, use the 'rule of 9s': - arm = 9% - leg = 18% (9% both above & below the knee) - chest = 18% - back = 18% - head = 9% - palms = 1% - genitals = 1% - a major burn is any burn that requires IV fluid resuscitation (=10% surface area in kids & 15% in adults) or a burn to the airways
Resuscitation	when performing ABCs the key points to remember are: - Airway: due to hot fumes the upper airway maybe damaged, look for singed nasal hair, consider early intubation (call for anaesthetic support) - Breathing: smoke inhalation can $\Rightarrow$carbon monoxide (CO) poisoning (CO has a higher affinity for Hb than oxygen $\Rightarrow$carboxyhemoglobin HbCO which interferes with normal O_2 transfer), give high flow oxygen (15L = mask with reservoir bag) - Circulation: burnt skin $\Rightarrow$fluid loss, insert 2 large cannulas (through the burnt skin if needed) formula to calculate fluid loss: 1. muir & barclay: over first 36 hours (divided into 4, 4, 4, 6, 6 & 12 hour intervals), fluid (ml) each interval = 0.5 × %burnt × weight (kg), give colloid (e.g. gelofusine) 2. parklands: over first 24 hours (half over the first 8 hours, the rest over the next 16 hours), fluid (ml) = 4 × %burnt × weight (kg), give crystalloid (e.g. hartmann's) - *for more information on fluid resuscitation see the 'Fluids' section of the appendix*
Burn Management	- most hospitals do not have burns units so patients need to be transported, in these cases dressings (e.g. cling film) are needed to reduce infection, heat loss & water loss - a full thickness burn $\Rightarrow$skin constriction $\Rightarrow$escharotomy surgery (incision through the skin to expose the fatty tissue below) for circumferential burns to improve circulation to distal extremities or to allow chest expansion/breathing if the chest wall is burnt

Clinical Skills

Please remember that although the steps I have outlined are correct to my knowledge, each university may ask you to perform things slightly differently, so always check this when revising for an exam. The one bit of crucial advice I will give you is to make sure you have everything you need at your side before you start to perform any of these practical skills. I have on a number of occasions started, for example taking blood, and forgot to bring cotton wool or a second syringe just in case I missed the vein the first time. If you just spend 10-20 seconds running through in your head all the steps before starting you will be fine. Also do not forget to wash your hands before the start of each procedure & once you've finished each procedure.

Measuring Blood Pressure

1. Wash your hands & collect together the required equipment
2. Introduce yourself to the patient & confirm their identity
3. Explain the procedure & obtain verbal consent from the patient
4. Ask if they have had a large meal, a hot bath, smoked, or exercised within the last 30 minutes
5. Put patient's arm on a pillow/table, make sure it is approximately at the same level as their heart
6. Apply the cuff to the upper arm, make sure the brachial artery arrow is in the correct position
7. Palpate either the radial or brachial pulse to establish an estimation of the systolic pressure by inflating the cuff until the pulse can no longer be palpated, position the diaphragm of the stethoscope onto the brachial artery & inflate the cuff for a further 10–30mmHg
8. Deflate the cuff slowly until clear tapping sounds are heard (=systolic value), these will increase in volume as the cuff is deflated & will then suddenly get quieter before they disappear (=diastolic value)
9. Record your findings + whether the patient was sitting or standing
10. Perform 3 times & take the average

Giving Oxygen

1. Wash your hands & collect together the required equipment
2. Introduce yourself to the patient & confirm their identity
3. Explain to the patient your intended actions and gain their consent
4. Place mask onto patient's face + secure the elastic behind the ears, or make sure the prongs of the nasal cannula sit comfortably in the nostrils (N.B. no more than 4L flow rate can be given via nasal cannula)
5. Ensure the connection tubing is properly attached to both the mask & oxygen flow meter
6. Educate patient about the risks of using oxygen (e.g. fire, therefore NO SMOKING)
7. Set the flow rate as prescribed (if uncontrolled method) or if using a venturi mask (=controlled method) it should tell you how many litres O_2 is needed to be flowing

Peak Flow Measurement

Equipment

- Peak flow meter
- Disposable mouthpieces with filter

Procedure

1. Wash your hands & collect together the required equipment
2. Introduce yourself to the patient & confirm their identity
3. Explain the procedure & obtain verbal consent from the patient
4. Insert a clean mouthpiece into the meter& ensure the pointer is set to zero
5. Hold the meter horizontally, with fingers clear of the scale
6. Sit in an upright position & take a deep breath in, seal lips around the mouth piece & blow as hard & fast as you can
7. Record the reading, return the pointer to zero & repeat twice more, use the highest of the three readings

Performing an ECG

1. Wash your hands & gather the equipment
2. Introduce yourself + identify the patient (name, DOB, etc.)
3. Explain & discuss the procedure with the patient + gain verbal consent before asking patient to take their top off
4. Cleaning the skin with alcohol wipes & allowing to dry will help the electrodes stick, N.B. it may be necessary to shave hairy patients
5. Apply the electrodes & connect to leads *(see 'ECG Interpretation' chapter for electrode positions)*
6. Check the machine is set to normal (= speed 25mm/sec, gain 10mm/mv)
7. Ask patient to stay still & take the ECG tracing (before you remove the electrodes quickly check the ECG to see that it is an adequate reading, if patient has been moving around or one of the electrodes is not properly attached it may be difficult to interpret the ECG, if this happens recheck all the leads and redo)
8. Remove the electrodes (place neatly on the machine) & give patient time to dress
9. Record on ECG: patient's name, hospital number/DOB, date & time recording was taken, the operator & department/ward it was recorded

Naso Gastric (NG) Tube Insertion

Equipment

- NG tube
- Spigot & collection bag
- 50ml syringe (to aspirate gastric fluid) & pH indicator paper
- Tape
- Glass of water
- Gloves & apron

Procedure

1. Collect together the required equipment & wash your hands

2. Introduce yourself to the patient & confirm their identity

3. Explain the procedure & obtain verbal consent from the patient

4. Arrange a signal so the patient can say if they want to stop the procedure, e.g. raising the arm

5. Sit patient upright

6. Put on gloves + apron

7. To estimate the length of the NG tube to be inserted measure from the xiphisternum around the ear to the nose

8. Ask about previous nasal trauma + check they are patent by asking patient to sniff with one nostril closed then the other

9. Dip the NG tube into a cup of water to lubricate

10. Insert the tube horizontally & advance to the marked point, at same time ask patient to take sips of water, when tube in place seal the end with the spigot

11. Secure the tube with surgical tape at the patient's nostril and on the cheek near the ear

12. To check the tube is in the stomach aspirate & test fluid with pH paper (5.5 or below = stomach acid) &/or by performing a chest X-ray (NG tubes have a radio opaque substance on them so they will show up on an X-ray)

13. Attach a collecting bag

14. If the patient shows any signs of respiratory distress remove the tube immediately

N.B. do not insert if patient has suffered traumatic facial injury (basal skull fractures can $\Rightarrow$NG tube into brain)

Intramuscular (IM) & Subcuticular (SC) Injections

Equipment

-   The drug (may need fluid to dilute)
-   Syringe & needle (blue for IM, orange for SC) + a drawing up needle
-   Gloves × 2
-   Alcohol wipe to clean the skin
-   Tray to put the equipment on (clean beforehand), don't forget a sharps bin

Procedure

1. Wash hands & collect together the required equipment

2. Check the name, dose, route & expiry date of the drug selected

3. Put gloves on, draw up the drug, remove the drawing up needle & dispose into a sharps container, put sheathed fresh needle on & expel any air from the syringe

4. Remove & dispose of your gloves

5. Introduce yourself to the patient

6. Check the patient's name, hospital number & DOB (can look at wrist band)

7. Explain procedure to patient & obtain their verbal consent

8. Wash your hands & put fresh gloves on

9. Identify the area in which you are going to inject (if patient has regular injections e.g. insulin, rotate the injection sites)

    -   IM = upper arm into the deltoid muscle, lateral aspect of the thigh, or upper outer quadrant of buttock (N.B. the sciatic nerve & the gluteal artery lie on the medial part of the buttock)

155

- SC = usually abdomen (as lots of fat there), upper arms or thighs

10. Clean skin with alcohol wipe (start at the centre and use increasing circles) + allow to dry

11. For IM: using your thumb & index finger stretch the skin around the injection site, hold the needle/syringe perpendicular (at 90°) to the surface then quickly but gently insert into the skin (remember to leave a third of the needle visible, in case the needle breaks)

12. For SC: using your thumb & index finger pinch the skin around the injection site, hold the needle/syringe at 45° to the skin surface then quickly but gently insert into the skin (remember to leave a third of the needle visible, in case the needle breaks)

13. Pull back the plunger (if blood is seen, remove the needle/syringe & apply pressure to the site until bleeding has stopped & start again with a fresh set of equipment), if no blood is seen inject the drug slowly

14. Dispose of the sharps into the sharps bin & sign the drug chart

Venepuncture

Equipment

- Blood request forms
- Tray (clean beforehand) + sharps bin
- Tourniquet
- Alcohol wipe
- Blood bottles + needle
- Cotton wool + tape
- Gloves + apron

Procedure

1. Wash hands & collect appropriate equipment

2. Introduce yourself & check patient's identity (name, hospital number & DOB)

3. Explain procedure & obtain verbal consent

4. Stabilise the arm on a pillow or table

5. Wash your hands & put on gloves + apron

6. Apply tourniquet approx 5-10cms above antecubital fossa (anterior area of elbow), use your finger under the tourniquet to avoid over tightening

7. Inspect/palpate the site + clean with an alcohol wipe (using increasing circles) + allow to dry

8. Remove the needle sheath

9. Anchor the skin by applying traction a few centimetres below the site

10. Warn the patient ("sharp scratch") then insert the needle with the bevel pointing upwards (bevel =opening at end of needle which is cut at an angle) at an angle of approx 30-45° following the vein

11. When attaching & removing the blood collection tubes to the needle make sure you do not push the needle further into the vein or pull it out

12. When all blood has been collected release the tourniquet

13. Place cotton wool over the puncture site, remove the needle then apply pressure, ask the patient to maintain the pressure

14. Discard the needle into the sharps

15. Label samples before leaving the patient and place into appropriate laboratory bags

16. Inspect the site then put tape over the cotton wool

17. Remove gloves + apron & put into clinical waste bin & wash your hands

Cannulation

Equipment

- Gloves + apron
- Tray (clean beforehand) + sharps bin
- Cannula (should have a bung on the end of the needle which you can screw off then attach to end of cannula once it is inserted, these bungs can also come separately, find out which type you will be using)
- Alcohol wipe
- Tourniquet
- Sterile cannula dressing
- Syringe, drawing up needle & flush (usually saline)

Procedure

1. Wash your hands & gather equipment together

2. Introduce yourself & check patient's identity (name, hospital number & DOB)

3. Explain procedure & obtain verbal consent

4. Stabilise the arm on a pillow or table

5. Wash your hands again & put on gloves + apron

6. Apply the tourniquet about 5-10 cm above the intended site, use your finger under the tourniquet to avoid over tightening

7. Inspect/palpate the site then clean with an alcohol wipe

8. Assemble equipment

9. Anchor the skin/vein using your thumb below the site & insert the needle through the skin at 20-30°

10. Once in the vein (there should be a 'flashback' of blood into the cannula chamber) flatten the angle of insertion

11. Insert the rest of the cannula whilst slowly withdrawing the needle (keep the end of the needle in at this point to stop blood pumping out)

12. Relax the tourniquet & apply pressure over the vein at the end of the cannula tip, take the bung from the end of the needle then remove the needle & discard into a sharps bin + attach the bung to the end of cannula

13. Secure the cannula with a sterile dressing

15. Before drawing up the flush into a syringe check its name & expiry date, once done discard the drawing up needle into a sharps bin & flush cannula slowly (via the one way port on top of the cannula), if patient complains of pain, you find it hard to flush, or you notice a raised area at end of cannula it may not be within the vein, if this is the case remove & apply pressure + cotton wool to area & start again somewhere else

16. Document in the notes the date, time & area of insertion

17. Wash your hands

Arterial Bloods Gas (ABG) Sampling

Equipment

- Gloves + apron
- Tray (clean beforehand) + sharps bin
- Alcohol wipe
- An arterial blood sampling kit (=syringe that contains heparin, needle, bung & filter cap)
- Cotton wool to place over the puncture site + tape to secure dressing

Procedure

1. Introduce yourself, identify the patient & explain the procedure with the patient + gain verbal consent
2. Wash your hands and put on gloves & apron
3. Perform allen's test (to assess blood supply to hand):
   - ask the patient to make a fist & find their radial & ulnar arteries/pulses
   - whilst pressing on the arteries ask the patient to relax their hand & observe its blanched appearance
   - remove pressure from the ulnar artery while maintaining pressure on the opposite side of the wrist, make sure patient's hand flushes with colour (if it does the ulnar artery is patent, if not there maybe damage to the artery in this case switch to the other wrist & start again)
   - perform test again but this time remove pressure from radial artery (as with the ulnar artery if there are any signs of damage switch to other wrist)
4. Stabilise the arm on a pillow or table
5. Find the artery & clean the site with an alcohol wipe
6. Expel the excess heparin from the ABG syringe (these syringes contain heparin to prevent the collected arterial blood from clotting, any excess needs to be expelled before the syringe is used)
7. Palpate the artery again but keep your fingers above & below the site you intend to insert the needle
8. Hold the syringe like a pencil, keep the needle's bevel pointing upwards (same as venepuncture) & insert at 45°
9. Finding an artery is sometimes tricky, if you don't get it first time withdraw the needle but keep a small section of it still below the skin, realign then advance again, you can repeat this several times each time making sure you do not remove the entire needle from the skin
10. Once in the artery the syringe should fill itself due to the pulse pressure of the vessel, N.B. some ABG syringes do not glide as easy as others so you may need to pull the plunger slightly to help it extract the arterial blood
11. Remove the needle & apply pressure to the site for 5 minutes using cotton wool (you can ask the patient to apply the pressure)
12. Inserting the needle into the rubber bung (is a safety measure to stop you getting a needle stick injury), then remove the needle using the attachment on the sharps bin (disposing of the needle at the same time) & attach the filter cap
13. Gently push the plunger (hold the filter cap whilst on you do this, I've had blood spray everywhere in the past) = expels any excess air
14. Roll the syringe for 10 seconds in the palm of your hand to ensure the heparin is mixed
15. Label specimen & transport to the lab immediately (if >10 minutes put on ice)

Urinary Catheterization

Equipment

- Gloves + apron
- Sterile dressing pack + sterile gloves (usually in dressing pack)
- Appropriate sized urinary catheter
- Sterile anaesthetic lubricating jelly
- 10mls sterile water & syringe to inflate the catheter's balloon (this is sometimes found in catheter packaging)
- Saline to clean area + alcohol wipe to clean the saline packet
- Urine drainage bag & stand

Preparation

1. Clean & dry trolley
2. Collect together the required equipment, checking all is within date & place on the bottom of the trolley
3. Introduce yourself, check the patient's name, hospital number & DOB
4. Explain the procedure to the patient & gain verbal consent
5. Put apron on & wash hands
6. Open the sterile dressing pack onto trolley, to form a sterile field unfold the dressing pack by only touching the edges of the square sheet
7. Using an aseptic technique open all the packs onto the centre of sterile field (=you only touch the outer rapping not the contents, this can be tricky & my need some practise), swab the tear area of the saline sachet with an alcohol wipe open & pour into the small plastic cup found in dressing pack, N.B. sometimes the items in the dressing pack cover each other, to keep area sterile you can use the sterile sheet as a barrier by putting your hand under it & moving the items by grabbing them through the sheet
8. Wash hands & put sterile gloves on (this must also be performed using an aseptic technique which needs practise, especially because in your exams your hands will probably be sweating which makes this task stressful, just take your time & make sure they are on correctly)
9. You can now touch & assemble the sterile equipment

Insertion

N.B. you will be using one hand for picking up from the sterile field (=clean) & one hand for touching genitalia (=dirty)

1. Ask patient or assistant to pull down their pants (I know you are always told to have a chaperone but sometimes in the real word you are often left on your own & the patient is unable to remove their pants, so you will need to do this before you perform task 8 above, just put on some non-sterile gloves and prepare the patient so they are ready to have the procedure performed)
2. Put the towel (contained within the dressing pack) onto the patient without your hands directly touching them, this will create a sterile field on the patient, N.B. if at any time your 'clean' hand becomes unsterile just remove the gloves and open a clean set (it is always good to have a spare set on your trolley)
3. Clean around the urethral orifice with saline using single downward strokes
   - for men your dirty hand should be used to retract & maintain the foreskin + support the penis
   - for women your dirty hand should be used to separate the labia

4. Holding the penis vertically (& slightly stretching it to straighten the urethra) insert the nozzle of the anaesthetic lubricating gel into the urethral opening, leave tip of syringe in urethra for a few seconds (to stop the gel fluxing), then if you wish you can milk the lubricating gel down the urethra by rubbing side of syringe along underneath of penis

5. Leave the gel for a few seconds so the local anaesthetic can take effect then insert the catheter

Now this is the difficult part, you basically need to get the catheter into the penis using an aseptic technique, which is easy on a dummy but in reality can be very tricky. In your exams they want you to insert the catheter bit by bit whilst keeping the rest of it sterile in the long bag it comes in. Some hints I can give you are: once your 'dirty' hand has hold of the penis in step 4 do not let go, this will stop lubricating gel getting under your grip because once it does your hand will not be able to control the penis properly, secondly each time you thread a small section of the catheter into the penis gently squeeze the urethra against the catheter with your 'dirty' hand to stop it coming out whilst you reposition your 'clean' hand. There are lots of small steps here that I cannot explain as everyone performs things slightly different, just keep practising until you have a clear mental picture in your head & stick to it.

6. In men resistance maybe experienced due to the prostate, positioning the penis horizontally under slight traction helps

7. Once fully inserted (urine may appear out of the end of the catheter), inflate the balloon with the sterile water (usually 10mls, in a 3 way catheter = used for irrigation of the bladder in patients with severe haematuria this maybe 30mls)

8. Slowly pull the catheter out until the balloon causes resistance & connect the catheter bag

9. Return foreskin to normal position (important step!)

10. Dispose of all waste in a clinical bin

11. Document in notes: stick catheter label (is found on outer rapping of catheter & contains various information), date & time + reason for insertion, amount of water in balloon, amount of residual urine collected, aseptic technique used & any problems encountered

N.B. catheters are measured in charrieres (ch) = circumference of the catheter in millimetres, choose the smallest size of catheter necessary to maintain drainage, e.g. 12ch for clear urine or larger sizes for urine with debris/clots, if large clots use a '3 way' catheter which has an extra channel to allow for bladder irrigation

Urinalysis

Equipment

- Gloves
- A clean pot for the urine, labelled with patient's details
- Reagent sticks (store in a dark place, only remove from jar when ready to use + put lid back on straight away)
- A watch with a second hand

Procedure

1. Introduce yourself & identify the patient

2. Explain the procedure with the patient & gain verbal consent

3. Wash your hands & put gloves on

4. Obtain urine specimen from patient

5. Dip the reagent strip into the urine, then remove & tap against the side of the container

6. Wait the required time interval before reading the strip against the colour chart (=found on the outside of the reagent stick jar along with all the information you need to analyse the urine sample, so spend some time reading this)

7. Wash hands & record findings

Fluids

This is the thing you will be bleeped most about during your junior doctor years

Fluid types	1. crystalloid: contain substances that are isotonic (in balance with those in the blood), when these are given not all the water stays in the blood vessels, most of it will diffuse into the intracellular (inside cells) & extracellular (between cells) compartments types of crystalloid: - normal saline (0.9%): water + salt (sodium chloride) - 5% dextrose: water + sugar - hartmanns: contains water + sodium chloride, potassium, lactate & calcium 2. colloid (e.g. gelofusine): contain water + proteins, these proteins are large molecules so they hold more of the water within the vessels than crystalloids, use if you need to raise a patient's BP quickly
Prescription	- a normal healthy person requires ~2,500mls maintenance fluid per day, the best way to supply this if the patient cannot drink is by: 2 litres 5% dextrose + 1 litre 0.9% saline every 30 hrs (run each bag 10 hourly) + add 20mmol potassium into each bag - patients who have an infection/fever, have lost blood (via surgery or trauma), have high output stomas, are vomiting, etc. need more fluid on top of their maintenance fluids to compensate, perform a clinical exam (BP, HR, urine output, amount vomited, etc.) to assess dehydration & alter their fluid regime to compensate - heart failure: be careful when giving fluids to patients with heart failure, their heart cannot pump the excess fluid efficiently, can $\Rightarrow$pulmonary oedema (*see 'Cardiovascular Revision' section*), perform regular cardiovascular & respiratory examinations - liver disease: although blood results may show $\downarrow$Na it is usually due to dilution by retained excess water (patient will have oedema), i.e. these patients generally have increased total body Na, therefore do not give IV saline to resuscitate - remember to assess the patient & take bloods regularly then alter their fluid prescriptions if needed
Children	- maintenance fluids (ml/day) = (100ml/kg/day for first 10kg body weight) + (50ml/kg/day for 10-20kg body weight) + (20ml/kg/day for >20kg body weight) - fluid deficit (ml) = weight (kg) $\times$ %dehydration $\times$ 10 dehydration assessment: 1. mild (<5%) = dry mucous membranes 2. moderate (5-10%) = as mild + slight $\uparrow$HR, $\uparrow$CRT, sunken fontanelle, $\downarrow$urine output & lethargic 3. severe (>10% shock) = as moderate + $\downarrow$BP, very sunken fontanelle, virtually nil urine output, irritable or in coma

GALS Screening

This examination is used as a screening tool for the musculoskeletal system, if an abnormality is detected a more focused exam should be performed *(see 'Musculoskeletal Examination' section)*

GALS grading: each section (<u>G</u> = gait, <u>A</u> = arms, <u>L</u> = legs, <u>S</u> = spine) is graded (normal or abnormal) under 2 categories (appearance & movement)

Introduction	- approach politely and introduce yourself - patients name & DOB - expose patient after asking - explain to patient what you are going to do
Inspect standing patient	- spinal curvature, muscle bulk & symmetry, carrying angle of arms, hip or knee flexion/extension deformity
Observe walking gait	features to look for: 1. spasticity = stiff & jerky movement on a narrow base 2. parkinson's disease = shuffling gait 3. cerebellar ataxia = broad base, unstable & tremors 4. sensory ataxia = broad base & high stepping 5. foot drop = high stepping gait 6. hemiplegia = plantar flexed foot with leg swung in arc
Put 2 fingers on adjacent lumbar spinal processes and ask patient to touch toes	- fingers should move apart, if not it may signify a lower back disease e.g. osteoporosis or ankylosing spondylitis
Palpate down spinal column for boney tenderness	
Place ear on each shoulder then chin on chest + extend neck	- tests neck range of movement
Hands behind head, elbows back	- tests external rotation & abduction of shoulder joint
Thumb as high up back as possible	- tests internal rotation of shoulder joint
Arms out, elbows locked	- tests for synovitis, osteoarthritis, soft tissue conditions & trauma
Touch hand to shoulder on same side	- elbow should flex to 150 degrees
Supinate & pronate hand with arms at side, elbows at 90 degrees	
Inspect hands & wrists	- look for joint swelling, muscle wasting, skin/nail changes - rheumatoid arthritis (inflammatory) or osteoarthritis (degenerative)
Squeeze across 2nd to 5th metacarpals	- tenderness = MCP synovitis
Make prayer sign & inverted prayer sign	
Make a tight fist	- joints should be at 90° to each other
Lie on back & flex each knee	- look for range of movement & feel for crepitus (osteoarthritis)
Rotate hips internally & externally	
Test knee for effusion	
Squeeze across metatarsals for tenderness	
Inspect soles for calluses	- shows abnormal weight bearing

Secretions of the GI system

Cells	Secretions	Excited by	Inhibited by
Stomach			
Mucous/Globlet	Mucus & Na bicarbonate		aspirin
Parietal/Oxyntic	HCl and vitamin B_{12} intrinsic factor ($\Rightarrow$absorption of vitamin B_{12} in terminal ileum)	HCl excited by histamine, gastrin, ACh (vagus innervation) & caffeine (via cyclic AMP)	somatostatin, gastric inhibiting polypeptide (GIP) & cholecystokinin (CCK)
Chief/Zymogen	pepsinogen (a digestive enzyme, activated by HCl & autocatalytic)		
Enteroendocrine	somatostatin (D cells), gastrin (G cells - causes gall bladder contraction) & vasoactive intestinal peptide (VIP)	somatostatin excited by HCl in duodenum	gastrin inhibited by secretin, gastric inhibiting polypeptide (GIP) & somatostatin
Duodenum			
K cells	gastric inhibiting polypeptide (GIP - stimulates insulin secretion) and cholecystokinin (CCK - causes gall bladder contraction & sphincter of oddi relaxation)	fatty acids	
S cells	secretin (released into blood)	HCl	somatostatin
Brunner's glands	mucus, Na bicarbonate & growth factor	chyme & acid	
Small Intestine Crypts			
Enteroendocrine	somatostatin, gastrin, motilin & vasoactive intestinal peptide (VIP)		
Pancreas			
α Langerhans	glucagon $\Rightarrow \uparrow$blood sugar		somatostatin (locally)
β Langerhans	Insulin $\Rightarrow \downarrow$blood sugar	gastric inhibiting polypeptide	somatostatin (locally)
δ Langerhans	somatostatin $\Rightarrow \downarrow$intestinal secretions		
Acini cells (exocrine)	trypsinogen (autocatalytic + enteropeptidase in duodenal mucosa converts it to trypsin) = a digestive enzyme	secretin and cholecystokinin (CCK)	
	Na bicarbonate	secretin and CCK	
	various digestive enzymes e.g. amylase & lipase	secretin and CCK	

- Gastric inhibiting polypeptide (GIP), cholecystokinin (CCK) and secretin are collectively known as enterogastrones because they effect gastric secretion
- Cholecystokinin (CCK) and secretin potentiate each others effects

Hormones & Their Effects

Hormone & where secreted	Effects

Hypothalamus (via post. pituitary)

Oxcytocin	stimulates milk ejection and uterine contractions
Vasopressin (ADH)	increases no. of water channels (aquaporins) in kidney tubules (V_2 receptor) $\Rightarrow \uparrow$water reabsorption + is a vessel vasoconstrictor (V_1 receptors)

Ant. pituitary (is controlled by hypothalamus via hypophyseal tract/portal system)

Follicle stimulating (FSH)	works on seritoli cells (men) & granulosa cells (women) by stimulating germ cell development $\Rightarrow$growth of follicles & spermatogenesis
Luteinizing (LH)	works on leydig cells (men) and theca cells (women), stimulates testosterone secretion, ovulation, corpus luteum development & oestrogen/progesterone secretion
Growth (GH)	stimulates body growth especially in bone
Thyroid stimulating (TSH)	stimulates secretion of thyroxine by thyroid gland
Prolactin	stimulates breast growth & milk production
Adrenocorticotrophic	stimulates melanocytes & secretion of adrenal cortical hormones (e.g. cortisol)

Adrenal cortex (has 3 zones/areas)

Aldosterone (from zona glomerulosa)	causes kidney's distal tubules, sweat glands & GI tract to absorb sodium (& therefore water) & excrete potassium
Cortisol (from zona fasciculate)	stimulates the formation of glucose in the liver
Oestrogen, progesterone & androgens (from zona reticulate)	involved in the menstrual cycle

Adrenal medulla

Adrenaline (80%) & Noradrenaline	controls fight or flight response

Thyroid gland

Thyroxine	regulates bodies BMR by increasing oxidation in cells
Calcitonin	inhibits Ca reabsorption by osteoclasts $\Rightarrow\downarrow$Ca in blood

Parathyroid

Parathormone	induces osteoclast activity ($\Rightarrow\uparrow$Ca in blood) & stimulates the release of $1,25\text{-}(OH)_2D_3$ (vit D)

Liver

$1,25\text{-}(OH)_2D_3$ (active vitamin D)	absorbs excess Ca and phosphate

Pancreas (endocrine)

Glucagon (via α islet of langerhans cells)	$\Rightarrow\uparrow$glucose in blood by binding to glycogen receptors on liver cell membranes $\Rightarrow$glycolysis (glycogen converted to glucose) and gluconeogenesis (amino acid to glucose)
Insulin (via β islet of langerhans cells 70%)	$\Rightarrow\downarrow$glucose in blood by increasing no. of GLUT carriers in cell walls $\Rightarrow$glucose from blood into cells, also it increases glycogen and other energy storage synthesis
Somatostatin (via δ islet of langerhans cells 5%)	local inhibition of insulin and glucagon

Cardiac atrial cells

Atrial natriuretic factor	decreases Na and & therefore decreasing water reabsorption (a natural diuretic)

Kidneys

Erythropoietin	increases rate of RBC cell production

Juxtaglomerular apparatus

Renin	converts angiotensin (from liver) to active angiotensin I → angiotensin II (vasoconstrictor & increases Na reabsorption in renal proximal tubes) → Aldosterone

Seritoli cells (men)

Inhibin	inhibits FSH secretion
Paracrine	effects leydig cell function
Androgen binding	binds testosterone
Mullerian inhibiting substance (MIS)	induced by SRY gene on Y chromosome ⇒ regression of female mullerian duct system (leaving only male wolffian ducts)

Leydig cells (men)

Testosterone	initiates spermatogenesis (via seritoli cells), sperm differentiation & proliferation, it also inhibits LH & GnRH secretion, stimulates bone growth, sex drive & erythropoietin secretion by kidney

Granulosa cells (women) in follicle phase then secreted by corpus luteum then if pregnant by the placenta's trophoblast cells

Oestrogen	inhibits LH secretion at low levels, at high levels increases LH secretion, increases oxytocin receptors in the uterine muscle layer + increases growth of uterine muscle
Progesterone	decreases GnRH ⇒ prevention of LH surge during pregnancy, inhibits uterine mobility
Inhibin	inhibits FSH secretion

Theca cells (women)

Androgen	⇒ oestrogen via granulosa cells

Placenta (in pregnancy)

Human Chorionic gonadotropin	prevents degeneration of corpus luteum and stimulates it to secrete steroids
Oxytocin	stimulates milk ejection and uterine contractions
Placental lactogen	acts like growth hormone and prolactin

Myometrium smooth muscle (in uterus)

Connexin	produces gap junctions between smooth muscle cells ⇒ contraction propagation during labour

Presenting Abdominal X-Rays

Abdominal X-rays are more difficult to make out than CXRs, just try to present in an organised way starting with the stomach & working down

Follow the steps below:

1. **patient details**: name, DOB, date X-ray taken
2. **stomach**: just below diaphragm, may contain air
3. **small bowel (duodenum, jejunum & ileum)**: found in the centre of the abdomen, has lines (valvaulae) that go continuously across the bowel, look for any signs of obstruction (dilatation or air-fluid levels)
4. **large bowel (colon)**: found around the edge of the abdomen, has lines (haustra) that are not continuous, look for dilatation (can be due to obstruction, strictures, toxic megacolon, etc.)
5. **rectum**: if contains faeces this is usually a sign the bowel is not obstructed
6. **lung bases**: quickly assess the lung bases & comment on any abnormalities

be aware of:
- hiatal hernias (air-fluid level above diaphragm)
- some gall stones or urinary tract/renal stones may show on a plain abdominal film, N.B. if you are concerned about a renal stone perform a KUB abdominal X-ray (=Kidneys, Ureters & Bladder imaged)
- air below diaphragm (on an erect chest X-ray) = bowel perforation (you should always perform an erect chest X-ray if you suspect bowel perforation)
- can get calcification in pancreas or liver due to chronic diseases of those organs

Presenting Chest X-Rays

Follow the steps below when presenting a CXR:

1. **patient details**: name, DOB, date X-ray taken
2. **PA or AP view**: heart magnified on AP therefore cannot comment on heart size
3. <u>**A**</u>**lignment**: are the clavicles horizontally in-line with each other, if not the patient may have been rotated
4. <u>**P**</u>**enetration**: look at the lower part of the cardiac shadow, the spine's vertebral bodies should only just be visible at this point, to understand penetration imagine the X-ray plate as being totally white before the X-ray is taken & the longer the penetration the darker it becomes, therefore under penetrated films look whiter & over penetrated look dark, *N.B. I have underlined A & P so you remember they come after step 2*
5. **heart size**: should be < ½ the thoracic cavity diameter
6. **bones**: check ribs & clavicles for fractures
7. **soft tissues**: look for calcified masses, air in soft tissue (surgical emphysema) & breast shadows (in women)
8. **diaphragm**: are the angles clearly defined, is there free air beneath the diaphragm (possible bowel perforation, do not mistake this with air in the stomach)
9. **lungs**: just say what you see (e.g. increased opacity/shadowing at base of R lung = possible infection)

Lobes of the Lungs

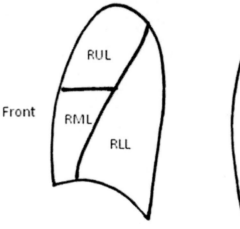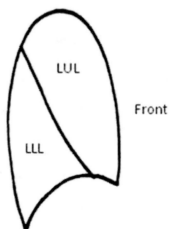

Presenting Orthopaedic X-Rays

Follow the steps below:

1. **patient details**: name, DOB, date X-ray taken
2. **type of film**: AP, lateral, etc.
3. **Adequacy**: is joint above & below fracture visible
4. **Bones**: describe fracture + bone quality/density
5. **Cartilage & soft tissue**

Fracture description:

1. skin & soft tissue damage: is it an obvious open/closed fracture
2. site: name bone + position on bone, i.e. proximal (end of bone closest to the heart), middle, or distal
3. pattern of fracture: transverse, oblique, spiral, or segmental
4. deformity: are the sections of bone displaced, angulated, rotated, or a combination of these
5. joint involvement: intra-articular extension of fracture, subluxation or dislocation of joint

When ordering X-rays in orthopaedics follow the 'rule of 2s':

- 2 views (e.g. AP & lateral)
- 2 joints (above & below injury)
- 2 occasions
- 2 limbs for comparison (e.g. in arthritis)

CT & MRI scans

Computed tomography (CT)	- CT machines look like large 'polo' mints & are basically X-ray machines - the section of the body being scanned moves through the machine whilst it takes a number of X-rays, these are then converted from 2D to 3D by the computer - interpretation: is exactly the same as an X-ray, bones are white, air spaces are black, and soft tissue has varying degrees of opacity depending on its density
Magnetic Resonance Imaging (MRI)	- the hydrogen atoms in a water molecule have a property called 'spin', there are 2 different spin states they can be in, each spin has a different energy level, when the correct magnetic field is applied to these water molecules all the hydrogen atoms align into the same spin, changing the magnetic frequency makes them change spin/drop to the lower energy level ⇒every water molecule emits energy which can be detected & created into an image - when interpreting MRI scans remember that regions of the body with a large water concentration (e.g. blood) show up brighter than areas with a low water content (e.g. the lungs) - these scans have the advantage of imaging without using ionizing radiation - before ordering an MRI scan you should find out: if the patient is claustrophobic (the machine consists of a long narrow tube), if they have any implanted metal (the strong magnetic field attracts metal), if the patient is pregnant (this is a contraindication for most imaging) - N.B. both MRI & CT scans can be performed with contrast (a substance drank or given IV which highlights certain areas of the body)

Lump Examination

These are the properties used when describing a lump, you will probably not need to use all of them at the same time

- Site: exactly where & what it is related to
- Shape
- Size: measure it
- Surface: smooth or irregular
- Edge: well defined or infiltrating into surrounding tissues
- Colour
- Temperature
- Pain on palpation
- Fixed/mobile: deep/superficial
- Composition: can be found out by percussion = solid, fluid (stoney dull), gas (hyper-resonant)
- Consistency: soft (e.g. lipoma), firm (e.g. lymphoma), hard (e.g. carcinoma of breast) or bony
- Fluctuation: fluid confined to a cavity, 2 fingers either side press in middle, do this in 2 planes
- Fluid thrill (if mass is large enough)
- Translucency: shine torch through
- Pulsatily: expansile (e.g. AAA)
- Compressibility: does it empty on pressing
- Auscultation (e.g. bruit = turbulent flow in a vessel)
- Reducibility (e.g. hernia)

Medical Statistics

Some of these definitions may be asked in your exams

Randomised case controls	-	randomly allocated, one group has treatment the other does not
Case control study	-	group that has disease are compared with group that does not
Cohort study	-	group of people with certain characteristic (e.g. smokers) are followed for a long time
Cross sectional study	-	representative sample studied at single time $\Rightarrow$ snapshot
Delphi method	-	no face to face contact (e.g. questionnaires)
Epidemiology	-	causes, distribution, prevention & control of disease in populations
Incidence	-	number of new cases in population over specific time
Prevalence	-	total number of cases in population at specific time
Morbidity	-	can be either incidence or prevalence of a disease in a defined population
Mortality	-	number of deaths in defined population
Relative risk (RR)	-	probability of an event in specific group divided by probability of an event in control group
	-	e.g. 5 dead out of 30 in test group, 1 dead out of 30 in control, RR $= \dfrac{\left(\frac{5}{30}\right)}{\left(\frac{1}{30}\right)}$
Absolute risk (AR)	-	number of events divided by number in the group
Absolute risk reduction (ARR)	-	(number of events in active group divided by number in group) – (number of events in control group divided by number in group)
Relative risk reduction (RRR)	-	$1 - RR$
Specificity	-	proportion of negative results correctly identified
Sensitivity	-	proportion of positive results correctly identified
Likelihood ratio	-	$\dfrac{sensitivity}{\left(1 - specificity\right)}$
+'ve predictive value	-	proportion with +'ve test results correctly diagnosed
–'ve predictive value	-	proportion with –'ve test results correctly diagnosed
True –'ve	-	patient without disease who has –'ve test result
True +'ve	-	patient without disease who has +'ve test result

Nursing

When possible get to know the nursing staff, you will be working with these people for a while, they are the glue that holds hospitals together and have a unique and invaluable take on patient care. We are all part of the same team and to provide the best care possible it is important for doctors to be able to work alongside nurses and communicate their thoughts/plans in a clear way.

Some nurses will have worked on the same ward for a number of years so if you are unsure about any aspects of care, ask the nursing staff before calling your superiors. Don't forget that some nurses have skills that are advantageous e.g. blood taking, cannulation, catheterization, etc., if you are friendly and approachable and ask them for help, these skills will become available to you.

During your student years you will be expected to spend a small amount of time shadowing nurses, make the most of this time and try to cover all the areas below, this will help you more than you can imagine as a junior doctor.

Patient interaction	- look at the patient as a whole person, not just a diagnosis, patients have hopes, fears, thoughts & feelings, it is important that we embrace and understand these issues to enable the patient to make informed decisions on the care they receive - take the time to sit and talk to your patients and their carers, ask them how they are feeling and enquire if they have any questions for you, don't be afraid if you don't know all the answers, nobody has all of the answers and sometimes the patient just wants somebody to talk to
Assessing patients	- stay aware of your environment & keep yourself safe! - wherever possible request a nurse chaperone when examining patients (especially in situations when examining the opposite sex, aggressive patients or any patient where you have concerns for your own welfare) - remember your duty of care to yourself, you have the right to refuse to assess patients who pose a threat to you - document every interaction you have with the patient - follow trust policy with regards to correct moving and handling techniques and always remember to protect your back
Observations	- familiarise yourself with oxygen, suction, blood pressure machines, saturation probes, thermometers, blood glucose machines, bladder scanners, doppler machines etc. if you know how to use such equipment it will save time & effort when the nursing staff are busy - understand early warning scores (EWS) + observation charts and learn how to complete them correctly, remember if a patient is scoring a 3 or above a doctor needs to be called (check your hospital policy) - neuro observations should be used for head injuries, increased confusion, or ↓GCS - learn how to read/complete fluid balance charts & how to empty catheter/stoma bags correctly - pressure area monitoring is important especially in patients with existing pressure wounds, reduced mobility/bedbound or with increased waterlow scores (assesses a patient's risk of developing a pressure sore)

Medications	- correct patient, correct route, correct time - ensure patient has a nameband + ask if they have any allergies - prescribe in clear, concise CAPITAL letters (spending a little more time making you hand writing eligible is good practice & will save you time in the long run) - analgesia: the majority of patients are admitted into hospital with pain, aswell as their regular medications always ensure that they have some kind of pain relief prescribed, this will save you the time & effort of being bleeped to come back to the ward when the patient is in pain
Administering IV fluids	1. ensure fluids are prescribed correctly & the patient has a working cannula in-situ 2. prepare IV fluids using an aseptic non-touch technique (ANTT) 3. clean & prepare your aseptic field 4. snap off port at the base of the bag of fluid & spike with an IV giving set 5. prime the IV giving set, ensuring no air bubbles are present 6. hang bag of fluid on drip stand 7. at this point the giving set can be connected to an IV pump/drip counter (seek help and advice on how to use this from nursing staff) 8. connect to patient using the principles of ANTT 9. observe for any adverse reactions (if any reactions occur disconnect immediately)
Miscellaneous	- if the phone is ringing answer it - if the 'call' bell is buzzing and there are no nurses available go and see if the patient is OK - familiarize yourself with the ward especially the clinic (so you know where specific apparatus is kept & so you can dispense simple medication) and the sluice (if a patient needs a vomit bowel or commode, go get them one!) - when you remove a dressing to assess a wound, replace it as best as you can & inform the nurse - whenever you make changes to a patient's care inform the nursing staff

Pain Relief (The Analgesic Ladder)

Pain relief is a huge subject in medicine, alongside fluids this is one of the things you will constantly get bleeped about during your junior doctor years

Analgesic ladder	- paracetamol & NSAIDs (e.g. ibuprofen & diclofenac) → add codeine → add morphine at titrated dose (stop codeine)
Morphine	- has both short acting (immediate release) & long acting (slow release) forms - administration: for acute severe pain (e.g. MI, trauma, etc.) where you need to gain control quickly give IV, otherwise give oral, IM or via a patch - patient controlled analgesia (PCA): this is a new way of administering IV opioids for severe pain, the patient pushes a button when they are in pain which ⇒ a small dose of IV pain relief, the machine that controls this stops the patient overdosing by having a 5 minute lockout between doses - to counteract opioids (e.g. morphine or heroin) give naloxone, this works very quickly but only lasts a short time ~45 minutes - antiemetics (e.g. cyclizine or metoclopramide) are given as opioids can ⇒N&V calculating dose: - when giving morphine always titrate the dose = start low & work up slowly, can ⇒respiratory depression if too much given - to convert to long acting morphine (e.g. zomorph) add up the total amount of morphine used over the last 24hrs (short + long acting), divide by 2 & prescribe as the long acting form twice a day - for 'breakthrough pain' add up the total amount of morphine used over the last 24hrs, divide by 6 & prescribe as the short acting form (e.g. sevredol) 'when required' (PRN), a patient can usually have this every 3 hours if needed - example: patient has used 4 doses of 10mg sevredol + 2 doses of 10mg zomorph = 60mg in total over 24hrs, the next day prescribe 30mg long acting (twice a day) + 10mg short acting (when required, maximum of every 3 hours) - remember this is a constantly changing process, if more short acting has been used change the long acting & breakthrough to compensate, on the other hand if no short acting/breakthrough is being used & the patient is not complaining of pain think about reducing the daily dose - N.B. if you have any queries about pain relief each hospital should have a 'pain team' you can phone for advice
Neuropathic pain	- caused by a lesion or dysfunction anywhere within the nervous system, e.g. diabetes (⇒peripheral neuropathy), fibromyalgia (a disorder of chronic widespread pain), a stroke, cancer, etc. - this type of pain is very difficult to treat & can require a mixture of antidepressants (e.g. amitriptyline), anticonvulsants (e.g. gabapentin) & opioids (e.g. morphine)
Palliative care	- concentrates on decreasing the severity of disease symptoms rather than curing them, this field of medicine is growing larger each year - as a junior doctor you will see patients on the 'care of the dying' pathway who do require continual pain relief, in these cases a syringe driver can be used - syringe drivers are prescribed over 24hrs using the same calculations as above - N.B. relaxants can also be added to syringe drivers (e.g. midazolam a benzodiazepine) because patients can become agitated/restless near the end

Syndromes

Syndrome	Cause	Symptoms	Investigations	Management
Down's	Trisomy 21 (non-dysjunction of 21) ↑risk as mother gets older	Short stature, thick nuchal fold, ↓femur length, small ears, congenital heart disease (VSD, patent ductus, ASD), large tongue, duodenal atresia, broad hands/feet, hand has single palmer crease, mental retardation, ↑alzheimer's risk	Ultrasound Amniocentsis Chronus villus sampling Triple test (↓AFP, ↑βhCG, ↓estriol)	Multidisciplinary approach
Edward's	Trisomy 18 (unbalanced translocation) Rarer but symptoms are worse than down's	Growth retardation (IUGR), rocker bottom/club feet, wide spaced nipples, cleft lip/palate, polyhydramnios, clenched hands, small head, congenital heart defects, mental retardation	Ultrasound Amniocentsis Chronus villus sampling Triple test (↓AFP, ↓βhCG, ↓estriol)	Multidisciplinary approach Usually die in childhood
Patau's	Trisomy 13	IUGR, facial cleft lip/palate, ocular abnormalities, cardiac defects, polycystic kidneys, severe mental retardation	Genetic testing	Usually fatal in first year of life
Turners	Sex chromosomes 45 XO	Only in females, short stature, webbed neck, ovarian failure (⟹no secondary sex features & 1° amenorrhea), aortic coarctation, renal abnormalities	↓FSH, LH & oestrogen Genetic testing	Hormone replacement
Klinefelters	Sex chromosome addition ⟹XYY	Seminiferous tubule dysgenesis + loss of leydig cells ⟹testicular atrophy, gynaecomastia & no 2° sex development, also can ⟹↓IQ, is the most common cause of male hypogonadism ⟹infertility	↓testosterone Genetic testing	Testosterone replacement therapy
Duchenne muscular dystrophy	X-linked	Overdeveloped calves, proximal muscle weakness ⟹delayed walking, falls, wasting of affected muscles, waddling gait	↑↑CK, gower's sign (hands push against legs when trying to stand from seating position), muscle biopsy	Multidisciplinary approach Usually wheelchair-bound by teens & died before 20
Huntington's	Autosomal dominant	Symptoms gets worse with each generation Onset usually between 30-50 yrs of age Cerebral atrophy + ↓neuro transmitters ⟹symptoms that start with personality change & gradually worsening chorea (rapid, jerky involuntary movements affecting limbs, face & tongue), later stages =dementia akinesia & rigidity	Genetic studies	Multidisciplinary approach Treat symptoms e.g. depression, nursing care, genetic counselling Death occurs approx. 15 yrs post onset
Familial ↑cholesterol	Autosomal dominant	↑LDL ⟹early heart disease	Bloods, ECG, etc.	Lifestyle, statin treatment + regular CV review
Marfan's	Autosomal dominant	Connective tissue disorder Usually very tall CV problems (mitral valve prolapse & dilatation of the ascending aorta can ⟹aortic regurgitation) Ocular abnormalities (⟹severe myopia/short sightedness)	CV investigations (bloods, ECG, echo, etc.)	CV medication & may need valve surgery Ophthalmology intervention

N.B. there are hundreds of syndromes, I have only covered those which commonly arise in your exams, some others can be found in the revision sections of the book

Systemic Enquiry

General	- well being - fever - sleep - appetite - weight change - energy
CV	- chest pain - SOB (at night) - palpitations - intermittent claudication - ankle swelling
Respiratory	- SOB (exercise tolerance) - wheezing - cough/sputum - chest pain on breathing - haemoptysis
GI	- condition of mouth - swallowing difficulties - N&V - indigestion/heartburn - abdo pain - weight loss - change in bowel habit/colour
GU	- pain on urinating - frequency - colour - no. of sexual partners - prostate symptoms (men) + libido/impotence - periods (women)
Neurological	- headaches - fits/faints/dizzy spells - tingling/numbness - muscle weakness - hearing
Visual	- appearance of eyes - pain - visual problems
Locomotor	- joint pain/stiffness - muscle pain/weakness
Endocrine	- heat/cold intolerance - sweating - prominence of eyes - swellings in neck - excessive thirst

Visual Field Defects

(symptoms depend on the position of the lesion/trauma)

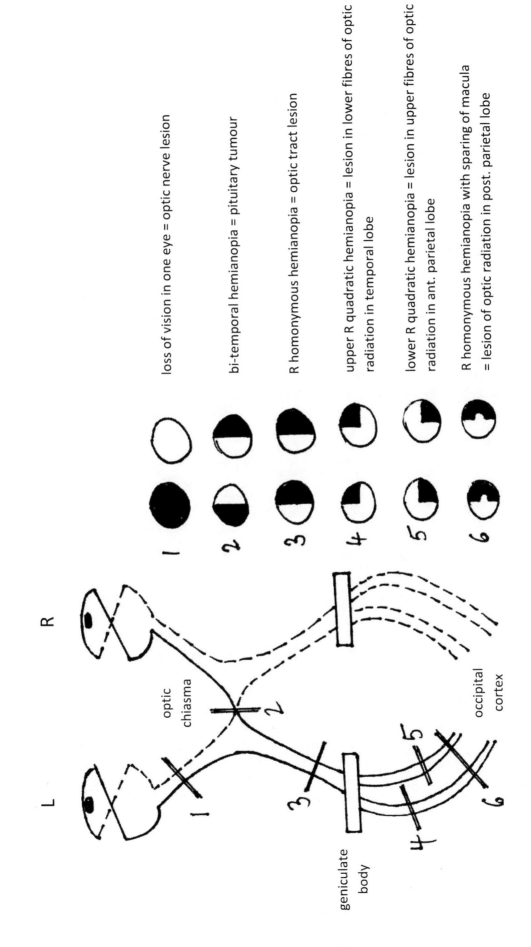

1 loss of vision in one eye = optic nerve lesion

2 bi-temporal hemianopia = pituitary tumour

3 R homonymous hemianopia = optic tract lesion

4 upper R quadratic hemianopia = lesion in lower fibres of optic radiation in temporal lobe

5 lower R quadratic hemianopia = lesion in upper fibres of optic radiation in ant. parietal lobe

6 R homonymous hemianopia with sparing of macula = lesion of optic radiation in post. parietal lobe

Viral Hepatitis Serology

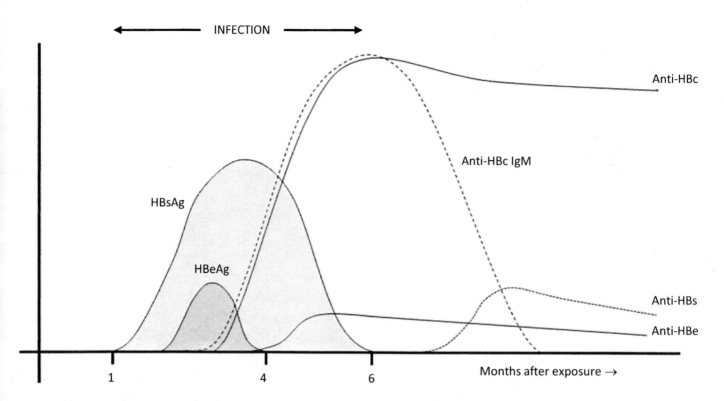

The above graph shows typical serology for a hepatitis B viral infection in which the patient has been able to clear the infection within 6 months, there can be chronic cases where this is not the case (the shaded areas do not reach zero again, patient becomes a carrier), a similar graph to this may come up in one of your OCSE stations or in the written exam

HBsAg	- hepatitis B surface antigen - as the virus replicates the amount of antigen in the body increases - surface antigen detection is used to screen for this infection, from the graph you can see that the patient is infected until HBsAg has been totally cleared from the body at 6 months - whilst a patient is infected they can also infect others - N.B. antigens are produced by the viral infection, the body's immune system then produces antibodies to fight these
HBeAg	- hepatitis B e antigen - the presence of HBeAg is associated with much higher rates of viral replication & ↑infectivity
Anti-HBs/HBe	- these are the antibodies to both the hepatitis B surface antigen & e antigen - as the body's defence mechanism replicates more antibodies against the virus the antigens will decrease, in people who are immunosuppressed this may not happen as fast or may ⇒chronic infection
Anti-HBc IgM	- this is the acute (IgM) antibody to the hepatitis B core antigen
Anti-HBc	- this is a long term antibody to the hepatitis B core antigen - if a patient is −'ve for HBsAg but +'ve for anti-HBs they have either cleared an infection or been vaccinated previously